THE ALBERT SHAW LECTURES ON
DIPLOMATIC HISTORY, 1907

———

International Law and Diplomacy

of the

Spanish-American War

By ELBERT J. BENTON, Ph.D.
Assistant Professor of History in Western Reserve University

THE LAWBOOK EXCHANGE, LTD.
Clark, New Jersey

ISBN 978-1-58477-665-9

Lawbook Exchange edition 2006, 2025

The quality of this reprint is equivalent to the quality of the original work.

THE LAWBOOK EXCHANGE, LTD.

33 Terminal Avenue
Clark, New Jersey 07066-1321

Please see our website for a selection of our other publications
and fine facsimile reprints of classic works of legal history:
www.lawbookexchange.com

Library of Congress Cataloging-in-Publication Data

Benton, Elbert Jay, 1871-1946.
 International law and diplomacy of the Spanish-American war /
 Elbert J. Benton.
  p. cm.
 Originally published: Baltimore : Johns Hopkins Press, 1908.
 Includes bibliographical references and index.
 Contents: Cuba and national policy -- American neutrality, 1895-
1897 -- Abandonment of non-intervention policy, October 1897 to
March 1898 -- Intervention -- Transition from neutrality to
belligerency -- Relations of the belligerents -- Relations between
belligerents and neutrals -- Negotiations of belligerents during war.
Restoration of peace -- Interpretation and fulfilment of treaty of peace.
  ISBN 1-58477-665-X (alk. paper)
 1. Spanish-American War, 1898--Diplomatic history. 2. United
States--Foreign relations--Spain. 3. Spain--Foreign relations--United
States. 4. United States--Foreign relations--1897-1901. 5.
United States--Politics and government--1897-1901. 6. Intervention
(International law)--History--19th century. 7. Belligerency--History
--19th century. 8. International law--History--19th century. I. Title.

E723.B47 2005
973.8'91--dc22   2005002920

Printed in the United States of America on acid-free paper

THE ALBERT SHAW LECTURES ON
DIPLOMATIC HISTORY, 1907

International Law and Diplomacy

of the

Spanish-American War

By ELBERT J. BENTON, Ph.D.

Assistant Professor of History in Western Reserve University

BALTIMORE
THE JOHNS HOPKINS PRESS
1908

PRESS OF
THE NEW ERA PRINTING COMPANY
LANCASTER, PA.

CONTENTS

5

decree, April 23. The treaty of 1795. Effect of war on payment of debts. The convention of 1834. Notification of neutrals. Legal field of operations.

Announcements regarding rules of international law controlling belligerent conduct. Adherence to Declaration of Paris. Privateering. The Spanish auxiliary naval force. The naval militia of the United States. Blockades. Closure of enemy harbors. Use of false flag. Use of non-organized, non-uniformed soldiers. Employment of savages. Operations of insurgents and the liability for failure to adhere to armistice. Bombardment of San Juan, Santiago, Manila and Manzanillo. Cable cutting and the status of cables under the Convention of Paris, 1884. Use of balloons. Newspaper correspondents in the field. Hospital ships and Red Cross. Geneva Convention. Treatment and exchange of prisoners. Private enemy property on land. Private enemy property on seas. Principles of prize law in the American decisions.

The declarations of neutrality. Sale of ships and munitions of war by neutrals. The use of neutral ports for asylum, repair, provisioning and coaling. Contraband of war. Severity of Spanish and American penalties prescribed for carrying contraband. The case of the *Restormel.* The blockade proclamation, April 22. Military blockade of Santiago, Manila, Guantanamo and Manzanillo. Blockade proclamation, June 27, 1898. Important decisions in prize law: the *Lafayette, Olinde Rodriguez, Adula.* Neutral cables in war. Use of neutral soil by belligerents. Neutral war-ships in belligerent ports; Admiral Diedrich and the *Irene.*

Preliminary negotiations begun July 18. Ambassador Cambon as mediator, July 21. Spanish mes-

sage of July 26 asking for terms of peace. Reply of
the United States, July 30, with three conditions of
peace. The peace protocol; terms and legal effects.
The suspension of hostilities, August 12. Subsequent
capture of Manila, August 14. American title to
Manila by conquest. Resumption of commerce between belligerents, August 22 and 23. Limitations
prescribed. Evacuation of Cuba and Porto Rico.
The Paris Peace Commission. Proceedings at Paris.
The Cuban debt controversy. The suspension of
conferences. Mediation of Ambassadors Castillo and
Porter. The demand for the Philippines in its bearing upon the peace protocol. Spain's position. Rights
of United States to Philippines from standpoint of
international law. Conclusion of treaty of peace.
Accessories of the treaty unconcluded until 1902-3.

The territorial cessions in treaty of peace. Status
of the Isle of Pines. Status of Cuba under American occupation. Obligations of the United States.
The Constitutional obligations during military government of territories. Rights of the Spanish roy-
alists. Public property and records. Private property and property guarantees. Effect of change of
sovereignty upon franchises granted by Spanish Government. Case of Manila Railway Company; of
Cuban Submarine Cable Telegraph Company. Industrial property under the treaty. Property right
in Spanish offices. The land dispute with the friar
orders. Settlement of land question. American-
Cuban claims. The Treaty Claims Commission.
The rules of guidance formulated on obligations of
United States. Establishment of independence of
Cuba. The Platt Amendment. Independent position of Cuba. Obligations and rights of United
States toward Cuba.

PREFACE

This work is intended as a study of the relations of the United States with Spain during the late Cuban insurrection and the resultant Spanish war. The history of the conduct of the belligerents from the standpoint of international law has been emphasized. The method of treatment is not without numerous precedents in recent monographic literature: Amédée Brenet, " La France et L'Allemagne devant le droit international pendant les opérations militaires de la guerre de 1870–71," Paris, 1902; Takahashi, " Cases on International Law during the Chino-Japanese War," 1899; Baty, " International Law in South Africa;" Smith and Sibley, " International Law as interpreted during the Russo-Japanese War," Boston, 1905; and Hershey, " International Law and Diplomacy of the Russo-Japanese War," are conspicuous and more or less ambitious undertakings of the same kind. The French writers have given this aspect of recent history the most careful attention. They have several monographs on the Spanish-American war: Viallate, " Essais d'histoire diplomatique américaine," Paris, 1905 ;[1] Lebrand, " La guerre hispano-américaine et le droit des gens," Paris, 1904, and Le Fur, " Étude sur la guerre hispano-américaine de 1898, envisagée au point de vue du droit international public," Paris, 1899. The latter by a well-known professor of international law at Caen, France, is the fullest study of the subject that

[1] Reviews in Am. Hist. Rev., XI, p. 423; Pol. Sci. Quar., 1906, p. 319.

9

has appeared, and in many particulars is an excellent
treatise. However, it was written before the publication of the " Foreign Relations of the United States,"
and is based almost exclusively on Spanish and French
sources, and correspondingly shares the severe anti-
American prejudices of an enemy. This fact, together
with its appearance before the problems connected with
the transfer of the islands had been met, makes it
inadequate. The custom, however, which M. Le Fur
has followed, of printing extended quotations from
the continental newspapers and Spanish Documents,
makes it an invaluable source book, and one which
has been very freely used. A study by Dr. Horace
E. Flack, " Spanish-American Diplomatic Relations
Preceding the War of 1898,"[2] has been very helpful
for the first part of the period. I take this opportunity to express my deep gratitude to Professor W.
W. Willoughby of Johns Hopkins University, in
whose seminar and under whose guidance this study
was originally begun; to my colleague, Professor
Henry E. Bourne of Western Reserve University;
and to the editor of this series, Professor John M.
Vincent of Johns Hopkins University, for criticism and
helpful suggestions that have been made in course
of the preparation. It is only fair to say that none
of these are in any way responsible for the conclusions
that have been reached or for the errors that appear.
Further particular acknowledgments are made throughout in the footnotes.

Owing to the greater resources and activity of the
American forces during the war, Spain was placed
upon the defensive from the beginning. The result

[2] Johns Hopkins Studies, series 24, nos. 1-2, 1906.

was to give comparatively few chances to test or criti-
cize Spanish practice except for the period of the
Cuban war. For the succeeding time the study becomes of necessity almost entirely a criticism of American usages in warfare. A serious effort has been
made to present the subject dispassionately, but the
point of view throughout is American, the greater
part of the sources have an American origin, and the
aim has been to exhibit the foreign policy and practice
of the United States during this period, both as a
neutral and as a belligerent. No pretension of doing
the same for Spain is made at this time.

CHAPTER I

CUBA AND NATIONAL POLICY

Every nation places its own interpretation upon the rights and obligations which belong to it under international law. This is to say that national policies constitute a strong and determining influence upon the principles or usages of international law which a state is willing to recognize and to observe in practice. On the borderlands of international law are disputed questions, and national interests influence the attitude toward such. England, with coaling stations at convenient intervals around the world, has held a doctrine of neutral obligations on coaling which France has been unwilling to recognize. Spain, without a large navy, has refused to accept the rule for the abolition of privateering after all the great powers have made it an established principle of action. Russia, placed at a disadvantage by the suddenness of the first acts of war inflicted by Japan, insisted upon the necessity of a preliminary declaration of war, even though such a position ran counter to opinion and practice. This principle of action, based on selfish national interests, has held true in all international affairs. Writers upon international law who are supposed to speak without bias are divided on controverted points along the line of national policies.

The history of American diplomacy forms no exception to the domination of national interests in national policy. This seems axiomatic, so fully is it recognized. The task undertaken in the present chapter is a survey of the influence upon American national policy of Spanish-American diplomacy respecting Cuba throughout three quarters of a century. The status of Cuba was one of the determinative factors in the evolution of the Monroe Doctrine. The political conditions in Cuba have continuously forced two tasks upon every American administration—the maintenance of a state of preparedness for any contingencies looking toward a change of sovereignty in Cuba, and the enforcement of the laws of neutrality in the face of the ceaseless troubles in Cuba and of the filibustering of American subjects in support of the revolutionary causes. On the surface these problems constituted no grievance of the United States against Spain. Governments under the prevailing régime of armed peace must be watchful of boundaries and strategic territorial positions, and must enforce their laws of neutrality during a contiguous war. But the long continuance of a galling diplomatic situation is a factor in the history of the Cuban question. Spain's well-known weakness as a state and her colonial embarrassments made it seem probable, fully a century ago, that Cuba must in the end fall to the most watchful of the rivals seeking her as a part of a constructive policy for the control of West Indian waters.[1]

The earliest American policy toward Cuba was in effect prompted by jealousy of England and France. From approximately 1823 to 1849 the dominant feature was a guarantee of Spanish sovereignty over Cuba, and every Secretary of State during these years

[1] Latané, Diplomatic Relations of the United States and Spanish America, p. 91.

expressed in some form the national purpose to prevent the transfer to any other power.[2] In 1825 the seizure of Cuba by Mexico and Colombia was thwarted by the position taken by the United States. Intervention at this time in favor of Spain prevented Cuba and Porto Rico from becoming independent. At other times, as in 1840 and 1843, the Government of the United States pledged the use of its military resources to maintain Spain in the possession of Cuba. Annexation to the United States was regarded as an ultimate probability, but American statesmen in those days were content to wait. " I would not," Jefferson wrote, " immediately go to war for it; because the first war on other accounts will give it to us, or the island will give itself to us when able to do so."[3] After the annexation of Texas and the Mexican war, the intoxication of military glory and foreign conquest, the old Cuban policy gave place to a new policy in which the chief end was the acquisition of the island. The annexation of California led to interoceanic canal projects and made the possession of Cuba of great importance to the United States. A wave of confidence in America's " manifest destiny " swept the country. It took the form of a crude belief in the universal superiority of " American institutions," a lofty contempt for the " effete monarchies " of Europe, and a strong sense of the righteousness of any aggressive action that the republic might undertake.[4] As a result American diplomacy became aggressive and intolerant. The change

[2] Moore, Digest of International Law, Vol. VII, pp. 447 ff. So Secretary Clay, 1825; Van Buren, 1829; Forsyth, 1840; Webster, 1843; Buchanan, 1848; Clayton, 1849; Marcy, 1853.

[3] Works, Vol. VII, p. 288.

[4] Smith, American Nation, Vol. XVII, p. 75.

boded ill for Spanish sovereignty in Cuba. The new militant foreign policy was in no sense strictly southern, but had its strong supporters in the North as well—for commercial reasons. However, a counter-influence checking the dangers of some aggressive measure came from a dread of increase of slave territory. On the other hand the anti-slavery party opposed Cuban annexation. In the South the enthusiasm for the annexation of Cuba was uncontrollable, and led to wide-spread filibustering.[5]

In 1849 President Polk offered Spain one hundred million dollars for Cuba, but the offer was promptly rejected.[6] The rankling of Spanish pride under the humiliation from the loss of other colonies showed clearly in the reply. "It was more than any minister would dare to entertain such a proposition, . . . such was the feeling of the country that sooner than see the island transferred to any power they would prefer seeing it sunk in the ocean."[7]

With the growth of factional strife over slavery the annexation of Cuba became more and more a party issue. The return of the Democratic party to power in 1853 committed its leaders to a renewal of diplomatic efforts for the acquisition of the island. Some of their number passed the bounds of international courtesy in a manifesto issued from Aix-la-Chapelle, October 18, 1854. Its methods were the methods of the highwayman,[8] but the Ostend Manifesto, as it was called

[5] De Bow, Review, September, 1854, Vol. XVII, p. 281; Callahan, Cuba and International Relations, pp. 217–56; Latané, pp. 98–114.

[6] Latané, p. 107.

[7] House Exec. Doc. 121, 32 Cong., 1 Sess., p. 58.

[8] Latané, p. 128; Callahan, pp. 284, 286.

from the first place of meeting, did not indicate a change in American foreign policy one way or another. It was in reality the work of a "hot-headed Frenchman, an avowed annexionist, and a sympathizer with filibusters," Pierre Soulé, the American minister at Madrid. The administration promptly repudiated the threat in the manifesto. The popular disapproval of the proposals of the manifesto which followed the publication in America revealed further that Cuba could not be taken by force with the support or connivance of the American people as a whole. But none the less the Democratic party hoped to bring about its acquisition. President Buchanan appealed to Congress in his second, third and fourth annual messages for united action on the part of the executive and legislative branches of government for the purchase of Cuba, but without success. A Senate bill of 1859 to appropriate thirty million dollars for that purpose, strongly urged by the President, and a strictly Democratic party measure, was allowed to drop through the evident hopelessness of pressing it in the face of the violent Republican opposition to the annexation of slave territory.[9]

After the Civil War domestic problems, especially economic ones, and industrial recovery absorbed national energies in the United States, and little interest was taken in Cuban affairs until the insurrection of 1868–1878. Such interest as there was became more humanitarian than territorial. Thought was less of annexation and more of the abolition of slavery and of liberal

[9] Richardson, Messages and Papers of the Presidents, Vol. V, pp. 511, 561, 642; Latané, p. 133. See Rhodes, History of the United States, Vol. II, pp. 350–54, for "debate in Senate."

2

political reforms.   The national policy from 1860 to
1898 was confined to efforts to secure humanitarian
reforms for Cuba and closer commercial relations.
Secretary Seward merely reflected the old feeling
toward Cuba when he wrote that the United States
" have constantly indulged the belief that they might
hope some day to acquire those islands [Cuba and
Porto Rico] by just and lawful means, with the consent of their sovereign."[10]

The Ten Years' War, ostensibly in favor of the
Republican Revolution in Spain, was in reality a war
of independence. President Grant attempted at the
beginning of his administration to mediate between
Spain and the insurgents,[11] and he found Spain ready
to accept mediation, though upon a different basis from
that proposed. Other incidents disassociated from
mediation gave offense to Spain, and the United States
was asked to withdraw its offer.

Great pressure was brought to bear upon President
Grant by interested parties to force a recognition of

[10] Moore, Digest, Vol. I, p. 589.
[11] He proposed to Spain:
   1. That Spain acknowledge the independence of Cuba.
   2. That Cuba pay Spain a sum to be agreed upon; future
payments to be secured by pledge of export and import duties.
   3. That the slaves in Cuba be emancipated.
   4. That Spain grant an armistice pending the final settlement.
The Spanish propositions in reply were as follows:
   1. That the insurgents lay down arms.
   2. That Spain grant simultaneously a full and complete
amnesty.
   3. That the people of Cuba vote by universal suffrage upon
the question of independence.
   4. That if the majority declared for independence Cuba
compensate Spain by a satisfactory payment guaranteed by the
United States.
Latané, pp. 140–41; House Ex. Doc. 160, 41 Cong., 2 Sess.

belligerency in favor of the insurgents. At one time he was saved from a premature recognition by his Secretary of State. The President signed a proclamation in 1869 for the recognition of belligerency, but his Secretary of State, Mr. Fish, whom he had apparently not consulted, placed the proclamation in safe keeping to await further instructions, which never came. Subsequently Fish explained his reason for so important an action in a private letter in which he said that the Cuban insurgents " have no army . . . no courts, do not occupy a single town or hamlet, to say nothing of a seaport." They are " carrying on a purely guerrilla warfare, burning estates and attacking convoys, etc. . . . There has been nothing that has amounted to war. Belligerency is a fact. Great Britain or France might just as well have recognized belligerency for the Black Hawk War."[12]

The unfortunate incident of the *Virginius* in 1873, the capture on the high seas of a steamer sailing under the American colors and the hurried execution of fifty-three persons taken on board, for a time strained relations and threatened to precipitate intervention and war.[13] But this, like the *Black Warrior* case, was no more than an incident in neighborly relations. During the last years of the great insurrection Grant addressed himself to new efforts to force Spain to settle the Cuban dissensions. In 1875 Mr. Fish ignored all former pronouncements about the purely American character of the Cuban question, and proposed joint intervention to the great powers of Europe. However, England held the time for intervention to be inoppor-

[12] Rhodes, Vol. VI, pp. 345–46.
[13] Latané, pp. 153 ff.

tune, and the plan fell through, as did all efforts to force Spain to end the Cuban war. Moreover, the latter disarmed the Government of the United States by the liberality of the concessions which were promised to the Cubans. Finally, in 1878, the insurgents laid down their arms upon the terms offered by the home government. Shortly afterwards, in 1885, Cuban slavery, one of the great causes for complaint by the United States against Spain, by gradual emancipation ceased to exist in the island.[14] On the other hand the earlier emancipation of slaves in the United States had removed one of the motives for the annexation of Cuba. Other influences lessened the need for Cuba as a part of the national military system so long advocated. The building of transcontinenal railroads turned American thought from an interoceanic canal and the necessity for the possession of Cuba for military reasons. From 1878 Cuba enjoyed seventeen years of rest and Spanish-American diplomacy a quiet disturbed only by some irritation over the Spanish-American commercial policy.

[14] Latané, p. 174.

CHAPTER II

American Neutrality, 1895–1897

The abolition of slavery by a process of gradual emancipation constituted the only important reform of the period following the Ten Years' War. The great colonial abuses remained unabated, and this at a time when the larger political relations of Spanish-American peoples and the increased commercial activities of Cuba in particular stimulated the natural political instincts of the people. Cuba, with a captain-general enjoying full and arbitrary power, without a legislative assembly and without true representation in the Spanish Cortes at a time when its neighbors were enjoying the form at least of a free and independent government, with an antiquated, restrictive colonial policy made doubly bad by abuses in the management of the insular revenues, with life, liberty and property at the mercy of an office-holding aristocracy—Cuba so placed had every reason for political discontent.[1]   The

[1] A. Mérignhac, "L'Autonomie cubaine et le conflit hispano-américain," in the Revue du droit public, Vol. IX, p. 237, shows that the constitutional liberties fell short of the aspirations of the Cuban people, that irregularities in administration annulled the considerable degree of nominal liberty granted in the decree of April 2, 1881, that arbitrary governors-general imposed vexatious limits on individual liberty, and finally that no true right of freedom of speech, thought or writing, nor the enjoyment of religious liberty or of freedom of assembly or association existed. The fundamental liberties were entirely subject to the caprice of the governing aristocracy. Another writer estimates that in a population of 13,000 not more than 500 were Spaniards, but

British colonies in America in 1776 had much less justification for rebellion. However, Cuba's main grievances were economic rather than political. It has been estimated that Spanish office-holders took from forty to fifty per cent. of the annual insular revenues. The census taken by the War Department of the United States in 1899 showed an average revenue for the five years, 1893–8, of $25,000,000. Of this $10,500,-000 was absorbed in paying interest on the Cuban debt, which in 1897 amounted to $400,000,000 or $283.54 per capita. Twelve million dollars was necessary for the support of the Spanish army and navy in Cuba, and the Government—state and church—in the island. Two million five hundred thousand dollars was devoted to public works, education and general improvement. Business was hampered by an unfortunate commercial system. The termination in 1894 of the reciprocal commercial agreement with the United States closed the natural market of the island, and set up again the old system of differential, special and discriminating duties against foreign trade, and forced back on the Cubans compulsory trade with Spain. High duties on sugar, coffee and tobacco imported into Spain closed the only remaining markets.[2] Wheat from the United States to Cuba was obliged to pass through the home ports of Spain, pay the duty, and then pass to Cuba. A letter written by Tomas Estrada Palma to Richard Olney, December

in the same community the electoral lists contained 32 Cubans and 400 Spaniards. There was not a single Cuban among the members of the Municipal Council of Havana. Lebrand, La guerre hispano-américaine, p. 24.

[2] *Ibid.*, pp. 12–14; Report of the Cuban Census for 1899, War Department, Washington, 1900, p. 38.

7, 1895, while an ex parte statement of the causes of
the insurrection, gives, there is every reason to believe,
in the main a true indictment. Palma writes: " The
causes of the insurrection of 1895 are substantially
the same as those of the former revolution lasting
from 1868 to 1878, and terminating only in the representation of the Spanish Government that Cuba would
be granted such reforms as would remove the grounds
of complaint on the part of the Cuban people. Unfortunately the hopes thus held out have never been
realized. The representation which was to be given
to the Cubans has proven absolutely without character;
taxes have been levied anew on every thing conceiv-
able; the offices in the island have increased, but the
officers are all Spaniards; the native Cubans have been
left with no public duties whatsoever to perform
except the payment of taxes to the government and
blackmail to the officials, without privilege even to
move from place to place in the Island except on
the permission of governmental authority.

" Spain has framed the laws so that natives have
substantially been deprived of the rights of suffrage.
The taxes levied have been almost entirely devoted
to the support of the army and navy in Cuba, to pay
interest on the debt that Spain has saddled on the
Island, and to pay salaries of the vast number of
Spanish office-holders, devoting only $746,000 for in-
ternal improvements out of the $26,000,000 collected
by tax. No public schools are within the reach of
the masses for their education. All the principal
industries of the Island are hampered by excessive
imposts. Her commerce with every country but Spain
has been crippled in every possible manner, as can be

seen by the frequent protests of ship owners and merchants.

" The Cubans have no security of person or property. The judiciary are instruments of the military authorities. Trial by military tribunals can be ordered at any time at the will of the Captain-general. There is, besides, no freedom of speech, press or religion."[3]

The direct cause of the insurrection was associated by the Cubans with the failure of the Cortes to pass the bill reforming the Government of Cuba, introduced in 1894 by Señor Maura, minister for the colonies. In fact, Spain had given Cuba many reform acts, such as the extension of the Spanish constitutional guarantees in 1881, the Spanish law of civil procedure in 1885, and the new Spanish civil code in 1889, but colonial politicians had perverted such concessions. For several years before the outbreak in 1895 Cuban leaders had been actively organizing revolutionary clubs and associating them into a revolutionary party. The soul of the movement was José Marti, a native of Cuba, who had had a varied career. He was educated in the law and had been for a number of years Professor of Literature and Philosophy in the University of Guatemala, for a time consul of the Argentine Republic, Uruguay and Paraguay in

[3] Senate Document 231, 56 Cong., 2 Sess., part 7, p. 96. These charges were denied by the former mayor of Havana, M. Alvarez, in an article in the North American Review, Vol. 161, p. 362, but his contention fails to convince the reader. Compare views of Le Fur, La guerre hispano-américaine, p. 8; Latané, pp. 137–38; Callahan, p. 367; Benoist, Rev. des deux mondes, Vol. 139, p. 553; Contemporary Review, Vol. 74, p. 1; North American Review, Vol. I, pp. 165, 610; Forum, September, 1895.

New York City, and in the same place publisher of a journal devoted to Cuban interests, La Patria. His associates were many of them veterans of other wars in Cuba and other parts of Spanish America. The supreme command in the rebel forces was assigned to Maximo Gomez, a Santo Domingan who had found service in the armies of Spain in his native island and Cuba and who had ably served the insurgents in the Ten Years' War. Before the outbreak of the revolt, the revolutionists had formed about one hundred and forty clubs or juntas in various states of North, South and Central America, Cuba and the other West Indies. Every member was a contributor to a fund to the amount of one tenth or more of his earnings. The greater sum was collected in the United States, but the aid from friends of Cuba, largely Cuban in blood, residents in other countries, was not inconsiderable. The agitators were supposed to have ready at the beginning of 1895 one million dollars.[4] The insurrection, it is acknowledged, was conceived on neutral soil by Cubans in exile, was prosecuted from the first through arms and ammunition supplied by Cubans in foreign lands, who had in many cases become citizens of the lands of their adoption, and was financially supported, in part at least, by funds raised abroad. By virtue of this dependence of the insurrection on aid from Cuban naturalized subjects of neutral states and other neutral sympathizers the war was destined to involve serious questions of neutral rights and obligations.

[4] See North American Review, Vol. 166, p. 560, for account of financial sources by H. S. Rubens, counsel of the American Delegation of the Cuban Revolutionary Party; also Senate Document 885, 55 Cong., 2 Sess., testimony of Mr. Guerra, Treasurer of the Cuban Delegation.

The insurrection, originally planned for six provinces, in reality was limited at the outset to three, Santiago, Santa Clara and Matanzas, all eastern regions, but it advanced steadily over the whole interior of the island. On September 16, 1895, the insurgents proclaimed the independence of Cuba and announced a provisional government.[5] During 1896 the insurrection spread into the western provinces, and Spain became convinced of the serious character of the contest before her. Marshal Martinez Campos, whose measured pacific policy failed to satisfy the Government at Madrid, was superseded by General Weyler, who had shortly before successfully quelled a Philippine insurrection. Spain put forth tremendous efforts to conquer Cuba. During the first thirteen months of war 121,326 soldiers and a vast quantity of military stores were transported 3000 miles by water for use in the island. The vigor and success with which the Government in Spain met that part of its problem was highly creditable; but in Cuba the army itself was obliged to meet geographical and climatic conditions which were probably well-nigh insuperable. The Cuban insurgents showed little respect in their conduct for the ordinary rules of warfare. They mercilessly plundered and robbed the plantations of loyalists, burned cane fields and closed sugar mills, or extorted large sums for exemption from depredations. Towns without garrisons were burned and loyal sympathizers driven into the forts which surrounded the cities. The object of the military policy of the rebel leaders was the exhaustion of Spanish wealth and of the sources

[5] The provisional government was scarcely more than a paper establishment. See Sen. Doc. 885, 55 Cong., 2 Sess.

of the Government's revenue, that the Spaniards might finally be driven from the island.[6]

General Weyler retaliated with an equally rigorous policy of repression, instituting the famous system of concentration by successive orders and proclamations.[7]

[6] Robinson, Intervention in Cuba, p. 44; Spanish Diplomatic Correspondence and Documents, pp. 32–33; House Document 405, 55 Cong., 2 Sess., p. 46; Sen. Document 25, 58 Cong., 2 Sess., p. 825; The Nation, Vol. 61, p. 73.

[7] General Weyler's *reconcentrado* proclamation of October 21, 1896, was as follows:

Havana, October 21, 1896.

Don Valeriano Weyler y Nicolau, Marquis of Teneriffe, Governor-General and Captain-General of this Island, and General-in-chief of its army, etc.

I order and command:

First. All the inhabitants of the country or outside of the line of fortifications of the towns shall within the period of eight days reconcentrate themselves in the town occupied by the troops. Any individual who after the expiration of this period is found in the uninhabited parts will be considered a rebel and tried as such.

Second. The extraction of provisions from the towns and their transportation from one town to another by land or water without permission of the military authority of the point of departure is absolutely prohibited. The infringers will be tried and punished as abettors of the rebellion.

Third. The owners of beeves should transport them to towns or their vicinity, to which end they will be given proper protection.

Fourth. At the expiration of the period of eight days, which in each municipal district shall be counted from the publication of this proclamation in the head town of same, all insurgents who present themselves shall be placed at my disposal for the purpose of fixing them a place where they shall reside, serving them as a recommendation if they furnish news of the enemy which can be made use of, if the presentation is made with firearms, and more especially if it be collective.

Fifth. The provisions of this proclamation are only applicable to the Province of Pinar del Rio.

VALERIANO WEYLER.

The inhabitants of the country districts, the producers upon whom the insurgents had depended, were given eight days within which to abandon their homes and repair to the fortified towns and cities where Spanish garrisons were stationed. All inhabitants found outside of the Spanish lines after the expiration of the eight days were to be treated as rebels, irrespective of age or sex. The decree contained an offer of pardon to insurgents laying down arms, and made clear the intention to devastate the abandoned country. The object was to draw distinctly the line between rebel and loyalist and to ensure the control of uncertain classes. The concentration of the producers was a signal blow to the resources of the insurgents. It was a military measure perfectly lawful in itself, provided the Spanish authorities could fulfil the corresponding obligations to protect the persons forced from their homes and could supply them with food. Concentration is not unknown in American practice in warfare. The most recent instances are the order of General Thomas Ewing, August 25, 1863, applied to the region around Kansas City, Missouri, and of General J. F. Bell, December 8, 1901, applied to Batangas, Philippine Islands.[8] In view of the mooted lawfulness of concentration it is quite noteworthy that no mention of it is made in the statement of the Laws and Customs of War on Land at the Hague Conference in 1899, so soon after the practice in Cuba had so forcibly brought the subject before the neutral powers.

The Spanish Treaty Claims Commission, having more recently to decide claims growing out of the insurrection, came to the conclusion that " concentra-

[8] Sen. Doc. 25, 58 Cong., 2 Sess., p. 125.

tion and devastation are legitimate war measures," but " when neutral foreigners are included in the removal or concentration of inhabitants, the government so removing or concentrating them must provide for them food and shelter, guard them from sickness and death and protect them from cruelty and hardship to the extent which the military exigency will permit."[9]

The real question concerns the conduct of the responsible military agents of Spain toward the obligations that the concentration of peaceably disposed inhabitants imposes. Upon the proclamation of General Weyler's orders the majority of the poorer peasants, women and children, with the helpless old men, accepted the enforced asylum of Spanish towns. Many able-bodied men joined the rebellion. Some escaped to the United States and neighboring countries, to become in time filibusters. No advance provision had been made for the care of the refugees or for the sanitation of their dwellings, and probably it was not within the power of the Spanish authorities under the circumstances to make adequate provision for such conditions. While the American consuls were convinced that the local authorities exerted all reasonable efforts to combat the evils of concentration, they were equally certain that the system produced great suffering of innocent non-combatants. The American press traced all the sufferings of the unfortunate indigent class, always large in Cuba, to the military system, and exaggerated the loss of population from concentration. The census report for Cuba taken in 1899 estimated the population in 1887 at 1,631,687, while the population in 1899 was 1,572,797. This was a loss of

[9] Sen. Doc. 25, 58 Cong., 2 Sess.

58,890 or 3.6 per cent. in 12 years of economic depression and a terrible war. If the increase of population remained the same as that for the more prosperous times before 1887, the population in 1895 would have been 1,800,000, which would give a loss of 200,000 from the combined results of starvation and death from disease incident to concentration, of loss in battle and in military operations, and of emigration. On the other hand, American opinion on the character of the war and the system of concentration in particular was based on current estimates of half a million. The loss of population was confined to the four western provinces, the two eastern making gains.[10]

Concentration as a military measure was an ill-advised expedient. Any system which forced able-bodied men into open rebellion, and which placed responsibility for the support of enemy dependents upon the Spanish authorities, was radically wrong. The complete success of the policy from the Spanish standpoint was dependent on the control of the interior of the island and the extension of fire and sword to the last resort of the insurgents. This Spain was never able to accomplish. Cuba was peculiarly fitted for insurgent warfare without a wide base of supplies. A few weeks in the tropical climate sufficed to secure fresh fodder and vegetables or fruits. To Spain the military benefits of concentration were slight as compared with the grave injuries. The concentration

[10] Report of Census of Cuba, War Department of the United States, Washington, 1900. See the results of personal study in the field by an English writer, Contemporary Review, July, 1898, Vol. 74, p. 1; Fortnightly, Vol. 69, p. 855; Foreign Relations of the United States, 1897, pp. 507 ff; Senate Document 240, 56 Cong., 2 Sess., " Consular Correspondence."

decrees continued the terrible retaliations and exacted needless sacrifices from the loyal portion of the Cuban population.

Any possible immediate military gains to Spain were more than offset by the moral effects of the inhumanity charged to her commanders and by the sympathy and —more tangible—the real legitimate aid from sympathizing persons from the nearby neutral states. Revolutionary agents in foreign countries gained vastly in their hold on public opinion, and in the end they were the only ones to profit by the system of concentration. In conclusion, Spain had full right to crush armed resistance, but on both sides there were certain elementary rights, among which was this one, that innocent non-combatants should not be needlessly illtreated or disturbed in their property rights and peaceable pursuits, but if this were unavoidable, at least they should not suffer untold misery as a result of an official military policy. From the standpoint of public law, only those in arms may be treated as enemies[11] and made to suffer the penalties of war. Not the system of concentration itself, but the administration of the particular military policy in Cuba violated this fundamental principle. That the decree was an extraordinary war measure, similar to the siege of a town, and justified by particular circumstances, or that the insurgents had previously violated similar rules, is no adequate answer.

The other aspect of the conduct of the war of which complaint was made concerned the character of the

[11] Hall, International Law, pp. 33, 412, 453; Wharton, Digest, sec. 338. Compare Laws and Customs of War formulated at Peace Conference of 1898, Holls, The Peace Conference, p. 157; Treaties of U. S. in Force, 1904.

forces employed by both the insurgents and Spain.
Each accused the other of resorting to the employment
of freebooters in warfare instead of properly organized, disciplined and uniformed men. A civil war
causes the most bitter animosities and retaliations, and
at the best irregularities are entirely too common.
But one is inclined to reject as without adequate evidence most of the current American stories of irregularities in this respect which were attributed to Spain.
War is always the opportunity of the lawless, and the
war in Cuba had a due number of criminal outrages,
but such outrages were in no way connected with the
official military policy. Guerrilla warfare in the sense
of fighting in small bands from hiding is not unlawful.
Only non-uniformed predatory guerrilla bands are
forbidden in civilized warfare. Governments regard
such persons as outlaws and may punish them as ordinary robbers and murderers. The essential requirements of a regular military force include a uniformed
soldiery, an army organization in form, using none but
permissible instruments in fighting, and then acting
only against similarly organized enemy forces.[12]

The military system employed to crush the rebellion
had more unfortunate results than those involved in
its lawfulness or unlawfulness. It increased the sympathy in America for the insurgents; a sympathy that
otherwise might have remained a sentiment became in
fact a moving impulse to be used by insurgent agents,
to be exploited by unscrupulous journals, and to be
appealed to by ambitious politicians. " Neither side
waged war with anything like the fury of the newspaper correspondents."[13] The name Spaniard became

[12] Wharton, Digest, sec. 351.
[13] The Nation, Vol. 62, p. 23.

undeservedly synonymous with butcher, and the contest was regarded as an outrage on modern civilization. The fact that all warfare is uncivilized and inhuman was lost sight of. The fact that it was to the interest of the Cubans to circulate inflammatory reports grossly exaggerating the cruelty of the enemy was not recognized, nor the equally significant one that the insurgents possessed a body of agents one of whose functions was to act through the American press in the interest of the Cuban cause.[14] The fact that the insurgents were more ferocious in their warfare than the Spaniards, and that whatever efforts were made to protect property and to ameliorate the conditions of the innocent inhabitants emanated from Spanish authorities, would surely not justify the violent attacks on Spain for the inhumanity of her methods of repression with which the American press teemed during the insurrection. There has been so much loose talk in the United States of recent years about the barbarous conduct of other states and about intervention that there is great need of some clearer conception of the relation of individual neutrals to the brutality of neighboring states. No one nation has been constituted by the others a sponsor for the morals of its neighbor in war or peace. Savage warfare, while condemned by international law, does not alone, except under unusual circumstances to be discussed later, warrant intervention by a neutral; and—which is the main fact in this connection—inhumanity of the

[14] Contemporary Review, Vol. 69, p. 41, Jan., 1896, " Five Weeks with the Insurgents." An Englishman's view. Shows false character of reports of the war from official sources on both sides.

belligerents does not in any manner alter the obligation of other states to maintain a strict and rigorous neutrality.

As American impatience with Spain in her failure to quell the Cuban revolt increased, and then gave place to a dislike for the people of Spain as a whole, a dislike very largely mistaken and unwarranted, the latter came more than ever to suspect the friendship and good faith of the United States, and this the more because of the alleged laxness in preventing its adopted citizens from furnishing aid to the rebels in Cuba. To Americans, Spain appeared to be able " neither to subdue Cuba nor to govern it; neither to keep the island nor let it go."[15] To Spaniards, the United States appeared no less lax in allowing its citizens to aid in prolonging the war.[16] There was, in short, a fundamental difference in the interpretation by two friendly powers of the obligations due one another in such a crisis. International law defines the obligations and rights of a neutral in time of war, but Cuba had no existence in international relations. The United States could not be a neutral in a strict sense until the belligerency of Cuba was recognized. The Cuban insurrection had not reached that point where the Government of the United States was willing to give it such recognition. The United States recognized a state of insurgency as existing in Cuba at an early date, but this did not make it a community recognizable in international law.[17] The recognition of independence, of belligerency or of insurgency each

[15] The Nation, Vol. 62, p. 389.
[16] Spanish Diplomatic Correspondence and Documents, p. 12.
[17] Insurgency recognized in President Cleveland's Proclamation of June 12, 1895, Richardson, Vol. IX, p. 591.

carries with it certain neutral rights and obligations. Those of the first two have been long understood and clearly defined, but insurgency is a new stage scarcely touched by the writers on the law of neutrality.[18] The recognition of insurgency, with the corresponding proclamation of neutrality that accompanied it, was a voluntary act of the United States, and was in effect an announcement to citizens of the United States that (a) an insurrection existed in Cuba temporarily beyond the control of Spain, (b) that the United States must have some relations with the insurgents, and (c) that in these relations the Government would enforce the municipal law on neutrality.[19] Spain could ask that the United States, a nation at peace with her, fulfill all treaty obligations and in a general way recognize the duties of amity and impartiality in relation to her internal affairs, and refrain from all official acts implying assistance, moral or material, indirect or direct, to the insurgents.[20]

The insurgents on their part acquired no rights over against neutrals when the United States recognized their insurgency, but they were no longer a mob from the standpoint of international law. The recognition of insurgency implied that in American opinion at least the insurgents were not *de facto* under the control of Spain, and it followed consequently that Spain could not be held liable to neutral citizens for their

[18] Professor Wilson, " Insurgency," in the American Journal of International Law, January, 1907, p. 49.

[19] Professor Wilson, Lecture on Insurgency at the Naval War College, 1900, p. 6.

[20] This does not affect the right to recognize the belligerency of insurgents under certain conditions, though doing so is naturally of moral, not to say material, assistance to any insurgent community.

acts. Insurgent depredations took the character of the unavoidable acts of warfare, which aliens residing in Cuba were forced to suffer.[21]

From early in 1896 there was a strong demand in the Congress of the United States for the recognition of Cuban belligerency. Such a resolution passed the Senate on February 28, 1896, and the House on April 6 following, but in American constitutional law the recognition of belligerency is an executive prerogative, and President Cleveland steadily opposed the step. He was in accord with a substantial number of Americans who believed at that time that the sovereignty of Spain in Cuba was essential to the welfare of the island, and who were content to hope that Spain could see its way to a grant of a larger measure of autonomy for the Cubans.[22] Spain at the time was confident of ultimate success, and insisted upon Cuban submission before making any extension of liberties.[23] In the United States, behind the Congressional sentiment favorable to Cuba, were an insistent few who had property interests in Cuba, owners of plantations, railroads and mines, estimated to be worth from $30,000,-

[21] Compare the rules of the Spanish Treaty Claims Commission with regard to the responsibility of Spain for the acts of the insurgents; Senate Doc. 25, 58 Cong., 2 Sess. See North American Review, May, 1906, p. 738, for Hannis Taylor, "The Spanish Treaty Claims." A view endorsed by a leading Spanish publicist, Marquis de Olivart, in *Revista de derecho internacional y política exterior,* Madrid, July, 1905. Other cases support the view. See Moore, Digest, Vol. VI, p. 972.

[22] Richardson, Vol. IX, pp. 719-20; Spanish Diplomatic Correspondence and Documents, p. 4; Sen. Doc. 56, 54 Cong., 2 Sess., for an examination of the constitutional power to recognize the independence of a new state.

[23] Spanish Diplomatic Correspondence and Documents, p. 8.

000 to $50,000,000.[24] With no less vigor merchants whose trade had been destroyed pressed for protection and intervention. A volume of commerce with Cuba which amounted to nearly $96,000,000 in 1894 fell to one half in 1896, and to still less as the insurrection progressed. Total exports estimated at $60,000,000 in 1895 were only $15,000,000 in the following year.[25] For this loss of trade the United States had no legal pacific remedy, nor had her subjects been specially wronged by Spain. One power has no ground of action if a friendly state with which it is in trading relations chooses to destroy by process of devastation incurred in a serious internecine conflict any part or all of the domestic industries. So long as public war is permitted to exist, neutrals must suffer with belligerents, non-combatants with combatants. That they should have to do so is, however, an anomaly of the age. Only when that process of devastation extended to American-owned property, fulfilled no useful military end, and when the innocent subjects of the United States were deprived of personal liberty and denied adequate protection, would the Government of the United States have had any occasion to address Spain for satisfaction, and then if denied redress, to resort to armed force. Where American subjects were in any way parties to the insurrection, and had forfeited all right to appeal to the United States for protection,

[24] American Investments in Cuba, For. Rel. U. S., 1896, p. 711; Richardson, Vol. IX, p. 718; An. Am. Acad. Pol. Sc., Vol. VII, p. 81; Forum, Vol. XXII, p. 371; Viallate, Revue historique, Vol. 82, p. 248.

[25] In more detail the effect of the insurrection on trade is indicated by the record of the production of sugar: Total produced, 1894–5, 1,004,264 tons; 1895–6, 225,221 tons; 1896–7, 212,051 tons; 1897–8, 204,123 tons; 1898–9, 25,098 tons.

treaties with Spain of 1795 and 1877 guaranteed them trial in civil courts, unless taken in open arms, and, whether taken in arms or not, the same treaties conferred the right to counsel, to witnesses in defense and to a public trial.[26]   However, personal claims for indemnity and commercial differences strained at all times diplomatic relations.

Owing to the absorbing character of domestic politics, American interest in the insurrection subsided considerably as the second year of the war drew to a close, but on December 7, 1896, the President's message recounted the grave interest of the United States in the prolonged conflict in Cuba.   On the subject of Cuban independence and belligerent rights the position of the administration remained unchanged.   President Cleveland noted that while the insurgents held two thirds of the island, their civil government had been a failure. Belligerent rights were, he said, no longer to be thought of.   The conclusion was that such an action would be untimely and injurious to American interests.[27]

Authorities have differed in their criticisms upon the conduct of the Government of the United States in withholding recognition of the belligerency of the Cubans at this time.   All agree that recognition is an executive prerogative; that neither Spain nor the Cubans could demand it of the United States; that if it had been accorded it must have been as an act of grace on the part of the United States, prompted by

[26] Treaties and Conventions of the United States, pp. 1008, 1030.
[27] Richardson, Vol. IX, pp. 717, 719. A Spanish criticism of the message in Revue de droit international public, 1905, pp. 469–92.

the consideration that the war affected its interests too greatly to be longer ignored.[28] It may be said here that from the standpoint of international law the recognition of belligerency legalizes, as it were, the hostilities of the new community and the military measures required to secure the final object, independence, and is, therefore, generally disadvantageous to the neutral conceding it. The neutral must then observe neutral duties toward two combatants. The parent state ceases to be responsible for the fulfilment of international obligations in territories under insurgent control, though in the latter respect the recognition of insurgency has the same effect. If possible the recognition of belligerency binds to stricter neutrality than does the recognition of insurgency. In the particular case in point, to grant belligerent rights to Cuba was to give Spain the right to search the merchant ships under the flag of the United States on the high seas for contraband goods, a right not otherwise possessed.[29] As Spain controlled the ports of commerce on the Cuban coast and the insurgents had no ships or ports of their own, the latter could not have shared the rights conferred by the new status. The insurgents were, on their part, in no position to take advantage of any belligerent rights in the way of blockade or restriction of contraband trade with their enemy. Their dependence on the importation of arms and munitions made it to their interest that the line of contraband trade, right of search to prevent such trade, and the like should not be more clearly drawn.

[28] Hall, International Law, p. 35; Wharton, Digest, Vol. III, sec. 381.
[29] Professor Wilson, the American Journal of International Law, Jan., 1907, p. 52.

The recognition of the belligerency of the insurgents could not have greatly affected belligerent relations. The obligation to carry on war under the reasonable humanities of modern warfare is binding on all civilized communities alike. Whatever advantages they might have reaped would have been in the nature of prestige and encouragement. It is by no means certain that these under the circumstances would not have been considerable. Such recognition would have implied that the United States thought the insurgents able to fulfill neutral obligations. It was doubt of the ability of the insurgent government to fulfil the obligations of neutrality which prevented President Cleveland from according belligerent rights. As recognition implies success to a certain extent, the insurgents would have gained a better standing for borrowing money, purchasing supplies and enlisting recruits. It is clear that recognition gives an insurgent body moral assistance, but the giving of such assistance is indirect and is the only kind that it is lawful for a neutral to give. In view of the effect on mutual rights it is eminently proper that a neutral granting belligerent rights should do so only for reasons adequate to itself. It is no offence to the parent state to take the step if the seriousness of the civil war warrants it, but to do so prematurely is a grave wrong. The reasons which will justify it vary with circumstances. Manifestly a neighboring state, intimately affected by the war, may do so when a distant power would not be at all justified. There should exist at least a regular de facto political organization capable of discharging the ordinary duties of a state, and a military organization acting in accordance with the rules and customs of war. These are essential conditions. If the insurgent government in addition possesses ports and a naval force on the high seas, the reasons for recognition become almost mandatory on the neutrals.[30] These tests, when applied to the Cuban insurrection, show convincingly that the little more than paper civil government which existed there was not enough. The military system which actually conducted the war was not a de facto government in the regular sense, and to have conceded belligerency at any time before American intervention would have been an instance of unwarranted haste.

After having examined in the light of international law the military system of concentration and the effect of insurgency, and having tested the obligations of the United States to accord belligerency to the Cubans, we may take up the task of examining American neutral conduct toward the parties to the war. The Cuban cause was largely dependent on its friends abroad. The insurgent organization included Cubans residing in the neighboring countries, and the strongest of these revolutionary societies had its headquarters in New York City.[31] The functions of the organiza-

[30] Hershey, Annals of the American Academy, Vol. VII, p. 450; J. B. Moore, Forum, Vol. XXI, p. 288; Woolsey, American Foreign Policy, p. 25; Hall, International Law, pp. 35, 36.
[31] The New York Delegation included: President Don Tomas Estrada Palma, who had served as President of the republic overthrown in 1878; Treasurer Benjamin Guerra; Secretary Gonzalo Quesada; Minister of War Roloff, who personally conducted at least four expeditions of relief; the Director of Supplies for the Cuban Armies, Brigadier-General Emilio Nunez, who personally directed some eight relief expeditions; and the Under-Secretary of the Treasury, Dr. Joaquin Castillo y Dussay.

tions wherever they existed were to procure funds by
contributions from those interested in Cuba, to invest
the money in supplies, and to transport both recruits
and supplies safely to Cuba.[82]

No less than seventy-one expeditions were fitted
out in the United States in aid of Cuba during the
insurrection. Of this number twenty-seven were
successfully landed in Cuba; of the forty-four failures
the United States authorities stopped thirty-three, the
Spanish five, storms thwarted four, and the English
interfered with two. Thirty-one separate vessels were
engaged more or less constantly in the services of the
Cubans. Among these the *Laurada*, the *Commodore*,
and the *Bermuda*, an English boat, made five trips
each. The *Three Friends* made eight, and the *Dauntless* twelve; the *Horsa*, a Danish boat, made two voyages, the *George W. Childs* two, the *Donna T. Briggs*
two, and the *Monarch* three. The captains constituted a sort of Cuban naval service. The commanders
and crew were generally American, with some English and Danish. The pilots were Cubans. The passengers taken to enlist in insurgent armies were also
generally Cubans returning from an exile.[83] The his-

[82] Cuban contributors to relief funds in the United States
are said to have numbered 40,000. Descriptions of methods of
raising funds in Carlisle, Report, Vol. II, pp. 35, 39. In Cuba
the insurgents prohibited the production of sugar except by
certain favored planters, who in return for the concession
advanced fifty cents per sack of their sugar on the estimated
crops. See Revue de droit international public, Vol. V, 1898,
pp. 358, 499, for two excellent articles by Marquis de Olivart,
ancien député aux Cortès, associé de l'Institut de droit international, on filibustering. The writer is very hostile to the
laxness of the American Government.

[83] Carlisle, Report, Vol. II, p. 34.

tory of the activities of the representatives of the Cuban insurrection in the United States and elsewhere is a monumental evidence of the efficiency of that service and of the abilities of the men engaged in it.[34]

[34] TABLE OF FILIBUSTERING EXPEDITIONS FROM UNITED STATES FROM MARCH, 1895, TO APRIL, 1898. COMPILED BY M. DE OLIVART IN REVUE DE DROIT INTERNATIONAL PUBLIC, VOL. V, 1898

Date	Name of Ship	Leader Where Known	Cause of Failure	Result Where Brought into Court
Mar. 1, 1895	Amadis, Lagonda, Baracoa		U. S. Revenue Cutters	
" 18, "	(Arms seized at Wilmington)		U. S. Revenue Cutters	
June 4, "	Geo. W. Childs	Roloff	Storm	Fined for violation of Passenger Act
July 9, "	Woodall	"		Dr. Luis condemned by U. S. Dist. Court, March 27, 1897, to 18 months' imprisonment. Roloff forfeited bail. Smith fled
Aug. 2, "	Geo. W. Childs	Maya and Rodriguez	U. S. Revenue Cutters	
" 14, "	Leon	P. Sanchez	U. S. Revenue Cutters	Case released Sept. 23, 1895
" 30, "	Laurada	P. Carrillo		
" 30, "	(Provisions seized at Cedar Keys)		U.S. Revenue Cutters	Released by order of the Attorney
Sept. 11, "	Commodore		U.S. Revenue Cutters	Released Sept. 22, 1895
" 17, "	Lark		U. S. Revenue Cutters	Released Sept. 22, 1895
" 18, "	(Expeditions to Florida)		U. S. Revenue Cutters	
" 20, "	Antoinette		U. S. Revenue Cutters	Released Sept. 20, 1895
Oct. 8, "	James Woodall		U. S. Revenue Cutters	
" 10, "	Delaware	" "	English Authorities	
" 21, "	Laurada	" "		Released Jan. 23, 1896
Nov. 9, "	Horsa	Cespedes		Wiborg and 2 sailors condemned by Dist. Court March 17, 1896. Affirmed by Sup. Court in case of Wiborg, May 25, 1896

TABLE OF FILBUSTERING EXPEDITIONS FROM UNITED STATES FROM MARCH, 1895, TO APRIL, 1898. COMPILED BY M. DE OLIVART IN REVUE DE DROIT INTERNATIONAL PUBLIC, VOL. V, 1898.—*Continued*

Date	Name of Ship	Leader Where Known	Cause of Failure	Result Where Brought into Court
Nov. 22, 1895.	James W. Forster		U. S Revenue Cutters	
Dec. 6, "	(Expedition from Cape Sable)	Carrillo	U. S. Revenue Cutters	
Jan. 25, 1896	Hawkins	C. Garcia	Shipwreck	
Feb. 4, "	Isaac N. Veasey		U. S. Revenue Cutters	
" 24, "	Bermuda	" "	U. S. Revenue Cutters	Released April 10, 1896
" 28, "	Three Friends			
Mar. 12, "	Commodore			
" 15, "	Bermuda			Released by disagreement of jury
April 20, "	Bermuda	Leite Vidal	Spanish Authorities	Released July 7, 1896
" 23, "	Competitor	Monzon	Spanish Authorities	
May 8, "	Laurada	F. Ruiz		Released by disagreement of jury
" 23, "	Three Friends	Leite		Liberated by D. C., Jan. 18, 1897. Remanded for new trial by S. C., Mar. 1, 1897
June 24, "	" "			
" 17, "	Commodore	Bethancourt		
July 17, "	Three Friends	Counspierre		
Aug. 5, "	Laurada and Dauntless	Roloff and Nunez		Hart condemned D. C., Feb. 23, 1897, affirmed S. C., Jan. 19, 1898
" 15, "	Three Friends	Castillo	U. S. Revenue Cutters	
Sept. 2, "	" "			
" 22, "	Unique		U. S. Revenue Cutters	
Oct. 5, "	Dauntless	"	Spanish Authorities	
" 6, "	Commodore		U. S. Revenue Cutters	
" 20, "	Dauntless		U. S. Ships of War	Fined $1200
Nov. 8, "	Three Friends		U. S. Revenue Cutters	
Dec. 4, "	Vaamose		U. S. Revenue Cutters	
" 26, "	Inca and Eighty-three		U. S. Revenue Cutters	
" 14, "	Three Friends	Arnao	Spanish Authorities	
" 31, "	Commodore	Pablo Rojo	Shipwreck	
Jan. 2, 1897	Dauntless	Arnao	Spanish Authorities	
Feb. 27, "	Laurada	Roloff and Castillo		

TABLE OF FILIBUSTERING EXPEDITIONS FROM UNITED STATES FROM MARCH, 1895, TO APRIL, 1898. COMPILED BY M. DE OLIVART IN REVUE DE DROIT INTERNATIONAL PUBLIC, VOL. V, 1898.—*Continued*

Date	Name of Ship	Leader Where Known	Cause of Failure	Result Where Brought into Court
Mar. 3, 1897	Monarch		U. S. Ship of War	
" 15, "	"	Amieba		
" 30, "	"		U. S. Revenue Cutters	
April 3, "	Bermuda	Sanguilly	U. S. Ship of War	
" 9, "	"	"	U. S. Revenue Cutters	
" 22, "	Expedition	"	U. S. Revenue Cutters	
May 20, "	Dauntless	Nunez		
" 30, "	Dauntless and Byscaine	"	U. S. Ship of War	Fined
June 16, "	Dauntless		U. S. Revenue Cutters	
" 26, "	"		U. S. Ship of War	
Aug. 6, "	Douglas (Horsa)		U. S. Revenue Cutters	
" 7, "	Blanche Morgan		U. S. Revenue Cutters	
Sept. 28, "	Sommers N. Smith and DonnaT.Briggs (Expedition from Tallahassee,Fla.)			
" —, "	(Expedition to Bahia Honda)		U. S. Revenue Cutters	
Oct. 9, "	Silver Heels			
" 19, "	Dauntless			
Nov. 19, "	"			
Dec. 4, "	DonnaT. Briggs			
" 6, "	——			
Jan. —, 1898			Spanish Authorities	
" 23, "	Tillie		Shipwreck	
" —, "	Cora M.		English Authorities	
Feb. 13, "	(Expedition 70 men with arms. "The World" states 6 others on same day.)			
" 20, "	Dauntless			
" 25, "	"			
Mar. 19, "	William J. Parker		U. S. Revenue Cutters	

The Cuban insurrection was in fact opened by expeditions loaded with arms and men which started from near-by neutral states. On March 1, 1895, the authorities of the United States intercepted three boats, the *Amadis,* the *Lagonda* and the *Baracoa,* ready to leave American waters.[35] A few days later the customs officials seized a quantity of arms at Wilmington, Delaware. These incidents occasioned a special proclamation by President Cleveland on June 12, 1895, calling attention to the civil disturbances in Cuba and warning American citizens of the penalties incurred in violating the neutrality laws.[36] The same admonition was repeated in his message to Congress, on December 2, 1895. There is no doubt, however, that during the war a continuous stream of supplies, arms, ammunition and reënforcements poured into Cuba.

Several of these expeditions became the occasion of judicial interpretations of the neutrality laws of the United States, and hence made clear American views of the obligations of neutrality during an insurrection not dignified by a recognition of belligerency.

On August 29, 1895, the tug *Taurus* left Wilmington, Delaware, with twenty passengers and twenty-seven cases of arms and ammunition aboard to wait in the main channel of the river for the *Laurada*. After waiting until late the following morning, the owners of the tug became alarmed and landed the arms and ammunition at Pennsgrove, New Jersey. The delay was fatal to the success of the expedition. The United States gunboat *Meteor* seized the *Taurus* and her cargo and forced the tug to return with her passengers to Wilmington, where the leaders of the party were indicted under the Neutrality Act, which[37] imposes a penalty upon " every person who within the

[35] Carlisle, Report, Vol. I, p. 28.
[36] Richardson, Vol. IX, pp. 591, 636.
[37] U. S. *v.* Pena, 69 Fed. Rep. 983, Sept. 23, 1895; Carlisle, Report, Vol. I, p. 28.

territory of the United States . . . sets on foot . . . any military expedition . . . against . . . any foreign prince or state . . . with whom the United States are at peace." The case was dependent on the interpretation of the expressions " within the territory of the United States " and " any military expedition." Judge Wales of the District Court for Delaware defined the latter as " a military organization of some kind, designated as infantry, cavalry or artillery, officered and equipped or in readiness to be officered and equipped for active hostile operations, and," he continued, " the preparing the means for such an organization would undoubtedly come within the inhibition of the law. But this would constitute only one element or part of the offense charged against the defendants. To complete the offense, it must be proved that the means were provided within the United States and that the expedition was to be carried on from thence against the dominions or territory of the king of Spain." Under this construction it was not surprising that the jury returned an acquittal for the accused. The *Laurada* came before the courts a second time early in 1896. She left New York on October 21, 1895, ostensibly for Kingston, Jamaica, but after passing Sandy Hook two tugs transferred to her thirty-five men, some boxes and three small boats. Apparently soon after starting the arms in the boxes were distributed among the men and some military exercises practiced. The expedition was safely landed on the Cuban coast, whence it joined the insurgents. The *Laurada* proceeded to Jamaica and on the return trip took a cargo of fruit to New York. Later in Charleston, South Carolina, the captain, Samuel Hughes, was indicted on the same charge that had been brought against Pena. The charge of Judge Brawley to the jury gave substantially the same definition of a military expedition that Judge Wales had given.[88] To him the elements—men and arms—were not combined in this case in so full a measure as to constitute a military expedition. "The uncombined elements," he said, "of an expedition may leave a neutral state in company with one another, provided they are incapable of proximate combination into an organized whole . . . It would be different if the men had previously received such military training as would have rendered them fit for closely proximate employment." In substance, in the acquittal which followed, the jury decided that the expedition which landed on Cuban soil was not in an effective state for hostilities until it had joined the insurgents and been incorporated into their ranks.

On February 24, 1896, the *Bermuda,* regularly signed for Santa Martha, Jamaica, with sixty unarmed men aboard, was lying at anchor a little below Liberty Island. With the *Bermuda* were the *Hawkins* and the tugboat *MacCaldin Brothers,* each having on board passengers, mostly Cubans. Farther down the bay the tug *Stranahan* was stationed with military arms and equipment. Calixto Garcia was in charge of the whole. Before the expedition could get under way a revenue cutter seized several of the passengers, among whom were Calixto Garcia, Hart, Hughes, Guerra, Bueno Brabanzon and Micchaleno, all leading Cuban agents in the United States, and they were charged with violation of the neutrality laws. The

[88] 70 Fed. Rep. 972; 75 Fed. Rep. 267.

accused were acquitted in the Circuit Court of the United States, April 9, 1896.[39] Judge Brown's charge to the jury enumerated five elements which in his opinion were essential to a military expedition. These were (1) soldiers, (2) officers, (3) arms, (4) action as a body bound together by an organization under a definite command, and (5) a determined hostile purpose of attack or defence. Not all the elements need be present from the outset, but it is especially necessary that the elements should be combined before reaching the scene of action. Here again the jury was not convinced that in the particular case enough of the elements were combined to constitute more than a legal commerce in arms and transportation of passengers.

The *Bermuda* made two expeditions in quick succession in March and April, 1896, and in both instances on the return of the leaders to the United States they were arrested, but finally released. In the second trial the statement of Judge Wilson, July 7, 1896, made the case turn on the point that the juncture of the elements had been made outside of the territorial waters of the United States. This feature was carefully noted by the Cuban leaders, and the majority of the subsequent expeditions started as separate elements to be joined at some point on the high seas.

This latter phase of filibustering came up for special adjudication as a result of an expedition of the *Lau-*

[39] U. S. *v.* Hart et al., 74 Fed. Rep. 725. Hart was the charterer of several vessels, American and foreign, engaged in the Cuban service. He was tried four times on filibustering charges and only once convicted. Carlisle, Report, Vol. II, p. 33.

4

rada, May 8, 1896. Several tugs met the *Laurada* at Montauk Point, where men, arms and munitions of war were duly transferred. Once on the high seas the expedition was placed under the command of General Ruiz, arms were distributed, and the men drilled as much as the ship's quarters would permit. The expedition ultimately joined the forces of the insurgents in Cuba. The organizer, Nunez, returned to New York, where he was indicted and tried. The essential question was whether the arms and men were combined and in a state to offer war without further organization. Judge Brown said that if the men, " when they landed in Cuba landed with arms in their hands, which had been provided for their use; and were then organized together in such a way that they could stand by each other and fight their way if necessary and defend themselves, or make attack, as the case might be, that would be in fact a military descent upon the Island of Cuba, and the organization or combination would be a military combination—a military enterprise."[40]

Some months before this decision, however, another case had been carried before the Supreme Court and a judgment secured which had a greater influence on filibustering methods. The *Horsa,* a Danish steamer sailing under the Danish flag, left Philadelphia, November 9, 1895. After passing Cape May she turned northward, proceeding as far as Barnegat. At a safe point three or four miles out in the high seas a steam lighter from Brooklyn transferred to her some cases of goods and thirty or forty passengers, mostly

[40] 82 Fed. Rep. 599. Circuit Court, S. D. New York, Nov. 19, 1896. The jury failed to agree on a verdict.

Cubans. The expedition was organized on board in the usual manner, by distributing arms and drilling in squads of three to seven. The steamship followed the usual course to Jamaica, only turning aside as she passed the Cuban coast to disembark the filibusters and their munitions of war. On the return to the United States, Wiborg, the captain, and Petersen and Johansen, the mates, were indicted and tried in the Federal District Court for Eastern Pennsylvania.[41] Here it was decided that the expedition constituted a military expedition or enterprise within the meaning of the law, and the defendants were sentenced to pay fines and to serve terms of imprisonment. It should be noted that the expedition differed in no particular from preceding cases where the Government failed to convict. The defendants appealed to the Supreme Court on a writ of error. According to Chief Justice Fuller,[42] in order to constitute a military organization it was not necessary that the men be drilled, put in uniform, or prepared for efficient service. It was sufficient that they had combined and organized to go to Cuba to make war on the Spanish Government, and had provided themselves with the means of doing so. This view destroyed the contention of the defence that filibustering enterprises were not in an efficient state until they had been incorporated into the insurgent army. To convict Wiborg and his associates it became a material question to determine whether they were responsible for the *Horsa's* undertaking. The court had said that it was necessary that

[41] 73 Fed. Rep. 159; Carlisle, Report, Vol. I, p. 30.
[42] Chief Justice Fuller delivered the opinion of the court, Justice Harlan dissenting. May 25, 1896. Wiborg v. United States, 163 U. S. 632.

the defendants should know when they started from Philadelphia that they were carrying a military enterprise. The conclusion was that the act of getting ready to sail and of taking aboard the two boats at Philadelphia constituted a preparation within the meaning of the law. Such an opinion gave a new and more rigorous interpretation of the question of what constituted a " preparation." A distinction was made in the cases of the mates—Petersen and Johansen —on the ground that there was little evidence that the subordinates knew of the real character of the enterprise. The decision of the District Court in the case of the mates was reversed and the causes were remanded for a new trial.

The significance of the *Horsa* decision was succinctly stated in the Nation: " The decision   is not primarily against the Cubans nor in favor of Spain. It is simply an interpretation and application of municipal law—known as the neutrality laws. Those laws are meant for the protection of our own Government and people. They do not relate, by direct intent, to our duty under international law, but are meant to prevent our citizens, or aliens under our jurisdiction from involving us in war with other countries. The principal point in the decision is the clear definition of what is meant, in the neutrality laws, by a military expedition. The lower courts have held conflicting opinions, but now, of course, will be bound by the definition of the Supreme Court."[48]

The practical consequences toward preventing further organized expeditions in aid of the Cubans were less than might have been expected. The following

[48] The Nation, Vol. 62, p. 408.

letter from Tomas Estrada Palma to the Insurgent Secretary of Foreign Affairs, dated from New York, September 10, 1896, is self-explanatory:

" I have the pleasure of enclosing a copy of a letter which Colonel Nunez has sent me from Key West since his return from Cuba. Three large expeditions, carrying 3900 guns, 1,250,000 cartridges, 12 cannon, 22 mortars, a park of artillery, 600 machetes, 1000 pounds of dynamite, electrical batteries, etc., have been successfully dispatched. Realizing the importance of employing the month of August for expeditions, Castillo and Nunez, of Rubens' staff, and myself have taken the necessary measures to carry them through, in spite of the temporary interruption caused by the arbitrary attitude of the government at Washington. The plan is to send in one vessel engaged for the purpose two thirds of the cargo, in a second the last third with some men, and the greater part of the force in a third. The second and the third, after meeting the first, are to take the cargo of the latter and proceed, one of them to Pinar del Rio and the other to Camaguy."[44]

The Supreme Court decision in the *Horsa* case inspired President Cleveland's message of July 27, 1896, in which the recent construction of the neutrality laws was quoted and enforcement accordingly ordered.[45]

What was intended by the New York Junta as the expedition *par excellence* occurred in August, 1896. The *Laurada* left Philadelphia on the last day of July for Wilmington, Delaware. There she took out

[44] De Olivart, Revue de droit international public, Vol. V, 1898, p. 399.
[45] Richardson, Vol. IX, p. 694.

papers for Port Antonio. Up to this point the voyage
had been perfectly innocent in form, and there were
on board neither arms nor men. From Wilmington
she proceeded into the open sea off Barnegat, where
three tugboats from New York, the *Fox*, the *Dolphin*
and the *Green Point*, were awaiting her. The *Fox*
had on board a few passengers, among whom were
the noted filibusters, Nunez and Roloff. On the other
tugs were boxes of arms and munitions of war. The
whole was duly transhipped to the *Laurada*. The
expedition then sailed for the Island of Navassa, situated in the Windward Passage, between Haiti and
Jamaica. Here the *Laurada* expected to meet three
ships, the *Three Friends*, the *Commodore* and the
Dauntless. However, the *Dauntless* only was at the
rendezvous ready for her part, and she accordingly
made two trips to Cuba with the *Laurada's* load, thus
completing the expedition. Apparently in a technical
sense the *Laurada* had not carried a military expedition under the interpretation of that expression by the
courts of the United States. The *Laurada* completed
the voyage to Port Antonio and returned to the United
States. Hart, the president and manager of the J. D.
Hart Company, owners of the *Laurada*, and Murphy,
the captain, were in due time brought into court,
charged with violating the neutrality laws. Hart was
condemned to two years' imprisonment and a fine of
five hundred dollars. Murphy was acquitted.[46] An
appeal of Hart to the Circuit Court on a writ of error
resulted in an affirmation of the judgment of the lower
court.[47]

[46] 78 Fed. Rep. 868; 84 Fed. Rep. 619.
[47] Jan. 18, 1898, 84 Fed. Rep. 799; Moore, Digest, Vol. VII,
pp. 915–16.

Judge Butler's charge to the jury followed in general the definitions of the Supreme Court in United States v. *Horsa,* but went further toward making difficult all prevailing forms of aid to the Cubans. He said: " It is unimportant that the organization is rudimentary, imperfect and inefficient; it is enough to meet the requirements of the statute that the men have united and organized with the purpose above stated, voluntarily agreeing to submit themselves to the orders of such person or persons as they have selected. . . . Nor is it important whether the expedition intends to make war as an independent body or in combination with others in the foreign country." In the same case the court declared that " a combination of a number of men in the United States, with a common intent to proceed in a body to a foreign country and engage in hostilities, either by themselves or in coöperation with the others, against a power with which the United States is at peace, constitutes a military expedition, when they actually proceed from the United States, whether they are then provided with arms or intend to secure them in transit. It is not necessary that all the persons shall be brought into personal contact with each other in the United States, or that they shall be drilled, uniformed or prepared for efficient service." The decision clearly established the principle that to secure a conviction in the courts of the United States it would not be necessary to show that the defendant had provided the means for carrying the expedition in question to Cuba, but that if he provided the means for any part of its journey with knowledge of its ultimate destination and of its unlawful character he was guilty. The construction made unlawful the expedient of using some point like the Island of Navassa as a destination for the original expedition and forwarding it thence in another vessel. The final conviction of Hart, January 18, 1898, came too near the American intervention to affect filibustering appreciably.

Two cases of another character will complete the review of the judicial interpretations of the neutrality law during the Cuban insurrection. Section 5283 forbids fitting out and arming vessels in favor of one foreign prince or power as against another with which the United States is at peace. There were few complaints of the violation of this part of the law. A charge was brought against the *Three Friends* for an expedition of May 23, 1896, when it was claimed that the vessel was fitted out and armed in the waters of the United States with the intent of serving the Cuban insurgents. She was seized on November 7, 1896, by the collector of customs for the District of St. Johns, Florida, as forfeited, and a suit of libel in forfeiture was duly entered in the District Court for the Southern District of Florida for condemnation of the vessel. The case was not finally disposed of until after the declaration of war against Spain, May 10, 1898, when it was finally dismissed in the Circuit Court of Appeals, Fifth Circuit, on the ground that there was not sufficient evidence that the vessel had been equipped or armed in any degree within the limits of the United States. This was an affirmation of the decision of the lower court.[48] During the course of the trial the case was carried before the Supreme Court on a writ of certiorari, in this instance owing to the release of the *Three Friends* by the District Court during the trial.

[48] See 78 Fed. Rep. 175 and 89 Fed. Rep. 207.

The Supreme Court ordered the District Court to re-sume custody of the vessel and to proceed with the case.[49] Judge Locke of the District Court had ad-vanced the doctrine that Section 5283, where it forbids fitting out vessels to be " employed in the service of any foreign prince or state, or of any colony, district or people, to cruise or commit hostilities against sub-jects, citizens or property of any foreign prince or state or of any colony, district or people with whom the United States are at peace," referred to a body politic which had been recognized by the Government of the United States at least as a belligerent. Chief Justice Fuller, in discussing this question, gave the opinion that the recognition of belligerency was un-necessary, and that it was enough that a state of insur-gency existed. The repeated acts of the administra-tion in recognizing the insurgency of the Cubans were all that was required within the meaning of the statute in question.

A similar suit was brought against the *Laurada* after her expedition of February, 1897. The original intention had been to transfer her load to another ves-sel at San Salvador, but after waiting eight days she undertook to complete the journey alone. According to the charge several cannon in the cargo were " rigged up " on wheels at suitable places on deck for protec-tion " against the Spanish men-of-war," and the arms aboard distributed among the passengers. The libel was in the end dismissed through a lack of evidence to show an original intent to arm against Spain. The position was taken that forfeiture under Section 5283 could not occur unless it was shown that those in com-

[49] March 1, 1897. 166 U. S. 1.

mand, while within the limits of the United States, had planned to commit hostilities. The opinion, however, declared that the arming and fitting need not necessarily be done within the limits of the United States to come under the penalties of the law of neutrality. The essential element was the intent that it should be so fitted out and should ultimately commit hostilities.[50]

From what has been written it will be seen that there were two quite distinct periods of filibustering. In the first, which precedes the decision of the Supreme Court in the *Horsa* case, May 25, 1896, less effort was made to avoid the technicalities of the law, and men and arms were joined on the same ship, if not from the port of departure, at least before entirely leaving American waters. The ship made a false declaration as to freight and destination, pretending to carry fruit or furniture to some port of Jamaica or Mexico or Venezuela. In the second period the expeditions became more complicated. The men and arms were transported in separate ships to the high seas or even into Spanish waters, and in some cases leaders went so far as to provide a third ship to effect the junction of men and arms. Whenever the enforcement of the neutrality laws of the United States became too severe, Canada, Jamaica, Belgium or some one of a number of other neutral states became the starting point for supplies.[51]

The decisions during the Cuban insurrection established certain valuable principles in the interpretation of the act of neutrality of 1818 which had remained

[50] U. S. *v. Laurada,* March 1, 1898, 85 Fed. Rep. 760.
[51] Foreign Relations, 1898, p. 665.

obscure, in particular with reference to relations with insurgents not recognized as belligerents, and to the legal aid permissible for American subjects. It was established that a declaration of belligerency is not necessary to bring into force municipal neutrality acts; that they act against insurgent bodies not recognized as belligerent states. The several opinions present more satisfactory definitions and constructions of such important terms as "a military expedition," "a preparation of a hostile expedition," "a continuous expedition," "a combination with intent," and "limits of the United States" as applied to fitting out. Here the judiciary showed a laudable purpose to interpret the obligations of neutrality as rigorously as could be desired, and laid down rules which rendered illegal the whole elaborate system of filibustering operated from American soil. It would appear from the decisions that the neutrality act was in itself adequate to enable the United States to meet its international obligations to the fullest degree.[52]

The Spanish Government made frequent diplomatic complaints and protests on the enforcement of the neutrality laws of the United States. Their representations were especially insistent that the Cuban Junta, "sitting publicly in New York," should be prosecuted.[53] In American law the residence of individuals of Cuban sympathies and the giving of individual aid to Cubans, as well as the meetings of the Junta, were not only in no way a violation of the law of the United States, but just such acts constitute the fundamental

[52] Carlisle, Report, Vol. II, p. 48; Hall, International Law, p. 614.
[53] Spanish Diplomatic Correspondence and Documents, p. 76.

guarantees of the American system which international law may supplement without contravening.[54] This was the view of President Cleveland in his fourth annual message to Congress. " Many Cubans reside in this country and indirectly promote the insurrection through the press, by public meetings, by the purchase and shipment of arms, by the raising of funds, and by other means which the spirit of our institutions and the tenor of our laws do not permit to be made the subject of criminal prosecutions."[55] The war in Cuba did not alter the right of citizens of the United States to carry on trade with the Cubans, insurgents or loyalists, and to carry on trade even in war material, subject always, of course, to the risk that Spanish ships of war would seize and confiscate the cargoes within their coast seas. It is a well-established principle that no government can be held accountable for the traffic of its citizens in military supplies so long as they do not furnish these to a visiting man-of-war or an expeditionary force. The duty of the government is fulfilled when it warns subjects of the risk of loss which they incur by engaging in such trade.[56] It is well known that a few months later in the war with Spain the United States bought more than one million dollars' worth of arms and munitions of war in England, and that Spain did the same in Europe. The legality of this commerce all recognized.[57] Spanish complaint was, of course, directed against organized expeditions

[54] Moore, Digest, Vol. VII, p. 909. Spanish Diplomatic Correspondence and Documents, p. 92.

[55] Richardson, Vol. IX, p. 718.

[56] Woolsey, American Foreign Policy, p. 44.

[57] See North American Review, Vol. CLXXIV, p. 687; American Law Review, Vol. XXXI, p. 62.

fitted out on United States soil to aid the Cubans, a practice illegal by the municipal law of the United States. In this respect the number of prosecutions and frustrated expeditions indicated constant effort to enforce the restrictions on aid given by Americans, but lack of power to entirely control the situation. President McKinley admitted as much in his message, April 11, 1898.[58] The executive of a great state ought to have had better support from local agencies in enforcing laws undoubtedly regularly violated.[59] The laxness of local government is the scandal of the American system of government and a constant international humiliation. The interpretation of obligations by the higher courts was creditably rigorous. The sole burden of preventing filibustering was not, however, upon the United States. Spain could exact only reasonable vigilance on the part of the authorities, not perfect vigilance; the test of the Geneva award, 1872, made it " due diligence."[60]

If " due diligence " was not employed the United States was liable to damages, and Spain might have claimed reimbursements. No such clear cases as the *Alabama* occurred. The filibustering was so closely allied to legal commerce that it was more difficult to adjudge the responsibility of the United States in this period. The Cuban ports were under Spanish control, and the burden of prevention was on those in

[58] Richardson, Vol. X, p. 148.

[59] Compare the conclusions of Flack, Spanish-American Diplomatic Relations, pp. 22–30, " that there was laxity of duty somewhere and that just as in the case of our government against England, Spain could, in certain instances, have justly demanded damages."

[60] Wharton, sec. 402; Snow, Cases, 43.

command at those places. The commanders of the coast defences were alone responsible for the prevention of commerce between insurgents and private individuals, and, in conjunction with the American authorities, for the prevention of military and hostile expeditions. The burden cannot be shifted to neutrals entirely, nor can the welfare of belligerents be construed entirely to the disadvantage of neutrals. It is no longer legal or reasonable for states at war to impose all the burdens of that unfortunate state upon neutrals. Rather, on the contrary, the tendency is toward more decided limitations on the obligations of neutrality. It is not the purpose of the principles governing neutral aid to belligerents to make insurrection impossible or directly to aid governments in maintaining the *status quo*. No more are they formulated to throttle sympathy and to forbid such comforts and support as individuals may desire to give. They accomplish their purpose when they prevent what is technically known as " direct military aid," " armed expeditions," " ships of war fitted out," or use of soil for belligerent purposes in aid of either one of the belligerents. The contention at present is that there is a limit to the obligations of a neutral as to the enforcement of neutrality; that its duty is not one of perfect vigilance.[61]

The other aspect of the subject, the enforcement of

[61] Woolsey, American Foreign Policy, p. 37. The Institut de droit international at its meeting at Neuchâtel, 1900, adopted a series of rules suggested by questions raised in the Cuban war. One of them referred to filibustering. " It is especially forbidden to third powers to permit hostile military organizations to be organized in its domains." The article added nothing not already recognized by the United States. Annuaire XVII, pp. 181 ff, and 227.

law in the United States and the treatment by Spain of persons caught in filibustering expeditions, was a matter of domestic concern, not of diplomacy or international law. The mere act of transporting expeditions did not constitute a crime which Spain could punish except by seizure and loss of cargo and time, but the members of the expedition, captured by Spain in the act of giving aid and bearing arms, forfeited the protection to which they would otherwise have been entitled. They became in law, to all intents and purposes, pirates and brigands liable to such penalties and pains as the law of their captors prescribed for the offence.[62] Their lot was somewhat improved by the agreement with Spain concluded January 12, 1877, which guaranteed to American citizens committing offences within Spanish jurisdiction freedom from trial in any exceptional tribunal except when captured with arms in their hands. In any case, whether tried in a military court for any offence or in the ordinary civil courts, the American subject became entitled to certain fundamental rights, such as counsel with access at suitable times, a copy of the accusation, a list of witnesses for the prosecution, and the right to secure witnesses for defence. Reciprocal guarantees were made to Spanish subjects within the United States.[63]

The treaty rights of American citizens who were taken on the charge of assisting the insurgents were the occasion of constant friction between Spain and the United States.[64] The United States had no right in the circumstances beyond that of insisting on the

[62] Wharton, Digest, Vol. III, par. 381.
[63] Treaties and Conventions of the United States, p. 1030.
[64] Foreign Relations, 1896, pp. 631, 711, 746, etc.

form of trial guaranteed in the treaty of 1795 and the protocol of 1877. In many instances, on the merits of the case, any penalty to the accused would not have been too severe. They were American subjects only in name and for convenience. Their return to Cuba should have automatically worked the lapse of their American citizenship and revived that of their native land. The case of the crew of the *Competitor,* an American schooner taken in the act of landing arms for the insurgents in April, 1896, furnished one of the most important illustrations of this limited right of the United States to protect its citizens in trouble for filibustering. The accused were ultimately accorded a trial, in form at least, as required by the agreement of 1877. Inflammatory reports of Spanish procedure in such cases kept popular feeling among sympathetic neutrals at high tension throughout the early part of the insurrection. By November 28, 1897, no American citizen remained imprisoned in Cuba.[65] The testimony of American official sources exonerates Spain from injustice, and proves her most liberal and conciliatory in the treatment of Americans involved. Filibustering profoundly influenced public opinion in Spain. It was a ready expedient for administrative authorities responsible for the failure of the military operations in Cuba to foist the responsibility upon the so-called non-neutral conduct of the United States. The Spanish public came to believe unquestioningly in the partisan non-friendly attitude of this country. On the American side the prolongation of the war tried the patience of a naturally long-suffering public.

[65] Foreign Relations, 1898, p. 644.

CHAPTER III

ABANDONMENT OF NON-INTERVENTION POLICY, OCTOBER, 1897, TO MARCH, 1898

The change of administration in the United States in 1897 had at first no perceptible effect on American neutrality. President McKinley adhered closely to the time-honored pacific policy, traditional in American diplomacy, and the choice of Senator John Sherman as Secretary of State was indirectly a confirmation of such a policy. A financial secretary was chosen at a time when the monetary question, not an aggressive foreign policy, was held to be paramount.[1]

On June 16, 1897, General Woodford was appointed Minister to Spain, another appointment interpreted as a confirmation of pacific intentions.[2] However, General Woodford's instructions made it manifest that strained diplomatic relations might at any time be broken. His instructions were to press upon the Spanish Government the American view of the seriousness of the conditions, the limits of the moral obligation of a border neutral to maintain self-restraint and remain a passive spectator—limits the essence of which is the " reasonableness " of the delay in ending the struggle—and the impossibility of continuing the policy of inaction much longer. The adjournment of Congress made the diplomatic situation somewhat

[1] Viallate, Revue historique, Vol. 82, p. 250.
[2] Spanish Diplomatic Correspondence and Documents, p. 36; Revue historique, Vol. 82, p. 252.

easier to control by suppressing for a time the agitation for the recognition of Cuba. On the assassination of Mr. Cánovas del Castillo, August 8, 1897, General Azcanaga became President of the Spanish Council; he continued the policy of his predecessor, but within a little over a month he had fallen into the minority, and the liberal Mr. Sagasta had taken his place.[3] General Weyler was thereupon recalled, and General Blanco was despatched to the post in Cuba with instructions to abandon the policy of concentration.[4] A bando of November 13 partially revoked the military system of General Weyler. The Spanish concentration of non-combatants had called forth American sympathy and interest, especially by reason of the presence of from seven to eight hundred American citizens among those in the concentration camps.[5] Repeated protests from the Government of the United States, and the activity of American consuls in Cuban cities in behalf of such Americans, had greatly strained diplomatic relations.[6] The immediate result of the change of administration in Spain was to relieve the stress measurably. The aggressive attitude of the United States in the early summer, which seemed verging on intervention, yielded to one of expectancy in October and November.[7]

On November 25, 1897, three Spanish decrees extended to Cuba the provisions of the Spanish constitution with the fundamental guarantees contained in

[3] Spanish Diplomatic Correspondence and Documents, p. 36.
[4] *Ibid.*, p. 37; Foreign Relations, 1898, pp. 600, 602.
[5] Foreign Relations, 1897, p. 507.
[6] *Ibid.*, pp. 507–14; 1898, pp. 597–98; Spanish Diplomatic Correspondence and Documents, pp. 24, 26.
[7] Spanish Diplomatic Correspondence and Documents, p. 38.

it, applied the electoral laws of Spain providing universal manhood suffrage, and announced autonomy for the island.[8] The new constitution for Cuba provided for an insular parliament of two coördinate chambers and for a Governor-General representing the home government. The upper house of administrative council was to consist of 35 members, 18 elective and 17 life appointments made by the Governor-General. Representatives of the other house were to be elected by universal suffrage, one for each 25,000 inhabitants, and for a term of five years.[9] Annual sessions were made obligatory. The legislative power of the parliament was made residuary, and colonial legislation was extended to all subjects on insular concerns not specifically and determinately reserved to the home government. Commerce was reserved for the Cortes at Madrid. The apportionment of the debt, including that for the existing war, was likewise reserved. The final authority was vested in the Governor-General, who could suspend the publication of new laws pending final decision at Madrid, and who had in his hands the control of the military, the appointing power, the pardoning power, subject to instructions from the King, and finally the power to suspend the most vital guarantees of individual liberty whenever he might deem it necessary for the preservation of the peace. The judiciary was made entirely subject to the control

[8] Spanish Diplomatic Correspondence and Documents, p. 40; Foreign Relations, 1898, p. 616; Mérignhac, Revue du droit public, Vol. IX, p. 235. A plan of reform was under consideration by the conservative ministry before its overthrow. See Spanish Diplomatic Correspondence and Documents, p. 19.

[9] Suffrage was given to males of twenty-five years, and to residents in a commune of two years. This had been one of the main demands of the Cuban liberal party.

of the home government. The same decrees established an autonomous municipal and provincial régime.
Proportionate representation and the referendum on
municipal debts and loans, when demanded by a third
of the councillors, were included. Autonomy on the
lines laid down in the decrees was predestined to
failure. Cuban industries were in a state of ruin, and
yet the imposition of a crushing burden of taxes would
inevitably follow the conclusion of peace. If the plan
had been accepted and put in force in the best good
faith, discontent and future rebellion were certain.
The plan merely postponed the final settlement. Autonomy as laid down in the Spanish decrees bore no
resemblance to the Canadian constitution, for in Cuba
the sovereignty of Spain remained an active and controlling force, and all the concessions had in no wise
lessened or weakened it. Cuba possessed nothing like
the responsible ministry known to the British colonies.
However, justice to Spain requires the statement that
the concessions were put forth as preliminary to a
fuller liberty to follow the successful operation of
these. Recent events in Cuba have tended to justify
the view held in Spain that the Cubans were not at
the time ready for a fuller degree of self-government.[10]

President McKinley recognized in his message,
December 6, the efforts of Spain to inaugurate a new
military policy and system of government, and he expressed a disposition to give her a reasonable time to
develop the results of the new régime. A tendency to
question the ability of Spain to carry autonomy into

[10] Mérignhac, L'Autonomie cubaine et le conflit hispano-
américain, Revue du droit public, Vol. IX, pp. 235-36.

effect was, nevertheless, apparent in the language of the President. The occasion was taken to denounce the military system of General Weyler. The recognition of belligerency was declared inexpedient under the altered conditions of the moment, immediate intervention was rejected, and the recognition of independence was held to be indefensible because the Cuban Government, in the opinion of the President, lacked the essentials of a sovereign state. Forcible annexation was spurned as criminal aggression.[11]

The message made no appreciable change in the situation. The newspapers in Madrid criticized the expressions seeming to assert a right on the part of the United States to set a limit to the time to be given Spain for conquering her rebellious colony. The Ministry and the Ambassador in Washington regarded the message as favorable to Spain.[12] General Woodford supported the views of the President in a note of December 20 to the Government at Madrid, repeating the administration's expressions of sympathy with the recently declared principles and purposes of the liberal party and with the signal action reversing the inhuman warfare of the preceding year, but ending with the scarcely veiled threat of intervention. The whole note was a lengthy exposition of the impossibility of awaiting long the outcome of further experiments of Spain in Cuba.

Disturbing news continued to reach the United States of suffering in Cuba and of the inability of

[11] Richardson, Vol. X, p. 127.
[12] Recortes periodísticos de los diarios de Madrid, Vol. IV, No. 93, December 7, 1897; Viallate, Revue historique, Vol. LXXXII, p. 254; Spanish Diplomatic Correspondence and Documents, p. 52.

Spanish charity to deal with the situation. As early as May 17, 1897, the suffering of American' citizens in Cuba had prompted a special message to Congress asking for an appropriation of fifty thousand dollars for a relief fund, to be dispensed by the Secretary of State, a part to be used in transporting American citizens to the United States.[13] The appeal was granted by Congress with a promptness which indicated a ready interest in Cuban relief.[14] In December the scope of the relief was enlarged to include the sufferers in Cuba without regard to their nationality. On December 24, in a special proclamation, President McKinley appealed to the American people for voluntary contributions for relief funds, and a few days later a central Cuban Relief Committee was instituted with headquarters in New York. Previously to this the authorities at Havana had been consulted,[15] and they promptly coöperated to facilitate the work of relief, and admitted free of duties all articles sent for that purpose.

This aid given by the United States was not in itself unusual. It was in every way a friendly act, perfectly consistent with absolute neutrality. Spain, of course, possessed the legal right to refuse or accept outside aid. Such relief was, none the less, in a sense an interference in a domestic problem of another country adjudged incapable of bearing the burden. And with the appeal for relief came horrible reports of the suffering from famine and disease in the war-stricken

[13] Richardson, Vol. IX, p. 127.
[14] May 24, 1897. Senate Document 105, 58 Cong., 2 Sess., p. 113.
[15] Foreign Relations, 1897, p. 511; 1898, p. 655.

colony which accentuated a growing American conviction that the war was becoming intolerable.[16]

On the other hand, the success of the political reforms proposed for Cuba was dependent upon their
acceptance by the Cuban insurgents and upon the co-
operation of the loyal Spanish population. In fact the
constitutional unionists and the insurgents alike rejected the proffered autonomy.[17] The insurgent
leaders declared for absolute independence. The loyalists, or constitutional unionists, showed themselves
bitterly opposed to the new régime on the ground that
it conceded too much liberty to the insurgents. The
attempt to inaugurate autonomy, January 1, 1898, met
with the most vigorous resistance. Colonel Joaquin
Ruiz, sent by the Governor-General to make known to
the insurgents the concession of the Government, was
captured and summarily executed, in spite of his rights
of immunity as an envoy. Riots in Havana attested
unpopularity closer at hand. On January 12 mobs led
by Spanish officers attacked the offices of the three
newspapers advocating autonomy, and it became necessary to place an armed guard to protect the American
consulate. The rioters shouted " Death to Blanco and
death to autonomy!" After a day and a night of riot-
ing the authorities gained control, but such events
were unfortunate at the moment. A decidedly adverse
sentiment swept over the United States, and Spain
lost there that confidence in her future policy which
had been obtained with so much labor by her diplo-

[16] An eye-witness of the conditions estimates that 400,000 died
from starvation and disease. Contemporary Review, Vol. 71,
p. 1, July, 1898.
[17] The London Times, April 8, 1898. Mérignhac, Revue du
droit public, Vol. IX, pp. 249, 251.

macy of the preceding twelve months.[18] The American public was convinced that autonomy had come to nothing, and, what was more serious, the President and his cabinet began to share the changed sentiment, the loss of confidence. The Spanish Minister became greatly alarmed at the open hostility on every hand, while Consul-General Lee at Havana, alarmed at the disorders of January 12, and convinced that their repetition would place American residents in grave danger, advised his government to be prepared to send ships to defend American interests.[19] In response, the ships of the Atlantic squadron were concentrated in southern waters, and instructions were given to commanders to retain men whose terms of service were expiring. As a part of the same plan, on January 24 the *Maine* was ordered from Key West to Havana, where she arrived the following day.[20] Such a visit under ordinary circumstances would have had no particular significance, but for three years the custom of exchanging friendly visits to Cuban ports had been suspended. Other foreign ships were in Havana harbor at the time, but no courteous words about the resumption of friendly relations could conceal the real loss of confidence in the ability of the Spanish Government to maintain order in Havana which the visit betokened. The moment chosen was unfortunate in the light of subsequent events. Con-

[18] Spanish Diplomatic Correspondence and Documents, pp. 64, 65; Foreign Relations, 1898, p. 1024.
[19] Foreign Relations, 1898, p. 1025.
[20] *Ibid.*, 1898, pp. 1025–26; Spanish Diplomatic Correspondence and Documents, p. 68. Spanish newspapers called this the *blockade* of Cuban ports. Recortes periodísticos de los diarios de Madrid, Vol. VI, Feb. 7, 8, 1898.

sul-General Lee, on receipt of information concerning
the orders to the *Maine*, had promptly advised
a delay of six or seven days, but his telegram
reached Washington too late. The Spanish authorities received the *Maine* with all outward
forms of courtesy, promising to reciprocate in
kind at an early date, but they seem to have
suspected Consul-General Lee of sending home exaggerated reports of conditions in Havana, and to
have desired his recall.[21] The reply of the Spanish
cabinet, February 1, 1898, to the communication of
General Woodford of December 20, 1897, was a vigorous protest against the idea commonly expressed in
American diplomacy that " reasons of proximity or
damages caused by war to neighboring countries might
give such countries a right to limit to a longer or
shorter period the duration of a struggle disastrous to
all, but much more so to the nation in whose midst
it breaks out or is maintained." All possibility of
foreign intervention was denied, as was any right of
the United States to fix a date for the final end of the
war of suppression.[22] The paper was a firm, able statement of the position of Spain, the validity of which,
tested by the ordinary canons of international law
applicable under the circumstances, was scarcely open
to question.

On the other hand, an unfortunate event of the early
days of February aggravated diplomatic uneasiness.
On February 8 the New York Journal published the
facsimile of a letter attributed to Mr. Dupuy de Lôme,
Minister of Spain at Washington. The letter had
been written about the middle of December to Mr. José

[21] Spanish Diplomatic Correspondence and Documents, p. 69.
[22] *Ibid.*, p. 73.

Canalejas, a Spanish agent who was sent to the United
States to inform himself regarding public opinion, but
who had afterwards gone to Cuba, where the letter
was addressed. Emissaries of the Cuban insurgents
had intercepted the letter, and sent it to the American
press. Mr. Dupuy de Lôme, who admitted the author-
ship of the letter, had in it expressed himself very
confidentially to a friend. The offensive passages
were these: "The message [of December 6] has been
a disillusionment to the insurgents, who expected
something different, but I regard it as bad (for us).
Besides the ingrained and inevitable bluntness with
which there is repeated all that the press and public
opinion in Spain have said about Weyler, it once more
shows what McKinley is, weak and a bidder for the
admiration of the crowd, besides being a would-be
politician who tries to leave a door open behind himself while keeping on good terms with the jingoes of
his party. . . . It would be very advantageous to take
up, even if only for effect, the question of commercial
relations, and to have a man of some prominence sent
hither in order that I may make use of him to carry
on a propaganda among the Senators and others in
opposition to the Junta and to try to win over the
refugees." The Government of the United States
took the position that the publication of the letter
made it impossible for its author to remain longer the
minister of his government. His resignation was
offered to his own government and promptly accepted, all before the United States had an opportunity even to ask for his recall.[23] As the letter had

[23] Foreign Relations, 1898, pp. 1007, 1018; Spanish Diplomatic
Correspondence and Documents, p. 81. Recortes periodísticos

never been intended for publication, and as the means resorted to in order to intercept it were questionable, the publication in the United States was hardly a serious offence in international law. Spain in promptly recalling her minister made the fullest reparation for whatever real offence he had committed. But the criticism of the President aroused bitter feelings, and, what was more serious, revealed the apparent insincerity of the pending commercial negotiations. It became manifest at once that the great essential in prolonging peace much longer—confidence in the sincerity of the other—was lacking in each country. In both Spain and the United States antagonistic positions had been taken which gravely endangered peace. General Woodford wrote from Madrid: " Spanish feeling grows more bitter against the United States each day. . . . I still believe that the Spanish Government will make no further concession, and will insist upon their own time to crush the rebellion."[24] In the United States significant events indicated a dangerous increase of hostile sentiment. On February 14 the party leaders in both houses, to prevent an open rupture, carried a resolution asking for the correspondence of the American consuls regarding concentration and autonomy in Cuba. The publication of the consular communications in Congress took from the ad-

de los diarios de Madrid, Vol. VI, Feb. 10, 11, 1898, for Madrid newspaper version in defence; Lebrand, La guerre hispano-américaine, p. 22. The offence was not a new one in American diplomacy. Compare the case of Marquis de Yrujo, Spanish Minister to the United States during Jefferson's administration; Jackson, British Minister, 1810; Poussin, French Minister, 1849; Catacazy, Russian Minister, 1871; West, British Minister, 1888.

[24] Foreign Relations, 1898, p. 1011. February 12.

ministration all possibility of control. An ultimate pacific settlement had become improbable at the moment when the American world was startled by the blowing up of the *Maine,* February 15, 1898. It only required such an event as that in Havana harbor and the recriminations which grew out of it to fix the wavering convictions of both parties and render diplomacy impotent.

For several days after February 15 the consideration of national differences gave way to the sad rites of caring for the victims. It was extremely unfortunate that a hasty American public, encouraged by unscrupulous journals, early became convinced that the destruction of the battleship was a deliberate act of Spain. The true cause of the explosion—whether it was an untoward accident through an internal or an external explosion or through the premeditated intervention of some individuals to force war, or a pure act of insane vengeance—it has so far been impossible to determine with a satisfactory degree of certainty. One thing is clear, there was no real basis in reason or fact for holding official Spain to be the deliberate perpetrator of a crime of such magnitude.

The Spanish Government promptly proposed a joint investigation into the causes of the explosion and the responsibility, but the United States, preferring to act alone, rejected the proposed course. The utmost conceded to Spain was that a national board of inquiry might have facilities for a separate investigation. The result was that two military boards, assisted by such experts as could be obtained, conducted hurried investigations. The work was begun on February 20 and completed about a month later.[25] The two commissions arrived at very different conclusions. The 'American report found the cause in an external explosion caused by a torpedo or a submarine mine, but declined to fix responsibility in any further particular. The Spanish commission no less positively found the cause in an internal explosion, and denied all responsibility on the part of Spain.[26]

In reviewing the relations between Spain and the United States at the time certain questions arise: Why was the United States unwilling to investigate jointly with Spain, and what rights had Spain in the matter? In case the explosion was external, what was the degree of responsibility of Spain?

Under the prevailing theory as to the status of a ship of war, as long as the *Maine* was intact it enjoyed complete immunities on board in matters of police and justice, but this gave it no rights to jurisdiction over the waters or to the soil beneath where it was anchored. Such soil was under the absolute sovereignty of Spain. The *Maine* after the explosion was for practical purposes little more than a junk heap, though the property of the United States still. Did the United States lose its peculiar jurisdiction from that moment? In the opinion of some writers a wrecked ship loses the immunities normally conceded to its character.[27] The view rests on the effect of a wreck on the organi-

[25] Report received by the President of the United States, March 25, 1898.

[26] Foreign Relations, 1898, pp. 1038, 1044; Spanish Diplomatic Correspondence and Documents, 1896–1900, p. 95. An excellent narrative of the *Maine* and the evidence on the causes in Wilson, Naval History of the Downfall of Spain, ch. 1; compare the Fortnightly, Vol. 69, p. 640, where the writer shows the difficulty in determining the cause of disasters of the kind.

[27] Le Fur, La guerre hispano-américaine, p. 18.

zation of the crew which gave life to the ship. With
the departure of the crew also disappear the immunities they hold. The strength of the view is that it
makes the whole peculiar jurisdiction depend not on
sovereignty, that is, the fiction of extraterritoriality,
but on the necessities of security and the right of preservation. With the wrecking of the ship the occasion
of these passes, and along with them the immunities.
Under such a view Spain should alone have controlled
the inquest. Marshal Blanco advanced such a view,
but fortunately for a continuance of amicable relations
the Spanish authorities yielded the control to the
United States, accepting the continued immunity of
the ship from local jurisdiction. The authorities in
the United States took the position that the fact that
the ship of war had become a wreck did not destroy
the organization which gave life to the force and
therefore had not invalidated the immunities, and that
only final abandonment could cause the ship to lose its
character as a public ship. Under the necessities of
strong international rivalries on such occasions the
latter theory, while somewhat illogical, is probably
still the most practical solution. The mere absence
for the moment of the crew is not abandonment. The
whole affair forms an important precedent in international law. A somewhat similar case was that of
the United States frigate *Constitution,* wrecked on the
Welsh coast in 1879. Local wreckers got her off and
libelled her for pay. The Government of the United
States claimed that the ship was not subject to local
jurisdiction, and the British Government sustained
that view.

The report of the American Naval Commission
failed to fix the responsibility for the explosion in any

particular, but in the subsequent diplomacy Spain was held at fault on the ground that the accident had happened within her jurisdiction. No demand was made for any specific pecuniary indemnity, but Spain was left to offer a suitable reparation. This meant concessions in Cuba. General Woodford, Minister at Madrid, expressed the American position in a note to the Spanish Government, March 28, 1898. " Upon the facts as thus disclosed a grave responsibility appears to rest upon the Spanish Government. The *Maine,* on a peace errand and with the knowledge and consent of that Government, entered the harbor of Havana, relying upon the security and protection of a friendly port. Confessedly she still remained, as to what took place on board, under the jurisdiction of her own Government. Yet the control of the harbor remained in the jurisdiction of the Spanish Government, which, as the sovereign of the place, was bound to render protection to persons and property there, and especially to the public ship and to the sailors of a friendly power."[28] Granting the American contention of an external explosion, which is very difficult to prove with any degree of satisfaction in the light of our present knowledge of the effect of high explosives and which is rejected by the majority of European experts; granting that the Government of Spain had mined the harbor, which was emphatically denied by that power—then the *Maine* disaster presents the responsibility which attaches to mining harbors. The right of a state to place fixed mines (distinct from the floating torpedoes which ought never to be employed) in the national ports is one of its sovereign rights.

[28] Spanish Diplomatic Correspondence and Documents, 1896–1900, p. 105.

Mining harbors is as legitimate a method of defence
as placing cannon in fortresses, but owing to the important rights of access to ports acquired by friendly
states under commercial treaties the placing of mines
or submarine torpedoes carries grave responsibility.
The sovereign state which opens its ports to neutrals
owes in every case the greatest care in securing the
safety of a visiting man-of-war. The necessities of
international relations make perfectly normal the visits
on occasion of the naval vessels of friendly powers
both in defence of national interests and in the exchange of mutual courtesies and the peaceful conduct
of naval affairs. It is recognized that the ports of
civilized states are generally open to the warships of
friendly powers, subject to the restrictions imposed by
the sovereign authority of the port. It is perfectly
within the right of the state to refuse entrance entirely, to make restrictions and to watch and control
the actions of the visiting ship either from political,
military or sanitary considerations. The admission of
a visiting ship is at all times a concession made out
of courtesy or friendship.[29] But once having admitted
public ships to the use of its ports the sovereign power
assumes responsibilities. The visiting ship cannot
know of the dangers lurking in such ports as it may
be allowed to enter, nor is it compatible with the use
of mines in harbors that another power should know
of their location. If the local authorities choose to
give a visiting ship a berth over a mine they guarantee
its safety while there through such control of the mine

[29] Rivier, Principes du droit des gens, Vol. I, p. 156; Rule
adopted by L'Institut de droit international, 1898. Annuaire,
Vol. XVII, p. 273. Revue de droit international public, Vol.
V, p. 853.

as makes an accident absolutely impossible. They alone have the power to do this. It is not necessary in case of an accident to prove the complicity of the Government in order to attach a liability. But the essential questions involved in the *Maine* explosion had to do with the facts of an external or an internal explosion—whether the damage was caused by a mine —and second, if an external cause is found, the extent of damages. If the two questions cannot be settled by joint investigation and ordinary diplomatic proced- ure they are suitable subjects of arbitration. Today they would in all likelihood be referred to the Hague Tribunal. From the standpoint of international law it is greatly to be regretted that the *Maine* case was not settled apart from the Cuban question. In asking for a settlement by arbitration Spain had the better of the two positions.

Before the reports of the naval commissions en- gaged in the investigation of the *Maine* disaster were made the war party had gained considerable headway in spite of the pacific councils of President McKinley. Consul-General Fitzhugh Lee gave offence to Spain by his vigorous representations of the suffering of the rural population. It was represented that the distress of the classes concentrated in camps was only partially relieved by the withdrawal of the more serious restric- tions in the concentration system.[80] Relying on his statements, the Government of the United States had decided early in March to increase the succour for Cubans and to employ two ships of war, the cruisers *Montgomery* and *Nashville,* in its transmission. Spain protested and the United States yielded, substi-

[80] Foreign Relations, 1898, p. 673; Spanish Diplomatic Corre- spondence and Documents, 1896–1900, p. 66.

tuting transports for the service.[31] A few days later, however, the *Montgomery* was sent into Havana to take the place of the *Maine*. With the same purpose of preparing for any emergency President McKinley, after consultation with the Secretary of the Navy, the leader of the majority in the House, and the four chairmen of the House and Senate Committees on the Navy and Appropriations, decided to ask Congress for an appropriation of fifty million dollars for national defense. The money was immediately voted and placed at the disposal of the President without any restrictions and with a unanimity which astonished all Americans. The unmistakable indications of a full treasury and of national confidence in the Executive was no less a revelation to the Spanish court.[32] Other events of the time indicated a conviction in American political circles that preparedness for war was the necessity of the hour.[33] Ships were assembled at Key West. On March 14 two cruisers just built in England were purchased from Brazil, and auxiliary vessels were added as rapidly as possible. On March 21 Congress, still having an approaching war in view, exempted all war material from customs duties.[34] Such events make it very evident that the war party in Congress had won the contest, and that President McKinley with his small circle of advisers of peace had begun a change in policy.

[31] Spanish Diplomatic Correspondence and Documents, 1896–1900, p. 89; Foreign Relations, 1898, p. 677.

[32] Spanish Diplomatic Correspondence and Documents, 1896–1900, p. 90; Foreign Relations, 1898, p. 684.

[33] Spanish Diplomatic Correspondence and Documents, 1896–1900, p. 93.

[34] See London Times, March 17, 1898; Message and Documents, 1898–1899, Abridgment, Vol. II, pp. 902–3.

CHAPTER IV

INTERVENTION

The American commission inquiring into the *Maine*
disaster placed its report in the President's hands on
March 25. Several days earlier, on March 22 and again
on March 23, Spain had been notified that unless some
satisfactory agreement securing immediate and honorable peace in Cuba could be reached within a few days
the *Maine* report would immediately on its receipt be
transmitted to Congress, where the decision would
rest. The statement in the temper of the moment
was almost tantamount to a threat of breaking off
diplomatic relations.[1] A few days later, on March 27,
the demands of the United States were again transmitted to Spain in a more specific form. They included an armistice in Cuba until October 1, during
which time negotiations looking toward a permanent
peace should be undertaken; the immediate and total
revocation of the order of concentration, and relief
measures for those in the camps; and, as a secondary
suggestion for the American Minister, an effort to
gain Spanish consent to the appointment of the President of the United States as final arbitrator in case
the terms of peace were not settled by October 1.[2]
No mention was made of the *Maine* affair, but it was
apparent all through that Spanish concessions alone

[1] Spanish Diplomatic Correspondence and Documents, 1896–
1900, p. 95; Foreign Relations, 1898, pp. 696–713.
[2] Foreign Relations, 1898, p. 712.

would prevent the use of the adverse report of the
Naval Commission as a means of influencing Congress.
Three days later, March 30, the second demand of the
United States was conceded when General Blanco published a bando revoking the concentration orders
throughout Cuba.[3] It contained at the same time
valuable instructions regarding relief methods to be
employed for those without immediate means of support, either through lack of means, resources, or farming implements.[4]

[3] Foreign Relations, 1898, p. 725.

[4] " As, notwithstanding this ample authorization, there will
necessarily remain in the old centers of reconcentration a rem-
nant of country people and their families, who for lack of
means, resources, or farming implements may not be able to
make a living by agricultural labor, the cabinet council will
submit to me, with the urgency which the case demands,
means of initiating and establishing a system of public works
which, while seconding the aid afforded by the magistrates
and protective juntas and by the establishment of economical
kitchens, shall acccomplish the double purpose of bringing
reconcentration to an end and remedying its effects and consequences, thus restoring the normal condition of rural labor
and relieving the misery of the masses, as well as making
reproductive and of use to the country the expenses which
the fulfilment of these arrangements may occasion.

" With which purpose and in virtue of the extraordinary
powers which are conferred upon me as Governor and Captain-
General and general-in-chief of the army, I have proclaimed
in force the following:

" Article 1. From the publication of the present order in the
Gaceta de la Habana, reconcentration of the inhabitants of the
rural districts is abolished throughout the entire island, such
country people and their families being permitted to return
freely to the places which they may deem convenient and to
engage in all kinds of agricultural work.

" Article 2. The protective juntas and all the civil and military authorities shall facilitate by all the means in their reach
the return of the rural inhabitants to their former places of
residence or to those which they may newly elect, extending
to them all the assistance which they can respectively command.

On March 31 the Government of Spain replied to the United States with a body of counterpropositions, offering arbitration on the *Maine* catastrophe, announcing the revocation of concentration, and promising to give government aid to the suffering classes and to leave the matter of peace to the proposed Cuban parliament, which had been convoked for May 4. An armistice was assured, if the insurgents would ask for it. As the suggestion to leave the ultimate terms of peace to the President of the United States was not in the form of a demand at first, and as the substitute in the Spanish reply to leave them to the Cuban parliament came at the suggestion of Minister Woodford and apparently with the consent of President McKinley, that part could not have been a serious ground of difference.[5]   In short, the reply was a satisfactory concession in every particular save an immediate and unconditional armistice.   Arbitration for the *Maine*

"Article 3. Under direction of the cabinet council and through the secretary of public works shall proceed the preparation and immediate establishment of all public works necessary or useful to give employment and subsistence to the country people and their families who, for lack of resources, opportunities for work or farming implements, are not able to return immediately to the country; as also for the establishment of economical kitchens, which may make normal and cheapen these labors.

"Article 4. The expenses resulting from the execution of the regulations of the present order, so far as they may exceed the resources at the command of the protective juntas, may be charged to the extraordinary war credit.

"Article 5. All the orders heretofore published upon the reconcentration of the rural population, and all those which are opposed to the execution of this order, are hereby abolished." Foreign Relations, 1898, p. 738.

[5] Foreign Relations, 1898, p. 762; Spanish Diplomatic Correspondence and Documents, 1896–1900, p. 107.

dispute was reasonable and just, the revocation of concentration was final and complete, the relief measures were of the fullest character.[6] Woodford was at the time convinced that Spain would finally yield even that. He wrote on April 2: " I have worked hard for peace. I am hoping against hope and still I cannot bring myself to the final belief that in these closing years of the nineteenth century Spain will finally refuse, on a mere question of punctilio, to offer immediate and effective armistice. I still believe that immediate armistice will secure permanent and honorable peace with justice to Cuba and sure protection to our great American interests in that island. Men will not reason when their passions are inflamed. So long as they are fighting they will not negotiate. When they stop fighting they will begin to reason. Negotiations will follow and peace will come. If arms are now laid down on both sides they will not be taken up again."[7]

Already forces were at work to satisfy the one remaining demand of the United States. On April 2 Cardinal Rampolla, acting in behalf of the Pope, offered the services of the Holy See as mediator.[8] The Spanish Government sent a reply which indicated an eagerness to find a solution that would save Spain from a ministerial revolution and yet satisfy the United States. The reply of Spain to Cardinal Rampolla was as follows: " The moment the United States Government is disposed to accept the aid of the Pope, the Queen of Spain and her Government will gladly accept

[6] Revue du droit public, Vol. IX, p. 265; Foreign Relations, 1898, pp. 727–28.

[7] Foreign Relations, 1898, p. 731.

[8] Spanish Diplomatic Correspondence and Documents, 1896–1900, pp. 109, 110.

his mediation, and, in order to facilitate the high mission of peace and concord which His Holiness is attempting, promise further to accept the proposal that the Holy Father shall formulate a suspension of hostilities; informing His Holiness that for the honor of Spain it is proper that the truce should be accompanied by the retirement of the American squadron from the waters of the Antilles, in order that the North American Republic may also show its purpose not to support—voluntarily or involuntarily—the insurrection in Cuba."[9] The reasonableness of the request that the United States withdraw the fleet from Cuban waters is very apparent. On the other hand the informal offer of the Pope to mediate aroused great excitement in the United States. His action was unfortunately represented by some papers as an attempt to make himself the arbiter of the Spanish-American differences. The statement of the Spanish Minister of Foreign Affairs that papal mediation came at the suggestion of President McKinley increased the hostility throughout the United States, and necessitated a delay in the declaration of the armistice. A rabid press cried out against papal intermeddling in American affairs. Scare headlines of "no popery," etc., appeared. In part this attitude was due to a deep-seated anti-Catholic feeling, in part to a misunderstanding of the origin and purpose of the papal action, and in great part to the absence of a correct understanding of mediation. As a result of the attitude of the American people the simple and well-intentioned suggestion of mediation, which is not to be confounded with intervention, tended rather to make harder the maintenance

[9] *Ibid.*, p. 110; Recortes periodísticos, X, nos. 209, 210.

of peace.[10]   In fact the Pope had never gone farther
than to convey to the two powers in an informal manner through his representatives an ardent wish that a
conflict might be averted, and to place his counsel and
his influence at the service of the two governments.
Mr. Woodford included the excitement over papal
mediation in the unfortunate incidents—like the De
Lôme letter and the *Maine* explosion—for none of
which Spain was in any sense responsible, which were
among the direct causes of war.   Except for them, in
his opinion, war could have been prevented.[11]

[10] Le Fur, pp. 22–23; the London Times, April 5, 1898.

[11] William McKinley and the Spanish War. A paper read
by Mr. Woodford, late Minister to Spain, before the Hebrew
Young Peoples' Societies, New York, March 8, 1904, pp. 2–3.
"Out from all that correspondence stand these facts. The
Queen Regent of Spain and the President of the United States
were each and both sincerely desirous of peace. The Spanish
Government steadily, courteously, but surely receded from
position to position in the interest of peace until there seemed
reasonable hopes of peaceful adjustment. Then came occur-
rences which human foresight had not foreseen and could not
have foreseen. The singular and inexplicable letter from the
Spanish Minister at Washington to a correspondent at Havana; the destruction of the steamship *Maine* in the harbor
of Havana and the suggestion by the Spanish Minister of
Foreign Affairs that the request of the Pope for an armistice
was at the instance of the American President. The first
weakened the faith of our people in the sincerity of the Spanish
negotiations. The second evoked a passionate popular cry
for vengeance. The third compelled delay in the announcement of the armistice, which then came too late to arrest the
demands of the American people for immediate action.

"It is impossible to forecast contingencies or to say what
would have come to pass had not these unforeseen and unex-
pected incidents occurred. They did occur and war came.
But I have always believed, and now believe, that but for
these things President McKinley would have achieved the
desire of his heart, and would have accomplished the ultimate
independence of Cuba without war."

At the same time that Pope Leo recommended to the Spanish Government an armistice with the Cuban insurgents he sent Archbishop Ireland, an intimate personal friend of President McKinley, to Washington, in order to induce the American Government to take steps toward persuading the insurgents to accept an armistice. These measures formed only the starting point for a formal mediation, which did not occur and could not until both powers were prepared to accept it. The Pope's offer of his good offices was highly creditable to him and was well received in Europe, and should have been better received by American journals.[12]

On April 3 Mr. Woodford sent a personal message to President McKinley in which he repeated his confidence that Spain would make all necessary concessions. He gave in effect his endorsement of the Spanish condition that the American fleet should be withdrawn from Cuban waters as a response to the conciliatory measures of Spain.[13] Spain strained every diplomatic resource to bring about a protest of Europe against the American position. On April 6 the representatives at Washington of the six great powers, Germany, Austria, France, Great Britain, Italy and Russia, presented an appeal to President McKinley for a continuance of peace. In its final form as presented the address, instead of a threat and a protest as Spain had wished it, became a moderate appeal for peace. The modification was due to the influence of England. In only one respect was the event remarkable.

[12] See London Times, April 7, 1898; Spanish Diplomatic Correspondence and Documents, 1896–1900, p. 111; Revue du droit public, Vol. IX, p. 277.
[13] Foreign Relations, 1898, p. 732.

The ambassadors met President McKinley in a body, and their spokesman, Sir Julian Pauncefote, read the note of appeal.   It has been a traditional practice of the United States Government to refuse to receive representatives from a combination of European states. Two days later in a similar address the same parties supported the papal request at Madrid for an immediate armistice in Cuba.[14]   It should be noted that the powers went further at Madrid than at Washington, since at the former court they pressed upon the Spanish Government not merely the general considerations that make for peace, but the adoption of a specific course of action then demanded by the United States.[15]   The reply of the Spanish Government, on April 9, was a suspension of hostilities in Cuba without any definite limitation beyond that implied by the words " for such length of time as he [the Governor of Cuba] may think prudent to prepare and facilitate the peace earnestly desired by all."[16]   General Blanco's armistice proclamation was published in due course substantially as follows: " The Government of his Majesty, according to the wishes expressed on several occasions by the Pope and by the Ambassadors of the Six Great Powers of Europe, has decided, in order to prepare for and facilitate the establishment of peace in the island, to suspend hostilities, and has ordered me to carry this decision into effect and to make the following dispositions :—

" 1. Hostilities shall be suspended throughout the

[14] *Ibid.*, p. 710; Spanish Diplomatic Correspondence and Documents, 1896–1900, pp. 113–15.

[15] The Times, London, April 20, 1898.

[16] Spanish Diplomatic Correspondence and Documents, 1896–1900, pp. 114–15.

island in every locality on the receipt of this proclamation.

"2. Details of the execution of the proclamation and the duration of the suspension of hostilities shall be determined by special instructions to the general commanding."[17]

It is significant that the expressed wishes of the United States for Cuba had been fully covered by the several concessions of March 30, March 31, and April 9. Mr. Woodford evidently considered Spain's concessions adequate. He wrote in a personal message to President McKinley, April 10, " I hope that nothing will now be done to humiliate Spain, as I am satisfied that the present Government is going, and is loyally ready to go, as fast and as far as it can."[18] But neither the address of the powers, so influential in Madrid, nor the pacific overture of the Spanish ministry, nor the pleading of the American Minister for time, had any perceptible effect in the United States. The long-promised message went to Congress on April 11. It had been delayed from April 6, the original date set for its transmission, not awaiting Spanish action, but upon the urgent request of the American Consul-General at Havana, who was fearful for the safety of Americans in Havana.[19] It was a lengthy document of seven thousand words, reviewing the Cuban insurrection, the treatment of reconcentrados, the character of the Cuban mode of warfare, the recent efforts of the Government for pesce, and the unsatisfactory answer of Spain to the latest demand. Other por-

[17] Foreign Relations, 1898, p. 750.
[18] Ibid., p. 747.
[19] Ibid., p. 743.

tions dismissed as inexpedient the recognition of the independence of the so-called Cuban Republic, and as unnecessary and disadvantageous if the United States would ultimately intervene to pacify the island.[20] Much space was devoted to a discussion of the legal and historical aspects of intervention, and the grounds for such a step were summarized in the following words:

" First. In the cause of humanity and to put an end to the barbarities, bloodshed, starvation, and horrible miseries now existing there, and which the parties to the conflict are either unable or unwilling to stop or mitigate. It is no answer to say this is all in another country, belonging to another nation, and is therefore none of our business. It is specially our duty, for it is right at our door.

" Second. We owe it to our citizens in Cuba to afford them that protection and indemnity for life and property which no government there can or will afford, and to that end to terminate the conditions that deprive them of legal protection.

" Third. The right to intervene may be justified by the very serious injury to the commerce, trade, and business of our people, and by the wanton destruction of property and devastation of the island.

" Fourth, and which is of the utmost importance, the present condition of affairs in Cuba is a constant menace to our peace, and entails upon this Government an enormous expense. With such a conflict waged for years in an island so near us and with which our

[20] " In case of intervention our conduct would be subject to the approval or disapproval of such government. We would be required to submit to its direction and to assume to it the mere relation of a friendly ally."

people have such trade and business relations; when the lives and liberty of our citizens are in constant danger and their property destroyed and themselves ruined; where our trading vessels are liable to seizure and are seized at our very door by war ships of a foreign nation, the expeditions of filibustering that we are powerless to prevent altogether, and the irritating questions and entanglements thus arising—all these and others that I need not mention, with the resulting strained relations, are a constant menace to our peace, and compel us to keep on a semiwar footing with a nation with which we are at peace. . . . In any event the destruction of the *Maine,* by whatever exterior cause, is a patent and impressive proof of a state of things in Cuba that is intolerable. That condition is thus shown to be such that the Spanish Government cannot assure safety and security to a vessel of the American Navy in the Harbor of Havana on a mission of peace, and rightfully there."[21]

No reply was made to the Spanish offer to arbitrate the diversity of views on the *Maine* matter. The message closed with these paragraphs: " In view of these facts and these considerations, I ask Congress to authorize and empower the President to take measures to secure a full and final termination of hostilities between the Government of Spain and the people of Cuba, and to secure in the island the establishment of a stable government, capable of maintaining order and observing its international obligations, insuring peace and tranquility and the security of its citizens as well as our own, and to use the military and naval forces of the United States as may be necessary for these pur-

[21] Foreign Relations, 1898, pp. 757–58.

poses. And in the interest of humanity and to aid
in preserving the lives of the starving people of the
island I recommend that the distribution of food and
supplies be continued, and that an appropriation be
made out of the public Treasury to supplement the
charity of our citizens. The issue is now with the
Congress. It is a solemn responsibility. I have exhausted every effort to relieve the intolerable condition
of affairs which is at our doors. Prepared to execute
every obligation imposed upon me by the Constitution
and the law, I await your action." At the conclusion
the armistice offered by Spain was referred to with
the further comment that "yesterday, and since
the preparation of the foregoing message, official information was received by me that the latest decree
of the Queen Regent of Spain directs General Blanco,
in order to prepare and facilitate peace, to proclaim a
suspension of hostilities, the duration and details of
which have not yet been communicated to me. This
fact with every other pertinent consideration will I am
sure, have your just and careful attention in the solemn
deliberations upon which you are about to enter. If
this measure attains a successful result then our aspirations as a Christian, peace-loving people will be realized. If it fails, it will be only another justification
for our contemplated action."[22]

The pertinent fact in Spanish-American diplomacy
at this time was the deliberate and formal submission
of further action to Congress. It was the surrender
on the part of the President of diplomatic efforts to
legislative action. He had formally yielded to an impatient Congress and a strong popular demand of the

[22] Foreign Relations, 1898, pp. 759–60.

nation. For this European writers, little comprehending the genius of American institutions, have strongly
criticized him.[23] It was in no sense equivalent to an
abdication of power, but rather a declaration to Congress of the futility, in the judgment of the chief executive, of further use of his peculiar province—diplomatic negotiations. The President alone is the judge
of the time when it is no longer possible to accomplish
anything by diplomacy, and that he formally declared
by his message of April 11. Declaration of war, the
putting of the state on a war basis, the steps to be
taken toward intervention, are, by the American system, properly matters for Congressional action and not
for executive determination. The vital question is
whether the President did not yield prematurely and
whether he had exhausted the resources of diplomacy.
The testimony of the Minister at Madrid is against
him. Mr. Woodford's correspondence to the last indicated a firm belief in the possibility of peace in Cuba
without war. Except for an uncontrollable desire for
war on the part of the United States, diplomacy might,
within all human probability, have accomplished the
emancipation of Cuba.[24] He wrote, April 13: " I
know that the Queen and her present ministry sincerely desire peace and that the Spanish people desire
peace, and if you can still give me time and reasonable
liberty of action I will get for you the peace you desire
so much and for which you have labored so hard."[25]

[23] Le Fur, La guerre hispano-américaine, p. 26, and footnote 2.

[24] See same conclusion by Flack, Spanish-American Diplomatic Relations Preceding the War of 1898, pp. 92–95. Compare Mr. Woodford's paper on William McKinley and the
Spanish War quoted in footnote 11.

[25] Foreign Relations, 1898, p. 732.

But neither time nor liberty of action was allowed.
Step by step Congress forced the United States into
war.

The Cubans, acting for themselves, refused to accept an armistice unless Spain would at the same time
consent to evacuate Cuba. The following letter written by Maximo Gomez to Consul Barker, and later
sent to President McKinley, gave the insurgent view.
" A year ago we received a proposal from Spain for
an armistice. We refused it then as we must refuse it
now. The rainy season will soon be at hand and until
it is over Spain and her troops would like an armistice.
We will not, however, throw away the advantage. I
am anxious that hostilities should cease, but it must
be for all time. If Spain agrees to evacuate Cuba, I am
willing to agree to an armistice until October 1, when
loyal Cubans shall come into their own again. I am
writing this at the direction of the Cuban Provincial
Government, with whom the Spanish may treat directly if they so desire."[26] But the letter was a party
declaration in the face of rising fortunes in the United
States. Mr. Woodford was confident that Spain
could be induced to give peace to Cuba along lines
acceptable to all parties—autonomy, annexation to the
United States, or complete independence.[27]

The message antagonized—practically affronted—
Spain. On the day following President McKinley's
message to Congress an extraordinary council of ministers in session in Madrid closed with an almost
defiant denunciation of American intermeddling in the

[26] London Times, April 12, 1898.
[27] Foreign Relations, 1898, pp. 731, 732, 747.

internal affairs of Spain,[28] which created considerable
sensation in diplomatic circles because of its spirited
character. On April 13 the Committees on Foreign
Affairs in the two houses of the American Congress
submitted simultaneously their reports, both bellicose
in nature and both committing the Government to
intervention. Spain awaited the action of the Congress
of the United States upon these reports. On April
19 the final vote was taken on a joint resolution. The
main differences in the original resolutions of the
houses and the cause of the delay turned on the recognition of the Cuban insurgent government. Both
houses were agreed on the vital question of intervention, but the Senate went farther, advocating a full
recognition of the Republican Government of Cuba as
the true and lawful government of the island.

The final resolution took the following form:

" Whereas the abhorrent conditions which have existed for more than three years in the island of Cuba,
so near our own borders, have shocked the moral sense
of the people of the United States, have been a disgrace
to civilization, culminating as they have in the destruction of a United States battle ship, with two hundred
and sixty-six of its officers and crew, while on a
friendly visit in the harbor of Havana, and can not
longer be endured, as has been set forth by the President of the United States in his message to Congress
of April eleventh, eighteen hundred and ninety-eight,
upon which the action of Congress was invited:

" Therefore, resolved by the Senate and House of
Representatives of the United States of America in
Congress assembled,

[28] Le Fur, La guerre hispano-américaine, p. 27.

7

" First. That the people of the island of Cuba are, and of right ought to be, free and independent.[29]

" Second. That it is the duty of the United States to demand, and the Government of the United States does hereby demand, that the Government of Spain at once relinquish its authority and government in the island of Cuba, and withdraw its land and naval forces from Cuba and Cuban waters.

" Third. That the President of the United States be, and he is, directed and empowered to use the entire land and naval forces of the United States, and to call into the actual service of the United States the militia of the several States, to such extent as may be necessary to carry these resolutions into effect.

" Fourth. That the United States hereby disclaims any disposition or intention to exercise sovereignty, jurisdiction or control over said island, except for the pacification thereof, and asserts its determination, when that is accomplished, to leave the government and control of the island to its people."[30] The fourth article was the famous Teller Amendment, added and agreed to without a division, and intended to quiet apprehension abroad and in Cuba.[31] The legislative recognition of the insurgent government in Cuba was defeated, mainly because that function belonged to the Presi-

[29] The words " and that the Government of the United States hereby recognizes the Republic of Cuba as the true and lawful government of the island " were stricken out.

[30] Foreign Relations, 1898, p. 763.

[31] For an interesting account of the Congressional attitude at this crisis see article by Senator Lodge, Harper's, March, 1899, p. 505. Whitney, Yale Review, Vol. VII, p. 8, " The Cuban Revolt and the Constitution," discusses the constitutional aspects of the subject.

dent. The declaration in the first resolution—that the
people of Cuba are independent—is difficult to con-
strue, but it certainly did not constitute a recognition
of a new foreign state.

Meanwhile, Spain continued her hopeless efforts to
secure action from the European powers which would
checkmate the United States. A memorandum of
April 18 in the form of a circular to the powers re-
viewed the relations of Spain with the United States
during the entire Cuban insurrection and the more
recent action of both governments. It was a forcible
defense and justification from the Spanish point of
view. Its main argument depended on the sovereignty of Spain in Cuba and the right to prosecute the
war there free from United States intermeddling.[32]

The resolution of April 19 committed the United
States to forcible intervention. On April 20 President McKinley signed the joint resolution of Congress
and prepared an ultimatum to be presented to the
Spanish Government by General Woodford. It directed the Minister of the United States at Madrid to
communicate officially to Spain the joint resolution of
Congress, and to say that "if, by the hour of noon on
Saturday next, the 23d day of April, instant, there be
not communicated to this Government by that of Spain
a full and satisfactory response to this demand and
resolution, whereby the ends of peace in Cuba shall be
assured, the President will proceed without further
notice to use the power and authority enjoined and
conferred upon him by the said joint resolution to

[32] Spanish Diplomatic Correspondence and Documents, 1898,
p. 126; Revue de droit international public, Vol. V, p. 544.

such extent as may be necessary to carry the same into effect."[33]

The Spanish Government, considering that the notification of the ultimatum would constitute another insult, managed to evade it. On April 19 Gullón, the Spanish Minister of Foreign Affairs, instructed the Minister at Washington to ask for his passports and to withdraw to Canada when the President should sign the resolution of Congress,[34] and accordingly the next day M. Polo promptly asked for his passports.[35] Early on the morning of April 21, at seven-thirty o'clock, just following the receipt by the American Minister in Madrid of the President's ultimatum and before he could transmit it to the Government of Spain, the Spanish Minister of Foreign Affairs notified Woodford that the resolution of Congress approved by the President was viewed in Spain as equivalent to a declaration of war, and that in consequence diplomatic relations had been ended. There was nothing left for the American Minister at Madrid to do but ask for a passport and withdraw, entrusting the protection of American interests in Spain to the English Ambassador at the same court. The following Spanish circular telegram announcing to Europe the procedure on April 21 illustrates the mode of breaking diplomatic relations in this instance:

[33] Foreign Relations, 1898, p. 764. Edward B. Whitney, "The Cuban Revolt and the Constitution," Yale Law Review, May, 1898, Vol. VII, p. 8, concludes that the joint resolution, April 20, in the form of an ultimatum was unconstitutional as an entrenchment upon the duties of the President.

[34] Spanish Diplomatic Correspondence and Documents, 1896–1900, p. 134.

[35] Foreign Relations, 1898, p. 765.

" Madrid, April 21, 1898.

" The President having approved the resolution of both Houses, which, in denying Spanish sovereignty and threatening armed intervention in Cuba, is equivalent to a declaration of war, our Minister at Washington withdrew last night, with the personnel of the legation, according to his instructions. This morning Mr. Woodford was notified that diplomatic relations between the two countries were broken off and that all official communication between the respective countries had ceased. The Government of His Majesty, in acting in this manner, proposed to avoid receiving the American ultimatum, which would have constituted a fresh offence. The representative of the United States understood this, and limited himself to asking for his passport and will leave this afternoon on the express train for France.

Gullon."[86]

With this review of diplomatic relations preceding the outbreak of hostilities, the time has come to study more in detail the juridical aspects of American intervention with the purpose of testing in the light of current practices and the accepted principles of international law the validity of the grounds set forth. The United States took great pains to state clearly its reasons for forcible intervention, as Spain did its reasons for resistance. In the message of President McKinley to Congress, April 11, occurred the most formal statement for the Government of the United States.[87] The grounds were:

[86] Spanish Diplomatic Correspondence and Documents, 1896–1900, p. 136.
[87] See ante, p. 92.

1. In the cause of humanity.

2. For the protection of the lives and property of American citizens in Cuba.

3. In defense of commercial and financial interests involved.

4. For self-preservation.

5. For the *Maine* disaster.

Upon the cases where intervention is justifiable writers on international law are far from agreed. Intervention is an interference with the normal sovereign rights of an independent state by another state, but the sovereignty of a state seemingly would preclude any such thing as a legal interference. States, however, have obligations as well as rights, and intervention must be based on a violation of one or more of those obligations which stand before and above the rights of sovereign independence. Looked at from the standpoint of the injured state the international obligations of the other, or wrong-doer, are the rights common to states in their international relations. The principal inquiry becomes at once, What are these preeminent rights of states which, when endangered, warrant an infringement of the rights of independence of another? Many of the reasons which have been set forth in practice would no longer be tolerated, for example such as have been based alone on friendship for one of two parties in a civil war or on the preservation of a balance of power.

Modern writers are quite generally agreed that self-preservation justifies intervention,[38] but they state

[38] Hall, International Law, p. 199; Lawrence, Principles of International Law, p. 118; Rivier, Principes du droit des gens, Vol. I, pp. 392–93; Phillimore, International Law, pp. 467–68; Woolsey, International Law, p. 44.

clearly that the danger must be " direct and immediate, not contingent and remote, and, moreover, it must
be sufficiently important to justify the expenditure of
blood and treasure in order to repel it."[39] Many
would allow intervention where the right was conferred by treaty or convention. States frequently limit
their own independence of action by agreements of an
international character. The most important power of
the kind enjoyed by the United States is the right conferred by the Platt Amendment, and recently applied,
to intervene in Cuba under certain specified circumstances. But such a condition did not exist in the
Spanish-American differences, and though a valid
cause for intervention according to the best opinion,
it needs no further consideration here.

The only other ground on which writers are in general agreement is when some law of nations has been
violated and all the nations sanction intervention.[40]
But again the difficult problem is to determine just what
things are forbidden to states by international law.
Writers and practice are in conflict. In the opinion
of some writers it would include interventions on
humanitarian grounds, to stop acts of great cruelty or
persecutions or a prolonged and inhumane civil war.
Many writers, on the contrary, deny any possibility of
a legal intervention resting on the inhumanity of another state, but this seems to carry the sanctity of
national independence to an unreasonable extreme.
Great Britain, France and Russia intervened in Greece
in 1827 on humanitarian grounds, Russia in behalf of

[39] Lawrence, Principles of International Law, p. 118.
[40] Hall, International Law, p. 304; Wheaton, Digest, part 2,
chap. 1, par. 9; Rivier, Principes du droit des gens, Vol. I,
pp. 392–93.

Bulgaria in 1877, and the western powers advanced the same reasons in support of the proposed intervention in the more recent Armenian troubles.

It must be admitted that intervention by a single state on this ground is highly questionable and is generally inadvisable. It is a much better rule to require the sanction of a considerable number of the nations. The significant feature of the rule is, however, that the states which constitute the active international powers must consent to the particular instance and form of intervention contemplated. As the consent of all would be impracticable in many cases, a better rule would limit intervention to a coöperation of an " effective " majority. The word " effective " is used advisedly, meaning a large enough number to make impracticable any resistance of those opposed. The essential benefit of such intervention is the absence on the part of the intervening state of self-interest and ambition. If it is certain these are absent, intervention may become a high and noble act of self-sacrifice. Because it is so difficult to be sure of these points it would be much better for the state contemplating intervention to bring about, through diplomatic means, a concert and coöperation of action of its associated states. It might be said that the United States had this consent in 1898 through the failure of Europe to prevent intervention. Negative authority does not satisfy the rule. The authority to act ought to be positive and the results controlled by the same coöperation.

Of the grounds set forth by the United States in intervention in Cuba, taken separately and isolated from a century's history, not one could have warranted intervention. The consensus of opinion of writers would condemn all intervention on the second and third reasons set forth by the President.[41]

By the statement made by President McKinley himself in his message to Congress, December 6, 1897, that "not a single American citizen is now under arrest or confinement in Cuba,"[42] it is clear that no grave condition of this kind existed in the last months of the insurrection. As for American property in the island destroyed by the war—destroyed, be it remembered, by the insurgents more than by Spanish military operations—for a century the United States has been able to settle graver damages through arbitration and claims commissions. Moreover, the United States had never asked that Spain pay the claims of its citizens for damages done during the war. Every reason leads to the belief that all just claims could have been readily adjusted. Property directly destroyed by the Spanish arms would doubtless have been paid for as promptly as is usual in such cases, and Spain was not responsible in international law for any other. Intervention for the protection of property interests of the subjects of a state is particularly dangerous, and to be condemned. Equally the loss of commerce and the concurrent financial losses to the citizens of one state caused by a war in another state where their markets are located give no right to use force to keep them open.

War damages neutrals, but its disastrous results to the belligerent subjects are greater. Spain's attitude regarding the *Maine* has already been considered, with the conclusion that the Spanish contention for arbitra-

[41] See ante, p. 92.
[42] Richardson, Vol. X, p. 136.

tion was valid. From this it follows that it weakened rather than strengthened the American position. Yet this was without doubt the very event which was regarded by the masses of the Americans as justifying a resort to war out of pure revenge.

The first and fourth reasons advanced by the United States remain to be tested.[43] Both may under certain circumstances warrant a forcible intervention. Did such circumstances exist in April, 1898? That is, were the peace and security of the United States directly endangered? That the war was troublesome to the United States is not enough. That it increased the costs of government and greatly strained administrative resources would not satisfy jurists that an immediate danger existed. Likewise it has been held[44] that the war was little more inhumane than wars generally are; at least that the cruelty of the Spanish warfare has been grossly exaggerated. Its most serious phase was that it had been prolonged and that there was little reason for believing that Spain could ever end it. The fact remains that Spain had reversed Weyler's policy and several months before intervention had substituted a mode radically more humane. Concentration had been discontinued, efforts had been made to restore grinding and agricultural prosperity, and if the Spanish policy had failed the cause rested with the insurgents alone, who had systematically thwarted every effort of Spain in this particular.[45] Spain could look with little tolerance upon the American protests on the ground of inhumanity in Cuba.

[43] See ante, p. 92.
[44] See ante, p. 33.
[45] House Document 405, 55 Cong., 2 Sess., Affairs in Cuba.

The Madrid papers matched American stories with historical incidents, reviewing the Indian wars and the policy of concentration on reservations.[46] The American Treaty Claims Commission have decided since the war that the systems of concentration and devastation were lawful acts.[47] L'Institut de droit international in session at Neuchâtel, 1900, adopted the following significant rule:

"One cannot make complaint to a state in whose domain insurrection has broken out upon the measures of repression it applies in its defense against the insurrection if it applies the same measures to all those, who participate actively in the civil war, whatever their nationality. Reservation is made for exceptionally cruel penalties which evidently exceed the necessities of repression."[48] Here again the war did not present clearly and unmistakably such tyranny or cruelty as writers on international law seem to regard as justifying intervention. The resort to war by a single state on this ground has few if any advocates.[49]

If then intervention was not warranted on a single one of the grounds advanced by the United States when taken separately, it does not follow that it was not when all are taken cumulatively. Writers have not, to be sure, accepted the cumulative principle. One writer has recognized that there may be cases "above and beyond the domain of law," justifiable on

[46] Recortes periodísticos de los diarios de Madrid, Vol. X, April 3, 1898.
[47] See ante, p. 28.
[48] Annuaire XVII, pp. 181, 227.
[49] For an interesting study of same subject see Flack, Spanish-American Diplomatic Relations Preceding the War of 1898, Johns Hopkins Studies, 1906, nos. 1 and 2, ch. II.

exceptional grounds not within the ordinary rules of international law.[50] If it can be established that the American Government exhausted every resource of diplomacy to avoid war, there is some technical ground upon which to rest intervention. Cuba presented in one century an exceptional case of misgovernment, of unfulfilled promises, of prolonged internecine war, of neutrals burdened by border warfare. But in the light of the resort to war in the face of the full concessions of Spain the technical basis becomes very weak indeed. In the opinion of nearly all writers on international law the particular form of intervention in 1898 was unfortunate, irregular, precipitate and unjust to Spain.[51] The same ends—peace in Cuba and justice to all people concerned—in themselves good, could have been achieved by peaceful means safer for the wider interests of humanity.[52]

[50] Lawrence, Principles of International Law, p. 121. Compare Hershey, Annals American Academy Political Science, Vol. XI, p. 353.

[51] Mérignhac, Revue du droit public, Vol. IX, p. 286.

[52] Compare the methods by which the same power has carried the open door into China and was able to limit the field of military operations in the Russo-Japanese war.

CHAPTER V

The conduct of the Governments of Spain and the United States in the critical period of transition from peace to open hostility offers the first opportunity to · test the application of the rules of warfare by two powers that have been well outside the sphere of modern wars. To be sure the United States passed through a great civil war from 1861 to 1865 and Spain one of lesser moment in the second Carlist Insurrection of 1873 to 1876, but both of these were in a different category; both exemplified the conduct of governments in civil wars.

The phase of the subject that first presents itself concerns the declaration of war. The Government of Spain had declared that the signing of the resolution of Congress authorizing intervention would be equivalent to a declaration of war and would be so regarded. General Woodford was given his passports immediately on the information reaching Spain that President McKinley had duly affixed his signature. The Government of the United States at first took the same view, and by a blockade proclamation of April 22, by the capture of Spanish merchant vessels on the same day, and by other belligerent acts conducted itself in every way as though the announcements already made were adequate to warrant opening hostilities. However, on April 25, four days later, President McKinley sent a special message to Congress recommending a formal Congressional declaration of war, " to the end that the definition of the international status of the United States as a belligerent power may be known and the assertion of all its rights and the maintenance of all its duties in the conduct of a public war may be assured."[1] The Senate and the House of Representatives responded the same day with a joint resolution " that war be, and the same is hereby, declared to exist, and that war has existed since the twenty-first day of April, A. D. 1898, including said day, between the United States of America and the Kingdom of Spain."[2]

The most significant feature is the retroactive portion. Of just what international value a retroactive declaration can ever be it is difficult to conceive. The blockade proclamation of April 22 formally notified the powers of the existence of war, and would be taken as sufficient evidence to them that a state of war existed.[3] The act was equally a matter of slight moment in domestic affairs from either a political or a constitutional standpoint. The President was authorized on April 20 to employ the army and navy in behalf of Cuban independence. The declaration of war merely repeated the same authorization, indeed in identical words.[4]

International practice and writers differ upon the

[1] Richardson, Vol. X, p. 155.

[2] *Ibid.,* p. 201.

[3] Cf. the view taken by writers on international law and the opinion of the Supreme Court of the United States, both to the effect that Lincoln's blockade proclamation was official and conclusive evidence that a state of war existed. 2 Black Sup. Ct. Rep. 665; Woolsey, International Law, p. 293.

[4] See Richardson, Vol. X, pp. 155, 201.

necessity of a declaration of war. Many French writers support the view of its necessity, while other European and most American and English writers hold the contrary view. Hautefeuille, Heffter and Calvo are the leading advocates of the old view of an obligatory declaration of war.[5] Le Fur holds the same opinion and asserts that the great majority of writers agree with him. He gives two reasons for his position: to avoid all possibility of surprise, and to give formal announcement to neutrals of the state of belligerency and the substitution of the laws of war for the principles, so different, which prevail in time of peace.[6] However, such European writers as Klüber, Twiss and Phillimore think that no obligation rests upon states to make a formal declaration of war to enemies.[7] Holtzendorff is of the same opinion, but a belligerent ought, he says, to give notice of some sort if he can do so consistently with his political interests and his military aims.[8] This seems to be the view of Rivier, who would require some form of public announcement, ultimatum, manifesto or circular note or dispatch or other official publication, but not necessarily a formal declaration.[9] De Martens, the Russian pub-

[5] See Hautefeuille, Vol. I, p. 102, 3d edition, Paris, 1868; Heffter, sec. 120; Calvo, Vol. II, p. 33.

[6] Le Fur, La guerre hispano-américaine, p. 49. Raspiller, "Du passage de l'état de paix à l'état de guerre," Nancy, 1904, pp. 34–67, argues for a formal declaration except (1) in a war of defence, (2) against pirates, (3) in a civil war, (4) in war with a non-organized state, and (5) in cases where belligerent measures are confined to means of constraint.

[7] Klüber, par. 238–39, Paris, 1874; Twiss, Vol. II, p. 65, Oxford, 1863; Phillimore, Vol. II, ch. 5.

[8] Holtzendorff, Handbuch, 1899, Vol. IV, pp. 334–38.

[9] Rivier, Vol. II, pp. 221–22.

licist, one of the most noted of the continental writers, considers that neither proclamation nor any form of diplomatic notice is obligatory, subject to the qualification that the relations of the parties are such that hostilities would constitute no surprise.[10] Hall,[11] the foremost English authority, says: " The doctrine of an obligation to declare war was never so consistently acted upon as to render obedience to it at any time obligatory. Since the middle of last century it has had no sensible influence upon practice." But, " partly for the convenience of the subjects of the state, and partly as a matter of duty towards neutrals a manifesto or an equivalent notice ought always to be issued, when possible, before the commencement of hostilities." Lawrence[12] regards the element of surprise as of slight importance in the state of modern diplomacy, and the first act of hostility is sufficiently definite for dating the legal effects of war. Oppenheim, Woolsey, Wheaton and Walker are in complete accord with the latter view.[13]

From the above review it would appear that the majority of writers outside of France take the view that a preliminary declaration of war is unnecessary. Practice has also varied greatly. The Franco-Prussian war of 1870 and the Russo-Turkish war of 1877 both began with formal declarations, though in the latter case Russia invaded Turkey on the day that war was declared. The Chino-Japanese war, 1894 to 1895,

[10] De Martens, Traité de droit international, Vol. III, p. 205.
[11] International Law, 398–99.
[12] Principles of International Law, pp. 299, 301.
[13] Oppenheim, International Law, Vol. II, pp. 103–6; Woolsey, International Law, pp. 189–90; Wheaton, International Law, p. 378; Walker, The Science of International Law, p. 242.

began without a declaration of war, and in the most
recent war between Russia and Japan hostilities began
with no declaration or manifesto of any sort.[14]

The United States in its foreign wars has generally
preceded active belligerent operations by a manifesto
or declaration of war by Congress, following a communication from the President. Hostilities were begun against Tripoli in 1802 upon the passage of an
act of Congress " for the protection of commerce and
seamen of the United States against the Tripolitan
cruisers," without a more formal declaration. Just
before the outbreak of the War of 1812 President
Madison wrote in a special message to Congress, after
reciting the grievances suffered at the hand of Great
Britain: " We behold, in fine, on the side of Great
Britain, a state of war against the United States; and
on the side of the United States, a state of peace toward Great Britain." The message ended without any
specific recommendation as to the course of action to
follow, but Congress passed a bill declaring war, and
the act received the President's signature. After a
brief delay England responded by a declaration of war.
However, in the mean time hostilities had begun. In
the case of the Mexican war President Polk declared

[14] Japan did not wait for the Russian response to her demands,
but ordered the Russian minister to leave Tokio and instructed
her own minister to ask for his passports. Under the circumstances the rupture in diplomatic relations was an adequate
warning to the enemy and to neutrals. Two days after the
beginning of hostilities the Japanese Emperor issued a formal
manifesto to his own subjects without the retroactive clause
so conspicuous in the American declaration, leaving the courts
to determine the moment when hostilities in reality began. See
for full discussion Hershey, International Law and Diplomacy
of the Russo-Japanese war, pp. 62 ff.

8

in a message to Congress, May 11, 1846, that American blood had been shed by the forces of Mexico on American soil, and that war existed by the act of Mexico. Two days later, May 13, Congress declared war and made provision for carrying on the conflict.[15]

The publicity and circulation of intelligence now make unnecessary what was the only safeguard against trickery in another age. No objection can be made to the practice of fixing a date for the benefit of neutrals and of belligerent subjects, but this is apart from an obligation to make a formal declaration of war. There is no justification in practice or in theory for a retroactive declaration. The act of Congress of April 20 authorizing intervention was sufficiently definite and public to acquaint neutrals, and the more so when accompanied by a proclamation of blockade two days later. The ultimatum and the breaking of diplomatic relations, on April 21, satisfied the necessities of warning to the enemy. The declaration of war, while it had no unfortunate results and was in itself not a contravention of any principles of law, was a useless formulary, out of accord with better opinion. If the declaration is at all a necessity, it ought to precede hostilities; if it is not necessary, why take a meaningless step several days after the first blows have been struck?[16]

[15] 2 U. S. Stat. 755; 9 U. S. Stat. 9; Moore, Digest, Vol. VII, pp. 168–69.

[16] The Institut de droit international at its session in 1904 at Edinburgh gave attention to declarations of war. The report argued for a period of ten days after the rupture of diplomatic relations before war could begin. Report of M. Rolin, Annuaire, Vol. XX, p. 64. Raspiller, Du passage de l'état de paix à l'état de guerre, pp. 24–25, condemns the retroactive resolution of the United States as incorrect in international law.

The extent to which neutral commerce has become immune in time of war and the universal practice of allowing belligerent commerce a period of grace still further overcome the need of formal declarations of war.

As a result of the captures by the American fleet made on April 22 before the declaration of war the courts were called upon to give an opinion upon the necessity of such a declaration. The Supreme Court stated in *Buena Ventura v.* United States what may be said to be the American doctrine:

" The practice of a formal proclamation before recognizing an existing war and capturing enemy's property has fallen into disuse in modern times, and actual hostilities may determine the date of the commencement of war, though no proclamation may have been issued, no declaration made, and no action of the legislative branch of the government had."[17]

The beginning of a war, whether through a declaration of war, a retroactive manifesto, or an unannounced overt hostile act, carries with it certain effects aside from the essential one of giving to the states involved the qualities of belligerents. These are the care of the interests of belligerents in enemy territory, the effect of war on treaties and conventions, the treatment of enemy subjects and property in enemy territory, and in the Spanish-American war an unusual subject—the status of Cuban and Philippine insurgents—had to be considered.

Ten days before the definitive breach of intercourse with Spain a sort of local rupture of diplomatic rela-

[17] 175 United States, 384; same in *Pedro v.* United States, 175 United States, 354.

tions occurred in Cuba. Consul-General Lee occupied a peculiarly delicate and difficult and, under the circumstances, semi-diplomatic position in Havana. On April 11, acting under instructions from Washington, he left Havana, taking with him such American citizens as availed themselves of the opportunity to leave the island. The care of American interests in the island was entrusted to the English consul at Havana. This curious partial breaking of relations between the two powers in that territory which was the particular cause of the differences was due in all probability to the American consciousness of the unpopularity of Americans in Havana and of General Lee in particular, and to the conviction that ultimate war was a certainty. It is, however, unusual to see relations interrupted in a particular part of one of the states involved when official efforts to preserve peace are continued in the capitals for many days.

The breaking of diplomatic relations in the Spanish-American war offers another unusual incident. It is the general practice for the belligerents, on withdrawing their own representatives, to entrust the care of the interests of their own subjects in the state abandoned to some single friendly power. The United States followed the common practice and entrusted its interests to the representative of Great Britain in Spain. Spain, however, chose to entrust the care of the interests of her subjects in the United States to two powers, France and Austria-Hungary, rather than offend by favoritism one of her closest friends.[18] Acting upon the request of Spain, the Ambassador of

[18] Foreign Relations, 1898, p. 785; Moore, Digest, Vol. IV, pp. 611–14.

France and the Minister of Austria-Hungary in Washington entered into an agreement to the following purport:

1. The archives of the Spanish legation were committed to the care of Austria-Hungary.

2. The consular archives and the protection of Spanish interests were entrusted to the consuls-general of Austria-Hungary in New York and Chicago, and of France in New Orleans, San Francisco and Philadelphia.

3. In the places where only one of the two countries had a representative that one was to assume the charge; in localities where both countries were represented by consular agents this duty was to devolve upon the French.

4. Questions requiring presentation before the Department of State were to be managed by the Minister of Austria-Hungary or the Ambassador of France according to whether an Austrian or a French consul should have the initiative.

In all other cases the Ambassador of France was charged with any proceedings which required to be made before the Government of the United States.[19] Later, upon the request of Mexico in behalf of Spain, the interests of the Spanish in the southwest of the United States, where there were no French or Austrian consuls, were entrusted to the Mexican consuls,[20] with the understanding that all communication from the Mexican consuls should be turned over to Ambassador Cambon.

[19] Foreign Relations, 1898, pp. 785–89.
[20] Ibid., p. 791.

The idea of a joint protection exercised by two or more states was not without important precedents. In the Greco-Turkish wars of 1869 and 1897 France was charged with the protection of the Greek Catholics, while the protection of orthodox Greeks was assigned after some difficulties to the ambassadors of France, Russia and England jointly. But in these cases peculiar conditions of religious differences existed which were wholly lacking in the Spanish-American war. The method of partition of protection is open to the grave danger of complications at a time when delicate diplomatic relations require the utmost care.

The commencement of a war raises the question of its effect on existing treaties between the belligerents. A decree of the Spanish Government dated April 23, 1898, stated in its first article that " the state of war existing . . . terminates the treaty of peace and friendship of the 27th October, 1795, the protocol of the 12th January, 1877, and all other agreements, compacts and conventions that have been in force up to the present between the two countries."[21]   This was of course good law as far as the termination of the treaty of peace and amity was concerned, and was possibly defensible as to those treaties regarding postal service and commerce and the conventions about property, though here opinion and practice differ very widely.[22] The

[21] Proclamations and Decrees, Washington, 1899, p. 93.
[22] Lawrence, Principles of International Law, p. 313, defends the proposition that treaties and conventions on postal service, commerce and property are simply suspended during the war; Hall, p. 404, holds it on the contrary " to be simplest to take them to be all annulled, and to adopt the easy course, when it is wished to put them in force again without alteration, of expressly stipulating for their renewal by an article in the

best opinion seems to advance the rule that treaties concluded between belligerents ought to continue in force in so far as they are not incompatible with a state of war.[23] However, Spain followed the prevailing European practice and expressly terminated all her treaties and conventions with the United States.

Among the treaty stipulations between Spain and the United States at the outbreak of the war were some that referred to a state of war. For example, Article XIII of the treaty of 1795 provided that if a war should break out between the two nations the merchants should be allowed one year for collecting and transporting their goods and merchandise. Another clause stated that privateers were not to be fitted out by one nation against the other.[24] Such provisions were obviously brought into operation by the war, and had no use or meaning except in such a time.[25]

Several weeks after the beginning of the war the rumor got abroad that the Spanish Government was contemplating issuing a decree of expulsion against enemy subjects in her dominion. The United States made inquiry through the British Ambassador at Madrid for the attitude toward the provision of the treaty of 1795 allowing citizens one year after the beginning

treaty of peace." Rivier, Principes du droit des gens, Paris, 1896, Vol. II, pp. 137-38, classifies treaties into (a) those which suppose a state of peace, in which case war terminates them, and (b) those which presuppose a state of war, in which case war does not terminate them. Oppenheim, International Law, Vol. II, pp. 107-8, is in substantial agreement with the above view.

[23] Consult the French jurist, Pillet, Le droit de la guerre, Vol. I, p. 304; Le Fur, La guerre hispano-américaine, p. 53.

[24] Treaties and Conventions of the United States, p. 1010.

[25] Moore, Digest, Vol. V, p. 376.

of war for preparation for departure. In reply the Government of Spain repeated its view that all the stipulations of the treaties were terminated, but offered, if the United States would propose it, to consider the question of adopting provisionally for the period of war the stipulations specifically relating to a state of war. The United States declined to make such a proposal because it considered the stipulations to be still in force.[26]

It is probably true that Spain was greatly desirous of escaping from provisions of treaties which had become galling. The treaties were the outgrowth of a time when conditions were very different, and they had established a sort of system of favoritism for the subjects of each of the states residing in the territory of the other. The natural consequence during the late Cuban insurrection was to render the repression of filibustering expeditions more difficult; and more, they had given a basis for interference with the free action of insular courts and for many claims for indemnity. Naturally, when war seemed to restore to Spain an opportunity to repudiate such odious restrictions, the proper authorities were not slow to take advantage of a seeming liberty of action.[27] Happily, Spain did not resort to a decree forcing citizens of the United States out of its dominions, nor did it in the end maintain the position on the termination of its treaties and conventions in their entirety.

A convention of 1834 between the two nations pro-

[26] Foreign Relations, 1898, p. 972. See for special treatment, J. B. Moore, Review of Reviews, Vol. XIX, p. 566; cf. same writer in Columbia Law Review, Vol. I, p. 2091.

[27] Le Fur, La guerre hispano-américaine, p. 54.

vided for the payment of an indemnity to the United
States for certain claims of its merchants against
Spain. This debt or the interest upon it was paid in
regular annual instalments of about $28,500. Spain,
in accordance with her proclamation of April 23,
stopped payment during the war. If the conventions
were not in force, then Spain was released from this
part of her debt, and acted correctly in stopping payment. The question is one of the effect of war upon
the debts of one belligerent to the other. The principle is established by publicists and by the practice of
nations " that the obligations of a state for the payment of its debts are not affected by war even though
such debts are held by citizens or subjects of the
enemy."[28] After the war, in December, 1899, the
Spanish Government paid not only the interest for the
year but also that for the year of the war, and recognized to the fullest extent the obligations under the
convention of 1834.[29] It may be said in conclusion
that by this action and the accompanying explanation
Spain acknowledged the debt and the convention as
surviving the shock of war, without any positive action
necessary to revivify them, and in so doing gave another precedent for the effect of war on conventions
involving fiscal obligations. During the negotiations
of the peace commissions at Paris the American members proposed an article by which all treaties in existence between the two countries at the outbreak of the
war were enumerated as continuing in force, but the
plan was rejected by the representatives of Spain on

[28] J. B. Moore, Columbia Law Review, Vol. I, p. 209.
[29] Foreign Relations, 1899, p. 708.

the ground that it involved subjects beyond the competence of the commission. The treaty of peace was concluded without any mention of the subject, and several years elapsed before action was taken.[30] In 1903 a treaty of amity, commerce and general relations formally abrogated all treaties concluded before 1898 except the convention of 1834. Naturally, with Spain eliminated from the West Indies, the exceptional agreements in the treaties of 1795 and 1877 disappeared in the new agreement. In 1902, however, by an interchange of notes the old arrangement on international copyright was restored.[31]

The report that Spain was contemplating a decree of expulsion against American citizens raises the question of the legality of such an action if taken. The report probably arose from the lack of faith which prevailed at the time in the United States on the humanitarianism of Spain, and which was fostered by the yellow journals. In fact, both Spain and the United States took the most advanced position in international usage upon the treatment of enemy subjects residing within their jurisdiction, and treated them with the utmost consideration. The expulsion in mass by one state of enemy subjects residing within its boundaries is no longer admitted in civilized warfare except in cases where the needs of defence necessitate their expulsion. In the Greco-Turkish war of 1897 Turkey ordered all Greeks residing upon Ottoman territory to be expelled in mass, but upon the representation of the great powers it consented to successive delays which in effect hindered the application of

[30] Columbia Law Review, Vol. I, p. 210.
[31] Treaties in Force, 1904, pp. 732, 741.

the proposed rigorous measure. The mere rule that enemy subjects are not to be ruthlessly, or without the strong necessities of defence, expelled from the boundaries of the other belligerent is not a sufficient safeguard. A belligerent is not free to hinder enemy subjects leaving its territories from rejoining their countrymen, even when their departure is for the express purpose of becoming incorporated into the army of the fatherland. Nor is it allowable to confiscate the property of such aliens on the outbreak of war.

The commencement of hostilities imposes upon the belligerents the obligation of notifying neutrals of the new and abnormal relations which exist. Courtesy due to friendly powers as well as legal rules of procedure under the circumstances would lead to the same requirements. In practice the notification is frequently joined with a manifesto or an announcement of a blockade or a statement of the rules of war to be adhered to in the pending conflict. The manifesto which accompanies this notification to the powers commonly gives some account of the causes of the war, and attempts to justify the course taken. This tendency is one of the most significant signs of the strength of public sentiment. States thus recognize the necessity of satisfying others of the justice of their pretensions, and there is in this way a curb upon hasty appeals to the arbitrament of war.

In the war between the United States and Spain the first official notification abroad from American sources was despatched on April 22, the day of the first overt act of hostility. It read:

"WASHINGTON, April 22, 1898.

"By proclamation to-day, under resolution of Cong-ress approved 20th President announces blockade of ports on north side of Cuba between Cardenas and Bahia Honda; also Cienfuegos, south side. Notify minister for foreign affairs.

SHERMAN."

This telegram was sent to all the legations abroad, and joined a sort of preliminary notification of the imminence of war with an announcement of a block-ade. Several days later, on April 25, immediately upon the formal declaration of war by Congress, Secretary Sherman sent a despatch to all the United States legations abroad stating the bare facts in the termination of diplomatic relations on April 21, and closing with these words: "Congress has therefore, by an act approved today, declared that a state of war exists between the two countries since and including April 21. You will inform the Government to which you are accredited, so that its neutrality may be as-sured in the existing war." The exceptional feature is the fact that there were in effect two American notifications to neutrals, one informal and expectant, on April 22, conjoined with a blockade proclamation, and the other formal and definitive, and distinct from any manifesto or other proclamation.[32]

On April 24 the Minister of State at Madrid, M. Gullón, sent the notification of war to the Spanish representatives and through them to the foreign gov-ernments having diplomatic relations with her. The

[32] Foreign Relations, 1898, p. 1171.

telegram united (1) the notification of the existing
state of war, (2) a brief manifesto setting forth the
justice of her cause, and (3) a statement of the rules
of maritime international law to which Spain would
adhere during the war.[33] From the facts set forth it
appears that those duties and liabilities of neutrality
connected in particular with the commerce of non-
belligerents with blockaded ports dated from the receipt of the American notification of April 22,
that probably this was adequate for all purposes,
but that there was no lack of more formal notification. From the wording of the proclamations of
neutrality it would appear that generally Europe
waited for the more formal notifications of April 24
(Spain) and April 25 (United States). The declaration of Great Britain was dated April 26, that of
France April 27. Italy and Belgium acted on April
25 before they could have received the final American
notification, but not until after open hostilities had
been continued three days. The practice indicates a
tendency to act slowly to avoid any premature step.

The beginning of a war makes it essential to determine the legal field of operations for the belligerents.
The Spanish-American war was no exception. It
may be laid down as a general principle that the legal
field of operations open to the belligerents comprises
all the territories over which they exercise full sovereignty, together with the territorial waters and the
high seas. The only exceptions are those cases where
by concert of the powers a state or portion of a state
has been affected by permanent neutralization, or

[33] Spanish Diplomatic Correspondence and Documents, 1896–
1900, p. 155; Revue de droit international public, Vol. V, p. 544.

where at the opening of war, as a result of mutual agreement between the belligerents, certain regions have been excepted. No such conventions limited the freedom of military operations of either Spain or the United States.

At the outbreak of the war the European powers made an effort to limit the field of military operations to Cuba or at most to the Spanish West Indies and the adjacent waters. Commercial countries most naturally opposed the baneful influence upon the trade of their subjects of a war carried on simultaneously over a large territory. However, in 1898 the actuating motive was undoubtedly continental hostility to the United States. The greatest maritime power was its strongest ally in preventing any concerted action against it. European success in imposing such limits must have seriously embarrassed the United States if not totally frustrated the objects of intervention. The Government of the United States demonstrated at an early date a determination to carry the war into all Spanish territories. On April 24 Commodore Dewey was ordered to carry the war into the Philippines, where he arrived May 1. Early in August Porto Rico was invaded, and the authorities at Washington decided to send a fleet to bombard the coasts of Spain; an eastern squadron was actually organized for the latter purpose.

During the invasion of Porto Rico in the early days of August, when the troops threatened San Juan, where were at the time many foreign residents, the foreign consuls requested the Spanish Governor, General Macias, to permit the establishment of a neutral zone between Bayamo and Rio Piedras, where in case of bombardment by the American fleet the foreign residents could take refuge with their families. The same arrangement was laid before the American authorities and accepted. The suspension of hostilities before the attack upon San Juan, however, prevented the consuls from carrying out their proposed plan of neutralization of a part of the belligerent territories.[34]

[34] New York Tribune, August 7; Foreign Relations, 1898, p. 800. It is clearly understood that the representatives of neutrals may take whatever steps are necessary to provide for the safety of the subjects of their countries, but this prerogative is always subject to the condition that the measures taken are not in conflict with any taken by the belligerents and do not hinder in any manner the success of the military operations of the belligerents. They can lawfully make provision for the subjects for whom they are responsible on board ships in the harbor, as was done at Santiago de Cuba, but they have no power to establish a neutral zone in any territory that is subject to military operations without the consent of both belligerents. But Le Fur is in error in his criticism upon the method used by the consuls. The publication of the Foreign Relations has shown that the American authorities were consulted and the neutralization was legally concluded. See Le Fur, La guerre hispano-américaine, pp. 57–58.

CHAPTER VI

Relations of the Belligerents

Great interest attaches to any announcements that the belligerents may make at the beginning of a war, declaring adhesion to this or that body of rules or special principles of international law. This is the more true when the war promises to be on the high seas and when the practice of the belligerents on unsettled principles of law is doubtful. As neither Spain nor the United States had given adherence to the Declaration of Paris of 1856, their attitude became a matter of concern to the great commercial powers. The rules of the Declaration of Paris, as is well known, are:

1. Privateering is and remains abolished.

2. The neutral flag covers an enemy's goods, with the exception of contraband of war.

3. Neutral goods, with the exception of contraband of war, are not liable to capture under the enemy's flag.

4. Blockades in order to be binding must be effective, that is to say, maintained by a force sufficient really to prevent access to the coast of the enemy.

Without entering here into a discussion of the reasons actuating the United States, Spain, Mexico and Venezuela in withholding acceptance of the declaration endorsed by all other states, it suffices to say that the rules as proposed were contrary to the interests of the powers rejecting them in 1856 because each had a long coast line and a weak navy.[1]

Rules 3 and 4 have been uniformly observed in American practice. Privateering, abolished by rule 1, had never been renounced as a right, but by 1898 had been abandoned. Of the second rule more must be said. American writers usually claim that in practice the Government of the United States has adhered to the principle advocated in rule 2 of the Declaration of Paris, but Professor J. B. Moore in an article in the Political Science Quarterly[2] has shown quite conclusively that it is not accurate to say that in American practice " the neutral flag covers an enemy's goods, with the exception of contraband of war," or that the Government had adhered to rule 2. " Our courts," he says, " except where a treaty prescribed a different rule, had uniformly confiscated enemy property, even when it was seized under a neutral flag." And moreover there were few treaties making any stipulation of exemption for enemy property that were in force in 1898. It has been a very common practice in negotiating treaties to include the contrary rule, that the goods of neutrals should be confiscated if taken on enemy ships, unless they were shipped before the declaration of war or within a stipulated time after war began and in ignorance of it. In our treaty of 1819 with Spain the principle of " free ships, free goods " was acknowledged, but only in regard to the property

---

[1] Stark, The Abolition of Privateering and the Declaration of Paris, Columbia University Studies, 1896, p. 366. See American Law Register, Vol. 37, p. 657, for a historical review of the policy of the United States toward the Declaration of Paris.

[2] Vol. XV, p. 402.

of enemies whose governments recognized the same rule.

On April 22, among the first acts of the Government of the United States in assuming the quality of belligerency, the State Department sent the following instructions to the diplomatic representatives abroad: " In the event of hostilities between the United States and Spain, the policy of this Government will be not to resort to privateering, but to adhere to the following recognized rules of international law." The instructions then included the second, third and fourth rules of the Declaration of Paris. Four days later President McKinley issued a proclamation which defined the position of the Government on questions of maritime law. The proclamation, after repeating the announcement that the Government of the United States would not resort to privateering, proceeded to state six rules for the guidance of its officers. The first, second and third of these were identical with the second, third and fourth rules of the Declaration of Paris. The fourth, fifth and sixth rules follow.

" 4. Spanish merchant vessels, in any ports or places within the United States shall be allowed till May 21, 1898, inclusive, for loading their cargoes and departing from such ports or places; and such Spanish merchant vessels, if met at sea by any United States ship, shall be permitted to continue their voyage, if, on examination of their papers, it shall appear that their cargoes were taken on board before the expiration of the above term; provided, that nothing herein contained shall apply to Spanish vessels having on board any officer in the military or naval service of the enemy, or any coal (except such as may be necessary for their voyage), or any other article prohibited or contraband of war, or any dispatch of or to the Spanish Government.

"5. Any Spanish merchant vessel which, prior to April 21, 1898, shall have sailed from any foreign port bound for any port or place in the United States, shall be permitted to enter such port or place, and to discharge her cargo, and afterward forthwith to depart without molestation; and any such vessel, if met at sea by any United States ship, shall be permitted to continue her voyage to any port not blockaded.

"6. The right of search is to be exercised with strict regard for the rights of neutrals, and the voyages of mail steamers are not to be interfered with except on the clearest grounds of suspicion of a violation of law in respect of contraband or blockade."[3]

From these rules it will be seen that the United States pledged itself to liberal dealing with enemy merchant vessels in its ports or vessels having set out for one at the outbreak of the war,[4] and with neutrals in exercising the right of search. The passage bearing on the voyages of mail steamers made it practically certain that federal officers would not repeat the *Trent* affair. In both respects the United States went farther than the letter of the rules of the Declaration of Paris required.[5] The rule of the United States,

[3] Proclamations and Decrees, pp. 77-78.
[4] It should be noted that the thirty-day allowance has been exceeded in several instances. In the Crimean war, 1854, the principal belligerents, England, France and Russia, gave merchant vessels six weeks for loading their cargoes and departing from ports. In the more recent Russo-Japanese war Russia allowed merchant vessels forty-eight hours. Japan allowed seven days. Hershey, International Law and Diplomacy of the Russo-Japanese War, p. 295.
[5] The Times, London, April 28, 1898.

liberal as it was, became further extended in its operation by the decision of the Supreme Court in the case
of the *Buena Ventura,* so that vessels having left port
before the proclamation were included.[6] The Spanish Government embodied the principles of action to
be followed by its officials in a royal decree of April
23.[7]

The first contrast apparent between the rules laid
down by the United States and those laid down by
Spain is in the degree of liberality shown to enemy
merchants at the opening of hostilities. Spain allowed
five days, but dated the beginning of the period from
April 24; the United States made it thirty days, but
started from April 21. Spain offered no specific immunity from capture during the voyage in cases where
enemy ships had already departed for her ports, and no
provision for their entrance and discharge of cargoes.
In practice Spain was more liberal than the letter of
the decree indicated, refusing to capture American
vessels leaving for Spanish ports before the outbreak
of hostilities and arriving in Spanish ports after the
expiration of the stipulated time limit.[8] The extended
period of immunity allowed to enemy commerce in
the Spanish-American war represented a distinct advance over former practice, and indicates the slight
extension necessary to bring about the total immunity
of private enemy property on the high seas.

The United States committed itself to the entire
Declaration of Paris, privateering and all. Spain

---

[6] See post, p. 166.
[7] Spanish Diplomatic Correspondence and Documents, p. 157.
[8] Cf. Le Fur, La guerre hispano-américaine, p. 115, note 2;
Revue de droit international public, Vol. V, p. 812.

expressly reserved for itself the right to issue letters of marque for privateers, but added that it would organize for the present a service of auxiliary cruisers made up of mercantile ships, to coöperate with the navy for the war and to be subject to the statutes and jurisdiction of the regular naval forces. An unnecessarily severe clause of the royal decree of Spain was directed against insurgents who might enter into the service of the United States. "Captains, commanders, and officers of non-American vessels or of vessels manned as to one third by other than American citizens, captured while committing acts of war against Spain, will be treated as pirates, with all the rigor of the law, although provided with a license issued by the Republic of the United States." Fortunately, as neither the Philippine nor the Cuban insurgents possessed a navy and privateering was renounced, no case arose under the threat. The insurgents coöperating with the United States must have been treated according to the usual laws of regular warfare. Experience has demonstrated the uselessness of such threats. The opportunities for retaliation in kind thwart attempts to resort to extreme measures of this sort.

The right to make use of privateers, while reserved by Spain, was not as a matter of fact exercised during the war. An auxiliary service was projected instead. The United States actually organized a sort of auxiliary naval force. In both cases the innovation was in response to a national consciousness of a need of a larger sea-fighting power than that furnished by existing public ships, and to a desire to avoid the resort to privateering, so unanimously condemned. The idea of an auxiliary service was not a new one. In the Franco-Prussian war Prussia was in the same situation, namely, with a merchant commerce which it was unable to protect with its naval force. As a means of protecting this commerce Prussia announced at the beginning of the conflict the intention not to capture private property at sea, hoping to force France into the same position. Failing in this respect, she later changed her policy and ordered the creation of a volunteer navy, and withdrew her announcement of immunity for private enemy property. The war closed before the next logical step came, namely, the authorization to the volunteer navy to capture private property. France protested vigorously, but without avail, against the proposed action of Prussia as a violation of the Declaration of Paris. The Prussian decree for a volunteer navy invited the owners of vessels to fit them out for attack on French ships of war, advanced ten per cent. of the assessed value of the volunteer, offered large premiums for the destruction of enemy ships and agreed to pay the owners the assessed value in case of loss. The owners of the vessels were to furnish the crews, and the officers were to be merchant seamen. The officers were to be uniformed as naval officers and under naval discipline, but the system was neither a part of the regular navy nor in any way attached to it beyond being subject to the general command of superior naval officers. Premiums were to be paid to the owners and the crews for the capture or destruction of enemy ships. The rule that the owner was to hire the crew and the state to give premiums for captures seems to have established a system which violated the spirit if not the letter of the Declaration of Paris.[9]

The Spanish auxiliary naval force, as projected on paper, was slightly different from the Prussian. The plan comprised a sort of marine militia to supplement the regular navy, coöperating with the latter and subject to its jurisdiction. In this way a service was to be created which would take the place of privateers without displeasing neutrals. The war ended before a single merchant ship had actually received authority to commit hostilities against the Yankees. By the Spanish system individual owners of ships suitable for the service could place them at the service of the Government, and retaining the ownership, could hire the crew subject to the law for recruiting merchant ships instead of the law of naval recruiting. Spain did not offer, however, the premiums for the capture or destruction of enemy ships as Prussia did. But the difference in favor of Spain was offset by the authority conferred on auxiliary cruisers, like ships of war, to attack and capture merchant ships as well as public ships of the enemy.[10]

[9] The Prussian system was not as a matter of fact carried out. Boissel, La course maritime, pp. 167–85, gives an account of the system of volunteer navies, and concludes that Prussia did not violate the letter of the Declaration of Paris, but he condemns Prussian duplicity of attitude toward enemy property. Calvo condemned the Prussian system. De Boeck and Geffcken endorsed it. Guiheneuc, La marine auxiliaire en droit international, Paris, 1900, p. 84, regards Prussia as violating the Declaration of Paris through the failure to provide for a bona fide and real incorporation into the regular navy. Stark, Abolition of Privateering, Columbia Studies, Vol. VIII, p. 377; Hall, International Law, p. 547; Oppenheim, International Law, Vol. II, pp. 93 ff.

[10] Calvo, Vol. I, par. 385, 4th ed.; Spanish Diplomatic Cor-

The United States created its auxiliary naval force for the war with Spain by a joint resolution on May 26, and it was in a real sense a part of the public naval service. The chief of the auxiliary naval force was a regular line officer of the navy detailed for the purpose of command. The rules of discipline, organization and emoluments were the same as those that applied to the regular navy. The enlistment and commissioning of officers were managed by the naval department and not by the original owners. The ships themselves became by purchase the property of the United States, and the Government made the contracts for transforming them for war service. In inaugurating the system resort was had to the existing naval militia of the states.[11] In the latter particulars the American system departed quite widely from that of Spain. The auxiliary cruisers of the United States bore less resemblance to privateers than did those of Spain. Both were an effective and, from the standpoint of the Declaration of Paris strictly construed, probably a wholly legal mode of incorporating the merchant marine into the regular navy. The practice appears to accord with the demands for a decrease in large regular navies and to solve the problem for the states with small navies, and to do so without the sacrifice of security for commerce. Some such means of reserve force must remain essential until the capture of private property at sea is abolished. The system of

respondence and Documents, p. 157; Le Fur, La guerre hispano-américaine, pp. 61–72; Boissel, La course maritime, p. 180; Bujac, Précis du quelques campagnes contemporaines, Vol. IV, p. 142.

[11] Message and Documents, 1898–1899, Vol. II, pp. 972 ff.

auxiliary ships was an application to the sea of the volunteer militia for land service. The danger in the Spanish plan, as in the Prussian, was in the use of the merchant crew without a transformation in its character assimilating it to the navy.[12] The vital part of any voluntary naval service which is to satisfy existing needs without contravening the Declaration of Paris and violating any essential principle of civilized warfare is that it be closely connected with the state, and constitute in spirit as well as in name a part of the public force.

The subject of blockade belongs rather to the relations of belligerents with neutrals than of belligerents with one another.[13] Blockades are primarily directed against neutral trade. Belligerent commerce is just as open to seizure whether there is a blockade or not, whereas neutral commerce, excepting contraband, is unaffected by a war except where a blockade closes the ports of the belligerents. It is only because a blockade becomes a means of excluding provisions from an enemy belligerent and hence a means of war that the consideration of the subject at this point is justified. The effect of a blockade upon neutrals and their consequent obligations can better be postponed to the following chapter.

[12] Both Russia and France have a volunteer service ready for incorporation into the regular navy in the event of hostilities, and differing only slightly from the American. Great Britain has a system similar in all respects to the American. See Hershey, International Law and Diplomacy of the Russo-Japanese War, p. 148 n. for the Russian use of volunteer navy; Oppenheim, International Law, Vol. II, pp. 94–95; Guiheneuc, La marine auxiliaire en droit international, pp. 21–22.

[13] Excellent statement of the subject by Paul Fauchille, Du blocus maritime, Paris, 1882.

A blockade proper is the fictitious closing of a harbor by the use of vessels of war so stationed as to be able to interrupt any neutral vessel attempting to enter. A blockade has no importance to the enemy state more than making it more difficult to secure the food supply of the region. The closing of a harbor by one of the belligerents as a means of defence or offence, whether artificially by the device of sinking obstructions at the entrance—a de facto blockade—or constructively by placing torpedoes, is quite distinct from a blockade proper. It has become a common practice for one or the other of the parties to a war to attempt to close the harbors by one of the latter devices. The legality of the practice can hardly be open to question at this time. A state has a perfect right in time of peace to forbid entrance to its harbors to any or all foreign powers; the more has it a right to do so when the abnormal conditions of war exist. The same sovereign right which allows it to open or construct harbors and improve them enables it to take away the privileges given. It may insure the enforcement of the closure by such means as are at hand. The damage is of its own doing and at its own expense, and the expense of removing the obstructions on the return to peace will be upon itself. That the act is done by an enemy exercising belligerent right does not alter the legality or change the responsibilities in the matter.[14]

The main obligation in closing a harbor in time of peace or war by a belligerent in self-defense, or of an

[14] Rivier, Principes du droit des gens, Vol. II, 292; Oppenheim, International Law, Vol. II, p. 190.

enemy port as an aggressive act of military operations, is that of due warning or notification to the neutrals. Both Spain and the United States resorted to the right in one form or another during the war. The United States mined many of its own harbors with torpedoes, but in such a manner as not to close the harbor completely. Naval Constructor Hobson and seven companions made an attempt, on June 3, 1898, to sink the *Merrimac* across the harbor of Santiago de Cuba in order to seal the outlet for the fleet of Admiral Cervera. Spain sank several barges in the harbor of Cardenas, and made a similarly ineffective attempt to close the harbor of San Juan.[15] In the case of the ports of Ferrol, Cadiz, Cartagena and Mahon, where submarine defences were laid, neutrals were forbidden entrance by night.[16] Neutral powers were greatly disturbed early in the war by the report that the United States intended to place torpedoes all along the blockaded coast.[17] The Government of the United States as a matter of fact never resorted to the expedient feared by neutrals, and the law of blockade as understood by writers today does not contemplate the use of such an auxiliary to public ships. It is doubtful, however, whether neutrals would interfere in any case where a powerful belligerent made the innovation. The several practices in the closure of ports and harbors of the enemy would appear to be perfectly natural applications of the changing character of modes in warfare, as long as they are limited to belligerent territorial waters or kept within the line of blockade.

[15] The Times, London, May 23, 1898.
[16] Wheaton, International Law, Atlay ed., p. 721.
[17] The Times, London, April 25, 1898.

Neutrals would be entitled to specific warning, that liability for indemnity might not attach to any losses suffered as a result. Where floating mines are employed the greatest care should be taken to prevent their drifting into the open sea. The same rules about the character of the warning should apply as in notification of a blockade proper.[18]

It does not seem necessary to class the closure of enemy harbors either by torpedoes or sunken ships or other devices as true cases of blockade in the usage of that term, but it should be judged upon its own merits as a distinct method of conducting the operations of war. No means of prosecuting war is more humane. The trifling expense of clearing the harbor on the return to peace, which has[19] been raised as an objection, is insignificant in comparison with the property losses which ordinarily result from the recognized modes of prosecuting war. Every method of warfare that throws the burden of the war upon the financial and commercial resources of the belligerents without increasing the dangers to life and limb of the combatants is distinctly to be sought. The de facto closing of enemy harbors is preëminently successful in this regard.

A great many of the early modes of conducting war have come to be considered as outside the pale of civilized warfare. Conspicuous among such is the rule

[18] Paul Fauchille, Du blocus maritime, especially pp. 133, 273; Rivier, Principes du droit des gens, Vol. II, p. 296; Hershey, International Law and Diplomacy of the Russo-Japanese War, pp. 124–35, for use of submarine mines and opinion of leading writers on international law.

[19] Le Fur, La guerre hispano-américaine, p. 82.

forbidding poisoned arms, and the rule against the use of guns loaded with nails or irregular bits of iron. The Convention of St. Petersburg, in 1868, agreed to give up the use of explosive projectiles weighing less than fourteen ounces, and any method of destruction which caused a loss of life or a needless suffering without a proportionately advantageous result.[20] In 1898 neither the United States nor Spain had acceded to the limitation, but the failure to join in so high a principle of humanity was due to other causes than any lack of sympathy with the objects of the St. Petersburg Convention. There was no occasion during the war to complain of the conduct of either belligerent. Both ratified the second convention adopted at The Hague the following year, 1899, and thereby subscribed to the general rule of not employing arms, projectiles or material of a nature to cause superfluous injury.

There are, on the other hand, certain so-called limitations on the justifiable means available for prosecuting war concerning which the agreement is not so uniform. The use of the false flag or other similar ruse to deceive an opponent may be instanced at the outset. The rule quite generally accepted for the use of the false flag may perhaps be stated in the following terms: the false colors may be used either to escape from the enemy or to lure a ship or a body of troops into a disadvantageous position, but the true colors must be raised before a first shot is fired. Hall says further: " Information must not be surreptitiously obtained under the shelter

---

[20] De Martens, Nouv. Rec. Gen., Vol. XVIII, p. 474.

of a flag of truce, and the bearer of a misused flag
may be treated by the enemy as a spy; buildings not
used as hospitals must not be marked with a hospital
flag; and persons not covered by the provisions of the
Geneva Convention must not be protected by its
cross."[21]   The Instructions for United States Armies
in the Field are in general agreement with the rule
here stated.[22]   The rule laid down in the proposed
Declaration of Brussels of 1874, repeated in the code
of the Laws of War drawn up by the Institute of
International Law, Oxford, 1880, and finally adopted
in the Hague Conference, 1899, and ratified by all the
great powers, forbade " improper use of a flag of truce,
the national flag or military ensigns and the enemy's
uniform, as well as the distinctive badges of the Geneva
Convention."[23]   But like the Instructions to the Armies
of the United States in the Field on the same subject
the statement adopted on the above occasion would
seem to lack explicitness.   Does it prohibit all use of
the enemy flag for the purpose of deceit?   Manifestly
from the language there is a distinct tendency toward
regarding the use of the enemy's flag as opposed to the
highest military honor and courtesy, without going
to the extent of an absolute prohibition.   In any event,
the United States commanders were bound, not by any
international convention, but by the instructions of

[21] Hall, International Law, pp. 557–58.
[22] Articles 101, 114, 115, 117 of House Document 100, 43
Cong., 1 Sess.
[23] Declaration of Brussels, Article 13, Annual Register, 1874–
1875; Manual of the Laws of War, Oxford, 1880, Article 8;
Second Convention of the Hague, 1899, Article 23; Treaties
in Force, 1904, p. 931.

their own government and by international law, not
to resort to the use of the false flag.

One complaint upon the conduct of the United
States forces in this respect came up during the war.[24]
On May 18 two American ships, the cruiser *St. Louis*
and the tug *Wampatuck,* in attempting to cut the near
shore cables, approached the entrance to the harbor
of Guantanamo. In doing so the commanders resorted
to the ruse of employing the Spanish flag, but raised
the national flag before the conflict began.[25] The
American ships were repulsed. Though the conduct
of the *St. Louis* was technically correct, Spain regarded the act as contrary to the spirit of civilized
warfare. Some days later the Minister of Foreign
Affairs included the use of a false flag in a circular
letter of protest against the conduct of the United
States which he addressed to the neutrals. With
characteristic irony, so common in history, the tables
were turning. The former complainant was before the
court of neutrals on the charge of inhumanity.

A further limitation upon belligerents universally
recognized is the employment of savages in the armies.
Here again the Spanish Government turned the charge
of violating usages of civilized warfare against the
United States. In this instance the question turned
on what constitutes savagery. Most naturally the
United States made use of the Cuban insurgents as
allies, and particularly as scouts and guides; the same
use was made for a time of the Tagals of the Philip-

[24] Spanish Diplomatic Correspondence and Documents, p.
165; Circular to the Powers, June 6, 1898.
[25] The Times, London, May 27, 1898; Annual Encyclopedia,
1898, p. 756.

pines, and its own negroes were largely employed in its regular and volunteer forces. The American commanders claimed no control over Cuban bands, but found them eager to coöperate and serve subject to American orders. In neither Cuba nor the Philippines were the insurgents allowed to share the fruits of victory and to take or plunder places captured by American forces for which American arms had become responsible. Indeed, the refusal of the United States to do so was the occasion of grave differences with the allies, which in one case resulted in a war between the United States and its own allies.[26] As long as Garcia's soldiers served under General Shafter they were furnished with rations and ammunition. An appropriation act of Congress late in May made possible such aid to the insurgents on a large scale,[27] but beyond informal relations with the Cuban and Philippine insurgents the Government of the United States steadfastly refused to go. It was hardly possible to ignore entirely those for whose sake the intervention was begun. The Cuban Government was not recognized before or during the war. But without regard to the relations of the United States with the insurgents and the peculiar status of the latter, it is difficult to see wherein the United States Government acted otherwise than in the strictest accord with its rights and with the obligations of international law. None of the allies or auxiliaries in Cuba or the Philippines

[26] New York Tribune, July 20 and 21, 1898; Message and Documents of the United States, 1898–1899, Vol. I, pp. 269, 297; Le Fur, La guerre hispano-américaine, p. 102.

[27] Report of Secretary of War, Message and Documents of United States, 1898–1899, Vol. I, p. 252.

belonged to the class of savages in the sense intended by the rule of international law. Much less did its own negroes. Spain had indirectly recognized the belligerency of the Cubans, and the Cubans from the standpoint of international law were as fully belligerents and entitled when captured to the treatment of prisoners of war as were the armies of the United States. The employment of the insurgents was not provoking them to arms or arming them against the mother-country, but was using favorable conditions, for which the United States was not responsible. It is a fact beyond dispute that the Cubans and Tagals committed acts condemned by the rules of civilized warfare, but these were exceptional cases and not due to inherent savagery. Any troops, however high in the scale of civilization they rank, become at times " savages " to a terrible degree. The acts are to be condemned, but their commission does not bring the government employing them or allying with them under the class of powers employing " savages."

The commanders of the armies of invasion of Cuba found themselves several times embarrassed by the failure of Cuban bands to respect armistice that had been made with captured Spanish garrisons. In such cases a grave responsibility rested upon the United States to force respect for the conventions with the enemy. Both Cuban and American commanders were at great pains to prevent an open rupture. The first obligation upon the United States in conquered territory was the preservation of order. It was not possible for the American authorities to meet the wishes of the Cubans by giving over to them the policing, garrisoning

10

and governing, and at the same time fulfil so paramount an international obligation. The feelings and
the natural aspirations, even the impatience of the
Cubans may well be comprehended, but a third power
had been invited to aid them, and much responsibility
passed to this power, which had responded by intervention. Its first duty was to preserve in its own control the conquered territory. Nor was this in any
degree a reflection on Cuban army discipline and self-
restraint, though the pillaging of Siboney, Baiquiri
and El Caney by insurgents before the arrival of the
American forces and the threats and continued acts
of persecution against Spanish planters were in themselves reason enough for the refusal of the ally to place
the natives in immediate charge of the island.[28]

The tendency to watch every act of the enemy and
to protest to neutrals upon the occasion of violation of
international law has been alluded to. Spain, the
weaker power, made repeated resort to appeals to
Europe. The protest of June 6, 1898, was the second
of the kind. On May 11 objections were raised to the
retroactive declaration of war and to the inefficiency
of the blockade. The second circular of June 6 added
bombardment without previous notification, the illegal
use of the Spanish flag, and the cutting of submarine
cables.[29]

In the matter of bombardment there is only the conduct of the United States to examine, as Spain had no

[28] Le Fur, La guerre hispano-américaine, footnotes to pages
102-4 have much valuable evidence on the subject of Cuban
pillaging.
[29] Spanish Diplomatic Correspondence and Documents, 1896–
1900, pp. 164, 165.

opportunity to resort to it.[30] It is the custom in treating of the law of bombardments to distinguish (1) forts and batteries separate from any town, (2) fortified towns, and (3) non-fortified towns. It is a good rule to say that the former may be bombarded at any time in time of war and without any notification; that the last should never be bombarded at all. In the

[30] The following table will exhibit the facts in the conduct of the United States:

TABLE OF BOMBARDMENT

Bombardment	Date	Nature of Fortification	Notification	Directed Against Fortifications Only
Matanzas	April 27	Detached batteries	None	Yes. Object to locate batteries
Cardenas	May 11	Detached batteries	None	Yes. Object to locate batteries
San Juan	May 12	Fortified town	None	Yes. Little more than practice drill. Small damage to town
Santiago	May 31	Against shore batteries	None	Yes. Slight damage
Caimanéra	June 10	Little more than garrison and batteries	None	Yes
Aguadores, Jaragua, Cabañas and Siboney	June 22–23	Detached fortifications and small towns scarcely more than garrison	None	Yes. Slight damage to private property
Santiago	June 11–12	Fortified town	Yes. July 3, with 24 hours warning; extended at request of foreign consuls to 48 hours. Repeated July 9 with 24 hours warning	Yes. Small damage to town and private property
Manzanillo	July 18	Small fortified town	None	Object, destruction of shipping in harbor
Nipe	July 21	Small fortified town	None	Yes
Manila	August 13	Fortified town	Yes. August 7, with 48 hours warning. Repeated Aug. 13, with 1 hour warning	Yes. Surrender immediate. Small damage to private property

second case opinion and practice alike vary widely. Some writers hold to a preliminary notification.[31] Others who are inclined to exalt belligerent rights admit the right to surprise, and therefore deny the necessity of any notification. All appear to agree that the fire should not be directed against private houses.[32] German writers of prominence, supported by the German military, defend bombardment without notification on the ground that the demoralization of the civil population will hasten the surrender.[33] In the Franco-Prussian war Paris was bombarded without a previous formal notification. The most recent statements of opinion—the Declaration of Brussels, 1874; the Code of the Institute of International Law, and the Second Convention of the Hague Conference—agree in making it the duty of military authorities to give notice to local authorities, except in cases of open assault, of an intention of beginning a bombardment.[34] But all admit the possibility of exceptions where a notification might not be necessary. The evident intention of recent statements has been toward making more binding the obligation to give some form of notification without going so far as to make the rule ironclad.

Instructions for the Armies of the United States, drawn by Francis Lieber, admit of surprise in bombardments. Article 19 reads: " Commanders, when-

[31] Claimed by Spain in Protest to Neutrals, June 6, 1898. Spanish Diplomatic Correspondence and Documents, p. 165.

[32] Hall, International Law, pp. 556–57.

[33] Revue de droit international et de legislation comparée, Vol. III, 1871, p. 300.

[34] Declaration of Brussels, Article 16; Code of Institute, Article 32; Hague Convention, Article 26, not applicable to naval bombardment.

ever admissible, inform the enemy of their intention to bombard a place, so that the non-combatants, and especially the women and children, may be removed before the bombardment commences. But it is no infraction of the common law of war to omit thus to inform the enemy. Surprise may be a necessity." The United States Code of Naval Warfare makes a very satisfactory statement of the law of bombardment in the following words: " The bombardment, by a naval force, of unfortified and undefended towns, villages, or buildings, is forbidden, except when such bombardment is incidental to the destruction of military or naval establishments, public depots or munitions of war, or vessels of war in port, or unless reasonable requisitions for provisions and supplies essential at the time to such naval vessel or vessels, are forcibly withheld, in which case due notice of bombardment shall be given. The bombardment of unfortified and undefended towns and places for the nonpayment of ransom is forbidden."[35]

The Spanish regulations for the guidance of commanders in the field, on the other hand, are more exacting and state that " by all means the besieger should previously announce the time of bombardment and give a term for the departure of the pacific inhabitants."[36] Most naturally Spain took every occasion to protest to the neutral powers against American bombardments which violated the letter of its more strict interpretation of the sanctity of notifications.

In the war of 1898 there were no bombardments of

[35] Quoted by Hershey, International Law and Diplomacy of the Russo-Japanese War, pp. 314–15.
[36] Spanish Diplomatic Correspondence and Documents, p. 165.

open or unfortified towns. In all cases of bombardment of fortified towns the rule to direct the fire only
against the fortifications was fully observed. There
were in fact only three cases of true bombardments
of fortified towns—San Juan, Santiago and Manila.
In the last two cases extremely liberal warnings were
given.[87] The bombardment of San Juan was begun
in the search for Admiral Cervera's lost fleet, and incidentally to locate batteries and test the enemy's prep-
arations for resistance, rather than for the purpose of
destruction or with any evident intention of an attempt
to take the town.[88] Under such circumstances the element of surprise was essential. The instructions of
the United States Government to its military commanders authorized such action. And it is by no
means clear that even the spirit of the second Hague
convention would condemn the conduct in such cases,
though it was on the occasion of the bombardment of
San Juan that Spain made an unheeded complaint to
the neutral powers. The attack on Santiago, June 22
to 23, belongs clearly to cases of bombardment during
open assault and against detached batteries, and is
admissible under the most rigid rules. The bombardment of Manzanillo, July 18, must be treated separately. The object was the destruction of the ship
yards in the harbor, and the town was not bombarded.
Such destruction of enemy property is always permissible.[89]

[87] See page 147, n. 30.
[88] Wilson, The Downfall of Spain, p. 196.
[89] Hall, International Law, p. 556, note 2; Rivier, Principes
du droit des gens, Vol. II, pp. 284-85. New York Tribune,
July 19, 1898; Wilson, The Downfall of Spain, p. 396.

Spain included the cutting of cables in her protest to neutrals on the conduct of the United States. The earliest belligerent acts of the United States were directed to the destruction of the cable communication of Cuba with the outside world, and the measure was a deliberate feature of the war operations. The complete isolation of large portions of the island of Cuba at an early date shortened the duration of the war. Cable cutting is a comparatively modern mode of prosecuting war; its legal aspects are far from being clearly defined by writers on international law. The International Cable Convention at Paris in 1884 imposed rules for the protection of cables in time of peace only, and expressly stated that belligerents should be free to act in time of war as though the convention did not exist. Cables connecting enemy ports or the ports of belligerents, whether neutral-owned or enemy-owned, have no protection in time of war beyond that which self-interest dictates to belligerents. The status of cables connecting neutrals with belligerent soil belongs to the relation of belligerents with neutrals rather than to the relation of belligerents among themselves, and it will be further considered at the proper place.[40]

The wireless telegraph had not come into use in 1898, and little use was made of balloons as accessories to military operations. The United States had but one balloon for service in the Santiago campaign, and so far as known Spain on her side made no use of them.[41] American authorities made two ascensions in

[40] See Holland, Journal de droit international privé, 1898, p. 651, " Submarine Cables in time of War." Rivier, Principes du droit des gens, Vol. II, p. 267.

[41] Message and Documents of the United States, 1898–1899, Vol. I, pp. 433 and 759 ff.

the short campaign around Santiago, and as no captures of those engaged in the operation of the one small balloon took place no opportunity arose to test the attitude of the belligerents on the subject. The balloon has a legitimate place in modern warfare, and its status in international law needs careful definition.

In the Franco-Prussian war, 1870, Germany showed a disposition to treat persons engaged in balloon service as spies. Though none of those captured were executed, they were harshly treated by severe imprisonment. The conduct of Bismarck, however, has met with general condemnation by writers on international law. Rivier, the Swiss publicist, classes aeronauts travelling openly as combatants.[42] The Declaration of Brussels, 1874, forbade the treatment of the operators as spies. The code drawn up by the Institute of International Law at Oxford, 1880, classes aeronauts charged with observing the operations of an enemy or with the maintenance of communications between various parts of an army as prisoners of war.[43] This rule was adopted in the second convention at the Hague Conference.[44] The Manual of France for the use of military authorities gives captured aeronauts the status of prisoners of war,[45] and the rule may now be said to be a fixed one in the law of war.

The use of balloons for throwing projectiles is another matter and involves different regulations. At the Hague Peace Conference of 1899 the use of balloons

[42] Principes du droit des gens, Vol. II, pp. 249, 283.
[43] Code of the Institute of International Law for Wars on Land, Article 20; Snow, Cases and Opinions, p. 557.
[44] Holls, The Peace Conference, Article 29, p. 441.
[45] Hall, International Law, p. 561.

for throwing projectiles or explosives was forbidden for a period of three years. This rule was made in the belief that balloons as at present constructed are not controllable and therefore cannot form an accurate dependable part of a conflict and commit injury or destruction of advantage to the army to which they belong. The short limit to the prohibition reflected the feeling of uncertainty as to the future development of the balloon as an auxiliary of warfare and the desire for liberty of action in the near future. The convention expired in 1904.

While aeronauts are in reality combatants and receive when captured the same treatment as soldiers, newspaper correspondents stand in a class by themselves. They are not combatants in the direct meaning of that term. They take no active part in the prosecution of war measures, yet they may at times by their communications menace or even thwart the plans of the enemy. It is necessary to distinguish (1) the correspondents of belligerents' journals who are subjects of the state whose army they accompany, (2) the correspondents of belligerents' journals who are neutral representatives of the state whose army they accompany, and finally (3) neutral subjects representing neutral journals. The first and second classes have a like status; neutrals serving enemy journals do in effect lose their nationality and become a part of the belligerent army in the same manner as neutrals enlisting as soldiers receive the enemy status and cease to be neutrals. The most severe treatment recognized is detention as prisoners of war. The Institute of International Law at its Oxford session made the limit detention " for so long a time as may be required by strict military necessity." A correspondent regularly accredited and conducting himself properly should meet with no harsher treatment.

During the Spanish-American war both governments treated correspondents of enemy newspapers as prisoners of war. Two reporters for the World accompanying the American forces were captured at Cabañas by the Spanish authorities and held in prison until the end of May, when they were released by an exchange for a Spanish colonel and a military surgeon.[46] The arrest of Wiggan and Robinson, who were attempting to land at Matanzas as the representatives of American journals, involved the treatment of neutrals serving the enemy. Both were made prisoners of war. The arrest of the correspondent of the New York Herald, an English citizen, and his condemnation to nine years' imprisonment arose out of his alleged photographing of the fortifications of San Juan, which was a criminal offence. He was once arrested and acquitted, and then rearrested on the same charge and the second time condemned as stated. The English Government intervened to demand his release on the ground that to arrest and condemn upon the same facts upon which he had once been acquitted was contrary to law and general usage.[47]

Neither Spanish nor American military authorities hesitated to censure or suppress completely the news sent from correspondents in their ranks or to expel the

[46] London Times, June 3, 1898.
[47] The Times, London, about July 23, 1898. Cf. New York Tribune, same date. Le Fur, La guerre hispano-américaine, p. 99.

undesirable correspondents from their armies. General Shafter expelled from Cuba the correspondents of the New York Journal because its reports were regarded as likely to excite an unwarranted feeling of revenge and hence as injurious to military discipline. Later in the summer, when the war was practically over, General Blanco refused to receive American correspondents on the ground that their presence would make it more difficult to restrain the passions of the enraged Spanish population.[48] The practice with regard to the treatment of correspondents was in general accord with the accepted rules of international law.[49] If newspaper correspondents have the right in one case of prisoners of war and in the other of innocent noncombatants, they too have important obligations. They are subject to the control of the military authorities, and violations of orders make them common criminals. The giving to the enemy of news may make them spies and subject them to the same treatment.

The introduction of wireless telegraphy since 1898 has presented to belligerents a new phase of the obligations of correspondents. In the recent Russo-Japanese war the Russian Government notified neutrals that the newspaper correspondents making use of wireless telegraph apparatus to communicate information regarding the war, if captured within the zone of operations of the fleet or near the coast of Kwantong, would be

[48] Le Fur, La guerre hispano-américaine, pp. 100–1.
[49] The most satisfactory treatment of the subject in the light of recent wars is to be found in three articles which appeared in the Revue général de droit international public, Vol. I, 1894, p. 60; Vol. III, 1896, p. 80, and Vol. IV, 1897, p. 698; Rivier, Principes du droit des gens, Vol. II, p. 249; Pillet, Le droit de la guerre, Vol. I, p. 217.

looked on as spies and that steamers furnished with wireless telegraph would be seized as prizes of war.[50] The declaration as to neutral ships equipped with wireless apparatus in effect declared such materials contraband. The declaration aroused at the time considerable excitement in newspaper circles, but there can be no question that Russia had a perfect right to prohibit the presence of correspondents within her territorial waters, and to take measures to expel them or to censure what news they were allowed to transmit. The same absolute control extended to the apparatus for wireless telegraph even on board neutral ships. The control of news is a vital element in the conduct of military operations, and the wireless apparatus would be no exception to the rules that have always obtained for cables and telegraph lines on land. Due notice of the prohibition ought to be given neutrals. However, wherever newspaper correspondents conduct their operations openly and without disguise the rigorous measures proposed by Russia would seem to exceed the offense. In the state of international law newspaper correspondents operating without the consent of the commander in whose lines they are taken ought to be treated as prisoners of war and not as spies. So far as known the Russian threat never came to an issue by an open violation. The Times (London) correspondent denied at the time having been in belligerent waters or having sent messages through other than neutral channels. This aspect bears an analogy to cables which are wholly or partly neutral, and follows the conclusions reached[51] on that aspect of

[50] The Times, London, April 22, 1904.
[51] Page 212.

the question. The right of neutral correspondents to transmit messages from neutral vessels on the high seas or in neutral waters cannot be questioned. Whether the message is carried by person, by wire, by cable or by wireless can make no legal difference.[52]

In the treatment of sick and wounded, and in the inviolability of surgeons, both belligerents fully respected the convention of Geneva, 1864, to which they were signatory powers, Spain in the first instance and the United States in 1882. The convention of 1864 only referred to the treatment of sick and wounded and neutralized the persons engaged in their service, hospitals, and other things like ambulances, horses, and medical and surgical stores needed for their care. An attempt was made in 1868 to extend the provisions of the original convention to the peculiar conditions of warfare on the seas, neutralizing hospital ships in addition. The latter failed of ratification, but in the Franco-Prussian war of 1870 it was accepted as a modus vivendi for the war, and again in 1898, upon the suggestion of Switzerland, both Spain and the United States did the same.[53] The Red Cross Societies of both belligerents served under the privileges secured by the conventions of Geneva. The American branch had undertaken to supply relief for reconcentrados in Cuba with excellent results, and was pre-

[52] For treatment of this aspect of the status of correspondents using wireless telegraphy, and particularly for the rule adopted by the Institute of International Law at its session, 1906, see Hershey, International Law and Diplomacy of the Russo-Japanese War, pp. 121–24.

[53] Hall, International Law, p. 419; Spanish Diplomatic Correspondence and Documents, pp. 143–54; Message and Documents of the United States, 1898–1899, Vol. I, p. 38.

pared for immediate coöperation with the American forces. The Red Cross Societies of England, France, Holland, Belgium, Switzerland, Denmark, Germany, Italy and Mexico aided by volunteers and money.[54] No cases of violation of the Geneva conventions arose during the war. The American Government fitted out a floating ambulance, the ship *Solace,* which was the first instance of a government vessel commissioned by any nation to coöperate with the volunteer service of the Red Cross.[55]

The largest number of prisoners taken during the war fell to the American forces upon the surrender of Santiago and Manila. There were 22,780 prisoners taken at the former and about 13,000 at the latter. The lot of the Santiago captives was fixed by the act of capitulation itself. The eighth article stipulated that the Spanish troops should be transported, together with all personal effects, to Spain. This was effected. The ships engaged in the service were neutralized through an agreement between the belligerents.[56] The capitulation at Manila occurred the day following the signature of the peace protocol, and the captured garrisons were left at liberty, and supplied with rations as though prisoners of war until their repatriation under the treaty of peace.[57] In the naval battle of Santiago, July 3, 1670 were made prisoners of war and sent to American fortresses. Aside from these cases the number of prisoners was small. Spain captured Hobson and seven companions on the occasion of the *Merrimac* episode.

[54] American Review of Reviews, 1899, Vol. XIX, p. 56.
[55] The Times, London, June 22, 1898.
[56] Foreign Relations, 1898, p. 989.
[57] Message and Documents, Vol. I, pp. 294, 898–99.

In general the treatment accorded the captured was as humane as the most advanced rules of war require. Some instances here and there occurred where commanders charged with the care of prisoners were no more liberal in privileges than the circumstances made absolutely necessary, but such were rare. Individuals complained at times of harsh treatment, but when investigated these complaints seem to be on the ground of close confinement. A commander is justified in incarcerating prisoners of war, and he rests under no obligation to do more than surround them with sanitary conditions and supply them with a wholesome and adequate food supply. Both governments attempted as far as local conditions permitted to fulfil the obligation. The complaints are more than counterbalanced by statements concerning the liberality of the captors. The Instructions for the Armies of the United States in the Field deal in detail with the subject, and represent the most liberal and advanced practice that obtains among the nations.[58] It would be difficult to say as much regarding the treatment of the prisoners taken by the insurgents in Cuba and the Philippines, where there is strong evidence of inhumane treatment of dead and captured,[59] though in the Philippines the instances of so-called cruelty that were investigated by the American commanders were attributed to neglect caused by the inability of the insurgents to supply proper food and medical attendance.[60] But for these instances neither the United States nor Spain had any responsibility.

[58] Articles 49–53, 55–56, 72–80, 105–110, 119–133.
[59] Cf. Le Fur, La guerre hispano-américaine, p. 95, note 4.
[60] Message and Documents of United States, 1898–1899, Vol. IV, p. 125.

There were only two cases of exchange of prisoners during the war. On May 20, 1898, upon the request of the English consul at Havana, a Spanish colonel and a surgeon on the one side were exchanged for two correspondents of the New York World held as prisoners of war. The other case was that of Lieutenant Hobson and the seven sailors made prisoners in the attempt to close the harbor of Santiago. The eight were exchanged for a Spanish lieutenant wounded at El Caney and fourteen subordinate officers and soldiers. No exception or unusual practice occurred in the exchanges effected during the war.

In turning to the conduct of the belligerents toward enemy private property it becomes necessary to distinguish enemy property on land and on the seas. The rules for the treatment differ radically. Private property on land is not subject to capture or destruction and indeed enjoys almost an inviolability. The only exception is the right to levy contributions and requisitions for the support of the invading army. Where time is lacking to effect a proper levy it is lawful to forage for food for horses and provisions for men. Rules of warfare regulate the exercise of these occasions of seizure of private property. The use of privately owned means of transportation and communication may be appropriated, but any damage except in urgent military necessity is forbidden, and the property must be restored upon the return of peace. State property of the enemy is subject to another series of regulations. In brief, movable state property, like war materials, ships of war, moneys, state railways, telegraphs, taxes and customs are always seized and used by the conqueror. Out of the incomes the local government is administered, and the excess passes to the new occupant. State lands and buildings pass into the possession of the new authorities, but the ultimate ownership awaits stipulations of a treaty of peace, though the profits accruing from real property become the absolute property of the occupant. Certain other property set apart for the maintenance of hospitals, educational institutions and scientific or artistic objects, archives and the contents of museums are in a sense now generally held to be neutralized, that is, to enjoy a complete inviolability. To this is added local taxes levied solely for local administrative purposes. Upon these rules there is scarcely any diversity of opinion. The American instructions in force in 1898 were in full support of the above regulations,[61] and the most recent European statements, as the Declaration of Brussels, 1874,[62] the Code of Oxford,[63] and the second convention at the Hague,[64] all support the same principles.

All captures and booty became the property of the Government. The right to prize money for the soldiers is unknown to international law and almost to local law as well.[65] Since Spain never succeeded in obtaining possession of any enemy territory, only the conduct of the insurgents and the United States forces can be examined. The American commanders care-

[61] Snow, Opinions and Cases, pp. 537–40; " Instructions for United States Armies," Section II.
[62] Articles 18, 38.
[63] 1880, Article II, pp. 50–60.
[64] 1899, Articles 16–56.
[65] Instructions for the Armies of the United States, Clause 45.

fully respected the rights of enemy property, and no
exception was taken by Spain to their conduct in this
respect. The American forces occupied Cuba, Porto
Rico and the Philippines, and in none of these places
did any case of pillage or unnecessary devastation, the
authorized work of American soldiers, come to light.
No one would dare assert that the American forces
were free of thieves or of licentious members who
violated all law. The utmost that can be said is that
any pillage or devastation or unlawful appropriation of
private property that occurred was in spite of rigorous
efforts to prevent it. The American armies resorted
on occasions to requisitions, but always guardedly and
within all lawful bounds. The limited resources of
the regions occupied, and of Santiago in particular,
prevented the resort in any great degree to foraging.
The main dependence was upon supplies from home
and upon the customs duties which were fixed by
Spanish law. No direct war taxes or contributions
were ever levied. The allies in Cuba and the Philippines were the worst offenders against the inviolability
of private property, and their licentiousness placed an
added burden on the occupying military authorities of
the United States. The insurgents were accustomed
in the heated passions of a long contest with Spain to
the ruthless destruction of private property. Whenever they entered a village of the enemy or crossed a
Spanish planter's estate they gave themselves over to
pillage. In both Santiago and Manila the American
commanders found in their exclusion the only safeguard for property. In Manila most rigorous meas-

ures became necessary to prevent the insurgents from pillaging.[66]

In connection with the status of property captured by the land forces an interesting and almost absurd episode occurred at Santiago. The land forces took several Spanish vessels in the harbor. The blockading vessels before Santiago, claiming the vessels as prizes, sent in a prize crew, and attempted to take them from the harbor, when the army authorities interfered. In the end, however, the ships, because they were the booty of the land forces, were held to be government property, and the enemy merchant vessels were restored to their owners.[67] A similar case arose on the taking of Manila. The Government declared that shipping, when taken in consequence of joint operations of land and naval forces, was not subject to condemnation as naval prize, and that private shipping belonging to the enemy might be taken for the use of the Government, but that the American policy was not to take it unless needed for public purposes.[68]

Enemy property taken on the sea, both public and private, is regulated by an entirely different body of rules. Great progress has been made of recent years toward the immunity of private property on the seas. In 1859 France restored the vessels captured from Austria; in 1860, in the war with China, England and France agreed to exempt merchant vessels and their cargoes not contraband. France restored in 1865 the

[66] Le Fur, La guerre hispano-américaine, p. 117.
[67] Law Register, Vol. 37, 1898, pp. 682–83.
[68] Message and Documents of the United States, 1898–1899, Vol. IV, p. 124.

Mexican captures; Austria, Italy and Prussia declared in 1866 for the immunity of private property at sea for the Seven Weeks' war, and Prussia announced the same principle in 1870 in the war with France. The United States has a treaty with Italy exempting private property from capture in case of war between them.[69] All Europe save England is committed to the immunity of private property.[70] The Spanish-American war offered the United States an excellent opportunity to put into practice a doctrine which it had so long attempted to advance. But practice fell short of pretensions.

The most noteworthy advance in the treatment of property in the recent war was the liberal concession by both belligerents of a period of days within which enemy ships could leave enemy ports at the beginning of hostilities. The thirty days granted by the United States was exceedingly liberal. On account of the early capture of the Spanish fleet and the small amount of American commerce with Southwest Europe, Spain had little opportunity to make captures at sea. The United States made on the contrary a disproportionate number of prizes in consideration of the shortness of the war. Altogether the American commanders reported one hundred and ninety-three enemy vessels captured. Of these thirty-two are known to have been condemned as lawful prize; ninety-seven were released; and thirty-six were for one reason or another destroyed. The fate of twenty-eight was unknown at the time the report was made. A great proportion of those released (eighty-six) were small lighters taken in Porto

[69] Treaties in Force, 1904, p. 453, Article 12.
[70] Stark, Abolition of Privateering, pp. 19, 265.

Rico just before the end of the war. Fourteen of those recorded as destroyed were armed ships of war destroyed in open battle. The record does not include the armed ships destroyed and captured in Manila on May 1 and August 13, nor the private ships that were taken but immediately released on the ground that the joint operations of the army and fleet did not make the captures lawful prizes, and that the Government desired to place no hindrance on the return of commercial activity.

The fleet of the United States captured two Spanish merchant vessels on April 22, the day the blockade was proclaimed and three days before war was formally declared by Congress, three on April 23, four on April 24, four on April 25 and one on April 26.[71] The Spanish authorities most naturally protested against captures before the formal declaration of war,[72] but the American prize courts held differently and condemned ten of them as lawful prizes. The commander in chief of the Atlantic squadron had immediately released two of them. The *Catalina* and the *Miguel Jover* were exempted by the prize courts under the President's proclamation, allowing ships that had set out from port before the beginning of war thirty days of grace, and later, after an appeal to the Supreme Court, the *Buena Ventura* was released for the same

[71] Message and Documents of the United States, 1898–1899, Vol. IV, pp. 316 ff.
April 22. *Buena Ventura, Pedro.*
April 23. *Miguel Jover, Sofia, Perdita.*
April 24. *Catalina, Tres Hermanos, Matilde, Caudita.*
April 25. *Panama, Sol, Paquette, A. Bolivar.*
April 26. *Argonauta.*
[72] Spanish Diplomatic Correspondence and Documents, p. 164.

reason. The decision of the court in the *Buena Ventura* illustrated the interpretation by the judiciary of the executive proclamation, with especial reference to the thirty days of grace for Spanish merchantmen in American ports.[73]

The *Buena Ventura* was a Spanish merchant vessel captured near Sand Key on the Florida coast on April 22. She had been chartered by a Liverpool firm on March 23, 1898, to carry a cargo of lumber from Ship Island, Mississippi, to Rotterdam. She left Ship Island on April 19 for Rotterdam by way of North-field, Virginia, where she was to take in bunker coal. This was in accordance with a permit obtained under the laws of the United States. The crew made no resistance when captured. The *Buena Ventura* carried neither military nor naval officers, nor arms nor munitions of war. There was no suspicion as to the legality of the papers or of the destination. The question for adjudication was simply whether she was entitled to exemption from capture under the rule regarding " Spanish merchant vessels in any ports or places within the United States." The proclamation, dated April 26, specifically referred to vessels in American ports. Another article of the proclamation made provision for vessels which had sailed from a foreign port prior to April 21. But the *Buena Ventura* when captured was on the high seas bound from one American port to another, having departed two days before the date of the proclamation. The United States District Court for the Southern District of Florida, sitting as a prize court in the first instance, condemned the

[73] Proclamations and Decrees during the War with Spain, pp. 77–78.

vessel on May 27, 1898, as enemy property "upon the high seas and not in any port or place of the United States upon the outbreak of the war," and therefore as a lawful prize of war. The cargo proved to be the property of neutrals and not contraband, and that was restored to the proper owners. The vessel was duly sold. The case was appealed to the Supreme Court, where the decision was handed down on December 11, 1898. The court stated that there were three possible constructions for the fourth clause of the President's proclamation. It might be held to include (1) "only those which were in such ports on the day when the proclamation was issued, April 26," or (2) "those that were in such ports on the 21st of April, the day that war commenced, as Congress declared," or (3) "not alone those vessels that were in port on that day, but also those that had sailed therefrom on any day up to and including the 21st of May . . . and were when captured continuing their voyage, without regard to the particular date of their departure from port, whether immediately before or subsequently to the commencement of the war or the issuing of the proclamation." The court adopted the last, the most liberal construction in favor of the enemy and of belligerent commerce. In doing so it followed the doctrine of the English courts.[74] The adherents of the movement for the exemption of enemy commerce from capture in war found their cause advanced a step nearer the goal. The court refused, however, to allow the owners damages or costs as demanded. " In this case," replied the court, " but for the proc-

[74] The *Phœnix*, Spink's Prize Cases, 1, 5, and the *Argo*, *ibid.*, p. 52.

lamation of April 26, the ship would have been liable
to seizure and condemnation as enemy's property. At
the time of the seizure, however, April 22, that proclamation had not been issued, and hence there was
probable cause for her seizure, although the vessel
was herself entirely without fault. The subsequent
issuing of the proclamation covering the case of a
vessel situated as was this one took away the right to
condemn which otherwise would have existed."[75]   The
Panama, the *Pedro* and the *Guido* all compelled interpretations by the court of the proclamation of the
President.

The *Panama* was a Spanish royal mail ship, bound
at the time of the capture from New York to Havana
with a general cargo, passengers and mail. On April
25, when within a short distance of Havana, she was
captured and sent to Key West. She had no military
officers, and her papers were correct. But the *Panama*
had a contract with the Spanish Government giving
the latter a right to take possession of her in case of
war, and requiring her to carry a certain armament
" for her own defense." There were on board when
captured an armament of five cannon, twenty Reming-
ton and ten Mauser rifles, and ammunition for all.
The vessel, however, had not been taken over by the
Spanish Government under the contract at the time
of capture. The defense claimed immunity as a mail
steamer and under rule 4 of the President's proclamation. The District Court condemned the *Panama* and
such parts of her cargo as were enemy property, re-
leasing the neutral-owned portions. The decision

[75] 175 U. S. 384. Cf. digest of decision in Political Science
Quarterly, Vol. XV, p. 406.

upon appeal to the Supreme Court was dated February 26, 1900.[76] Justice Grey in the opinion of the courts held that three features separated the case from that of the *Buena Ventura*: (1) the mails, (2) the arms carried, and (3) the contract with the Spanish Government. On the first he said: " No general rule of international law exempts enemy mail ships from capture as prize of war," and the opinion is undoubtedly the law today. The only exceptions to the principle arise where the belligerents are parties to postal conventions which provide immunity in case of war. The court denied any immunity from search and seizure to enemy mail vessels under the sixth article of the President's proclamation. That was held to refer specifically and to apply to neutral vessels only. Article 6 was in the following form: " The right of search is to be exercised with strict regard for the rights of neutrals, and the voyages of mail steamers are not to be interfered with except on the clearest grounds of suspicion of a violation of law in respect of contraband or blockade."

On the application of Article 4 of the President's proclamation the court's opinion was that " a Spanish vessel owned by a subject of the enemy; having an armament fit for hostile use; intended, in the event of war, to be used as a war vessel; destined to a port of the enemy; and liable, on arriving there, to be taken possession of by the enemy, and employed as an auxiliary cruiser of the enemy's navy, in the war with this country," could not reasonably be construed as included in the description of " Spanish merchant vessels which are to be exempt from capture." Justice

[76] 176 U. S. 535.

Peckham, who delivered the opinion on the *Buena Ventura,* dissented from the opinion here.

The *Pedro* and the *Guido* involved the interpretation of the law in the case of enemy vessels leaving enemy ports before the war and bound for other enemy ports. The *Pedro* was chartered, while in Antwerp loading a cargo of general merchandise for Cuban ports, to proceed after unloading at Havana and Cienfuegos to the United States for a cargo of lumber. The vessel arrived at Havana on April 17, where she remained five days, discharging part of her cargo and taking on some twenty tons of general merchandise for Santiago. She departed from Havana for Santiago on April 22, and was captured the same day, taken to Key West, and condemned by the District Court as lawful prize. The facts in the case of the *Guido,* captured near Havana on April 27, involved no significantly different question. She left a port of Spain for Cuba and intended to proceed to the United States for a return cargo, but was without specific engagement to do so. In the appeal to the Supreme Court[77] the defense advanced that the voyage from Antwerp to her American destination by way of the several Cuban ports was one continuous voyage, but Chief Justice Fuller held that since the *Pedro* left Havana, an enemy's port, on the day after war began, with no cargo for an American port and bound for an enemy's port, she must be presumed to have a knowledge of the perilous condition of affairs at the time of her departure; that the fact that she was under contract to proceed ultimately to an American port did not affect the character of her

[77] Decision, December 11, 1899. Four justices dissenting in *Pedro,* three in *Guido.* 175 U. S. 354, 382.

conduct; that she was an enemy vessel trading from one enemy port to another; and that under such circumstances the doctrine of continuous voyage did not apply. It is noteworthy that four justices—White, Brewer, Shiras and Peckham—dissented on the ground that the principal voyage of the *Pedro* was from Antwerp to the United States, and that the calling at Cuban ports was merely incidental; that it was neither conceived nor known on April 22, when she departed from Havana, that a state of war existed; that the President's proclamation had not intended to distinguish vessels having cargoes for American ports from those that had none; and they argued for a more liberal construction in accord with the enlightened moral purpose of the proclamation of President McKinley.

The other element of the defense—that the *Pedro* had been formerly a British ship, and that British subjects were the legal owners of part of the stock and equitable owners of the rest, and that she was insured against risks of war by British underwriters—compelled the court to define enemy property. The answer was that " the *Pedro* was owned by a corporation incorporated under the laws of Spain; had a Spanish registry; was sailing under a Spanish flag and a Spanish license; and was officered and manned by Spaniards. Nothing is better settled than that she must, under such circumstances, be deemed to be a Spanish ship and to be dealt with accordingly."

Two other cases upon enemy ownership came up for adjudication during the war. The *Benito Estenger* was captured off the south coast of Cuba on June 27, 1898, and taken into Key West, where she was condemned on December 7, 1898. From the represen-

tations of the claimants it appeared that previous to
June 9, 1898, the vessel was the property of Spanish
subjects residing in Cuba, and that on the latter day a
bill of sale was made to a British subject and she was
registered at Kingston, Jamaica, as a British vessel.
Much confusion existed in the testimony regarding
the facts of the transfer and the personnel of the crew,
but apparently Spanish subjects continued to officer
the vessel. The *Benito Estenger* was captured on
leaving the Cuban port of Manzanillo to return to
Kingston. The principal issue was upon the ownership and the legality of the alleged transfer. The
opinion of the Supreme Court on the appeal, given
March 5, 1900, laid down the ruling that merchant
vessels in time of war are " legitimate objects of trade
as fully as any other kind of merchandise, but the
opportunities of fraud being great, the circumstances
attending a sale are severely scrutinized, and the transfer is not held to be good if it is subjected to any condition or even tacit understanding by which the vender
keeps an interest in the vessel or its profits, a control
over it, a power of revocation, or a right to its restoration at the conclusion of the war." In the case of
the *Benito Estenger* the court said the burden of proof
of a bona fide transfer was upon the claimant, and
held that such evidence was lacking. Three justices,
Shiras, White and Peckham, dissented.[78]   As the
Cuban claimant advanced in defense a sympathy with
the American cause, the court turned to the status of
the Cubans with the conclusion " that in war the citizens or subjects of the belligerents are enemies to each
other, without regard to individual sentiments or dis-

[78] 176 U. S. 568.

positions and that political status determines the question of enemy ownership." The executive had refused to recognize their government and to do more than unofficially coöperate with them in the military operations of the war; the judiciary in its turn refused to recognize them as other than Spanish subjects.

In the case of the Spanish bark *Carlos F. Roses,* the ownership of the cargo came into dispute. The bark was captured on May 17 off the Cuban coast en route from Montevideo to Havana with a cargo of jerked beef and garlic. No appeal was made on the question of the condemnation of the vessel itself, but British merchants endeavored to establish that the cargo was their property on the ground that at the time of shipping they made advances upon it to the amount of about thirty thousand dollars, and that in consideration of this the bills of lading were endorsed in blank and delivered to them, with the intent that they should take title to the bills and the cargo, and on the arrival of the vessel at her destination hold the cargo as security, with the right to dispose of it and reimburse themselves with the proceeds. The British claimants contended that in this way they became the lawful owners of the cargo.

The Supreme Court refused to recognize that the cargo ever passed in good faith to the British merchants, but decided that it remained the property of a Spanish subject and was liable to confiscation like all enemy property. In deciding against the neutral claimants the court reversed the decision of the District Court. Two justices, Shiras and Brewer, joined in a vigorous dissenting opinion, well supported by American and European precedents, for a more liberal

interpretation. In brief they said that bills of lading
endorsed to neutrals acting in good faith, who have
advanced money to purchase goods shipped long before the declaration of war, create a right to property
in the goods.[79]   The cases of the *Benito Estenger* and
the *Carlos F. Roses* indicate that in American prize
law a transfer during the time of war from an enemy
to a neutral will be severely scrutinized, and that the
burden of proof of an innocent and bona fide action
will rest with the claimant.

A more important opinion from the standpoint of
influence on international practice was that of the
Supreme Court in the case of the Spanish fishing
smacks, *Paqueta Habana* and *Lola,* captured off the
Cuban coast on April 25 and April 26. Both left
Havana many days before the outbreak of the war,
and when captured were returning with cargoes of
fish. Both were condemned at Key West in the District Court and sold under prize law. The cases were
appealed to the Supreme Court and an opinion was
given by Justice Grey on January 8, 1900.[80]   The decision upheld the principle that coast fishing vessels,
with their implements and supplies, cargoes and crew,
unarmed and honestly pursuing their peaceful calling
of catching and bringing in fresh fish, are exempt from
capture as prize of war. This was no new principle.
Indeed, the practice of exempting such vessels is very
ancient, and seems to have prevailed in the mediaeval
wars between England and France.[81]   Both countries
have adhered to their ancient practice in recent wars.

[79] 177 U. S. 655.
[80] 175 U. S. 677.
[81] Hall, International Law, p. 467.

The United States refrained from capturing fishing vessels in the Mexican war. Though recent practice has inclined toward the immunity of fishing vessels, it cannot be stated as a settled doctrine of international law, and this fact makes it a satisfaction to find the highest court of the United States falling in line with the most liberal practice. Three justices of the Supreme Court, in dissenting, upheld the doctrine that the seizure of such vessels was proper in the ordinary exercise of executive discretion in the conduct of war, and that their exemption was a matter of grace and not of right.

In review, the decisions growing out of the war show the acceptance of the following principles as a part of its prize law:

1. Proclamations allowing vessels belonging to one belligerent to sail either from or for the ports of the other belligerents will be liberally construed.

2. If issued after the commencement of hostilities they will be considered to refer to the beginning of the war. Vessels in port before the proclamation, and those that had sailed in ignorance of the war, will be exempted from capture.

3. They will not extend to vessels adapted for use in warfare that are under contract with the belligerent government, although in point of fact never so used.

4. "Mail steamers as such are not exempt from seizure as prize of war."[82]

5. "Fishing boats engaged solely in domestic fishing are exempt from seizure as prize of war," as are

[82] Oppenheim, International Law, Vol. II, p. 195. England and France have treaty stipulations which concede immunity to mail steamers. Treaty of 1833.

also barges propelled by sweeps and by poling and non-sea-going floating derricks or wrecking boats without means of propulsion, which are the property of private citizens.[83]

6. "When a cargo consigned to an enemy is captured on an enemy's vessel, title in a neutral claimant will not be sufficiently established by proof that he has made advances for the purchase of the cargo, and has paid drafts drawn on him for the amount of the advances, which drafts are accompanied by bills of lading endorsed in blank."

7. A vessel owned by a Spanish corporation, having a Spanish registry and sailing under a Spanish flag and a Spanish license, and being officered and manned by Spaniards, must be regarded as a Spanish ship, no matter if some individual stockholders are neutrals or if the vessel was insured against the risks of war by neutral underwriters.

8. No damages accrue to the claimants of a released vessel where probable cause for capture existed at time of seizure, even though the right to condemnation has been taken away by a subsequent proclamation.

9. Where a nation intervenes in an insurrection and allies itself with the insurgents, merchantmen belonging to the latter will be considered as enemy property. Citizenship and not individual sentiments will be regarded as the test of enemy or non-enemy character.

10. The transfer of vessels *flagrante bello* cannot be sustained if subjected to any condition by which the vender retains an interest in the vessel or its profits, a control over it or a right to its restoration. And the burden of proof in respect to the validity of the transfer is on the claimant.

[83] U. S. *v.* Dewey, 188 U. S. 254.

11. Incidentally the decisions establish that the American courts regard the taking of prizes before a declaration of war by Congress as perfectly legal.[84]

The most important one showing an advance over general practice is the rule regarding fishing boats and small barges. It is noteworthy that in the execution of the proclamation the judiciary showed a greater liberality than the letter required, probably greater than the executive intended.

A great number of writers express regret that the United States did not go farther in the late war and deny to men-of-war the right to capture merchant vessels engaged in the peaceful pursuit of international trading as long as they carry strictly lawful goods and not contraband. They point to the state of almost complete inviolability of enemy private property on land, and to the steps that have been taken in the abolition of privateering, and to the well-known sympathy, expressed in 1856 and repeated since, for the immunity of private property at sea. As a matter of fact a movement was started in Congress to secure an application of the principle in the war with Spain. Mr. Gillett, of Massachusetts, proposed a resolution to that effect in Congress. It was referred to the Committee on Foreign Affairs, but failed owing to a belief that

[84] Cf. articles on "The Law of Prize as affected by Decisions upon Captures made during the Late War between Spain and the United States," Columbia Law Review, Vol. I, p. 141. Also "Recent Development and Tendency of the Law of Prizes," Yale Law Review, Vol. XII, p. 306, March, 1906; "Maritime Law in the Spanish-American War," Political Science Quarterly, Vol. XV, p. 399; Review of Reviews, Vol. XIX, p. 563.

Spain would not reciprocate and to an unwillingness to enforce a self-denying ordinance.[85]

Le Fur, the French publicist, takes exception to the conduct of the United States navy at the bombardment of Manzanillo on July 18. Three Spanish merchant vessels and four gunboats were destroyed during the engagements. The destruction of the gunboats and of one of the merchant vessels, the *Purisma Concepcion,* which had been employed as a transport of arms and munitions of war, was admissible, but he regarded the destruction of the others as unjustified. "These vessels," he says, "may be seized but not destroyed, when their destruction had no other result than to inflict a damage upon an enemy subject; such an act will be no more legal than the destruction or burning of a house belonging to an enemy subject, a deed clearly contrary to international usage."[86] The criticism would stand if the facts as to character were true. The United States authorities claimed, however, that three of the vessels destroyed were transports, one of them a harbor guard and storeship and the others gunboats.[87]

As a result of the legal controversies growing out of the captures during the war, Congress, by an act of March 3, 1899, abolished naval prizes and bounties for destroying enemy vessels.[88]

[85] Congressional Record, April 25, 1898.
[86] Le Fur, La guerre hispano-américaine, p. 116.
[87] Message and Documents, 1898–1899, Vol. IV, p. 261. Wilson, The Downfall of Spain, p. 395.
[88] 30 Stat. U. S. 1904.

CHAPTER VII

Relations between Belligerents and Neutrals

It is customary for neutrals, on learning that a war has begun which is likely to affect their interests, to announce to their own subjects the altered condition and to inform them and the belligerents concerning the particular rules of neutral conduct they wish observed. The announcement takes the form of a declaration of neutrality. A declaration of neutrality is an express statement of an intention to remain neutral, and is usually accompanied by a more or less detailed statement of the attitude the neutral proposes to assume on the several subjects which concern neutrals in time of war. In the Spanish-American war the majority of the powers issued declarations of neutrality, the only noteworthy exceptions being Germany and Austria-Hungary. Germany had made it a practice to abstain from the formality for at least a quarter of a century. While the imperial authorities deny the necessity of a formal declaration of neutrality, they uniformly publish in the leading imperial papers official notes of an intention to observe strict neutrality in all relations with the belligerents.[1] These notes have the effect of warning German subjects in a general way of their peculiar duties and obligations during the war. The importance of declarations of neutrality arises from the indefiniteness in international

[1] Le Fur, La guerre hispano-américaine, p. 126.

law of certain of the duties and rights of neutrality. It cannot be said that a declaration affects the status of the neutral, or increases or diminishes its rights and duties. In its main aspect the declaration announces to the world the particular state's municipal law of neutrality and interpretation of the law of nations upon those subjects where usage differs, is doubtful, or where a margin of liberty of action is admitted. Like a formal declaration of war, it has lost with increased facilities for communication much of its former significance and importance. Nevertheless, as long as there are great differences in the law of neutrality it has valid reasons for existence. It at least emphasizes for the benefit of subjects the effect of the war on their conduct, and makes clear the conditions under which they may expect protection in any conflict with a belligerent. It is true that the declarations of many states go no farther than a general prohibition upon non-neutral conduct without an attempt at special statement.

The declaration of neutrality does not in itself bring into life the law of neutrality. That, instead, dates from the first act of hostility committed by one of the belligerents. In the Spanish-American war the neutral status of the non-belligerents began April 22, while the declarations of neutrality bore dates all the way from April 23 to June 20.[2]

In general it may be said of the declarations of neutrality of 1898 that they differed little from those published on the occasion of other recent wars. The

[2] Archives diplomatiques, Vol. 66, pp. 249–53, 360; Vol. 67, pp. 209–11, 323 ff.

French declaration included the French protectorates
in the same category with France herself and her colonies, whereas the declarations published during the
Greco-Turkish and the Chino-Japanese wars did not.
The English declaration, in the main a recital of the
Foreign Enlistment Act, differed like the French from
its predecessors in making more emphatic the imperial
character, and specifically stating that the same obligations of neutrality were imposed upon all colonies and
dependencies.   In another particular it was more stringent, in applying the restrictions of neutrality to belligerent vessels in British ports at the date of the
proclamation as well as to those which should enter
them later.   The proclamation, moreover, for the first
time incorporated the rules appended to the treaty of
Washington, though as is well known the Foreign
Enlistment Act was in substantial agreement with
them.[3]

One of the fundamental obligations imposed upon
neutrals is that of giving no aid to either of the belligerents.   Any form of government assistance or
favoritism is inconsistent with neutrality.   It is also a
general rule that a state ought not to conclude treaties
in time of peace which will prevent its strict neutrality
in time of war; if it has done so it must accept the
consequences and expect to be treated as a belligerent.
No case of the kind existed in 1898, though a treaty
between Haiti and the United States has been criti-
cised as inconsistent with neutrality, but it is difficult
to see wherein the treaty infringes the obligations of
the most impartial neutrality.   Article 30 of the treaty

[3] The London Times, April 27 and 28, 1898.

of 1864 is as follows: " It shall not be lawful for any
foreign privateers who have commissions from any
Prince or State in enmity with either nation to fit their
ships in the ports, either to sell their prizes or in any
manner to exchange them ; neither shall they be allowed
to purchase provisions, except such as shall be necessary to their going to the next port of that Prince or
State from which they have received their commissions."[4] The treaty is positive and clear, and it cannot be construed to obligate the parties to grant one
another privileges which are prohibited to the enemies.[5]
The conduct of Haiti during the war belies such a
construction.   Her declaration of neutrality is in every
respect regular, and states specifically that the special
conventions with the United States in the treaty of
1864 will be put into practice equitably toward both
belligerents.

It is a universally accepted obligation upon neutral
states not to sell or furnish to belligerents any ships of
war during the actual continuance of hostilities.   Neutrals may sell ships to buying states up to the moment
when hostilities begin, but no longer, nor is it permissible for ships purchased by a belligerent to depart from neutral ports after war has begun.   Before
the outbreak of the Spanish-American war both the
United States and Spain, having reason to believe
that peace could not long be maintained, went into the
market for ships of war, but neither met with much
success.   The United States purchased on March 16
two vessels from the Brazilian Government, the *Ama-*

---

[4] Treaties and Conventions of the United States, p. 559.
[5] Le Fur, La guerre hispano-américaine, p. 131, holds a
contrary view.

zonas and the *Almirante Abreu.*[6] Both were being built in English shipyards. As neither was ready for service when war broke out, the English Government forbade the former, a torpedo boat nearly completed, to leave port, and stopped work on the other, a cruiser. As the transaction itself took place several weeks before war began, there was nothing irregular about it. On the contrary England's conduct was strictly regular. The right of neutrals to sell ships after relations have become strained is challenged by some writers, but the consensus of opinion does not condemn the transaction as long as war has not actually begun. In short, it may be said that it is a permissible commercial transaction until the first act of hostilities; after that moment it constitutes a violation of neutrality.

In a similar manner the sale of war supplies is held to be a violation of neutrality if it takes place after war begins, but perfectly legal before that time. The purchase of several torpedoes from Brazil in April, 1898, raised a vigorous protest in some European journals, but like the preceding case such sales are not inconsistent with neutrality until war has actually begun. The United States itself has not in the past been very scrupulous in observing its neutral obligation to abstain from aid through the direct sale of war supplies. It is recalled that in 1870 the Government sold at public sale in New York a quantity of surplus guns and other arms. A large part was bought by French agents, paid for through the French consul, and transported directly by French ships.[7] Probably

[6] Moore, Digest, Vol. VII, p. 861.
[7] See Senate Report 183, 42 Cong., 2 Sess., and House Report 46, 42 Cong., 2 Sess. Hall, International Law, p. 622; Moore, Digest, Vol. VII, p. 973.

such an act would not take place today with the increased international sentiment against acts in contravention of neutrality. Whereas neutral obligations forbid the sale of ships and munitions of war by a neutral government, and the rule is pretty well understood if not accepted in practice, confusion exists upon the legality of traffic in merchant ships or armed ships intended to be employed as ships of war on the part of individual citizens of neutral states after the beginning of war. Bluntschli made the distinction that a ship of war can be sold by the subject of a neutral state to a belligerent state as a purely commercial or industrial enterprise without violating the neutrality of the neutral.[8]   Of course in such a theory the ship or munitions would be classed as contraband of war and would be subject to confiscation if captured.

In court decisions and in executive declarations the Government of the United States has upheld the legality of the traffic by its citizens,[9] though to fit a vessel out as a ship of war armed and ready to serve one of the belligerents would violate the laws of neutrality in force. The illegal element is apparently the use of American harbors for fitting out vessels for the transport of contraband and not the act of sale itself.[10] The American doctrine would seem to leave much to be desired.

[8] Droit international, p. 766; Hall, International Law, p. 85.
[9] See U. S. v. Trumbull in 48 Fed. Rep. 99, where in 1891 it was held that to deliver arms and ammunition to Chilean insurgent vessels in American waters was not in contravention of the neutrality laws of the United States; Hall, International Law, pp. 83–84.
[10] Heffter, Le droit international de l'Europe, p. 408; Hall, International Law, p. 84.

Several states in their declarations of neutrality specifically forbade their subjects to trade in ships and munitions of war on any scale, large or small. Great Britain, Japan, Denmark, the Netherlands and Liberia included such acts among those forbidden their subjects.[11] Haiti forbade supplying privateers with arms or other munitions of war. The penalties varied from the mere forfeiture of protection to fine and imprisonment; in the declaration of England, to the confiscation of the ship with its cargo. Great Britain applied the restrictions upon belligerents to the sale of packet boats by the great steamship lines. At the outbreak of the war the United States had purchased in England the steamship *Ireland,* the largest and fastest of the English-Irish lines. The ship was fitted out and was on the eve of departure for the United States when the English Government intervened. Italy is said to have taken the same views of neutral obligations without any specific statement of the kind in the declaration of neutrality.[12] In conclusion, the war showed a distinct advance of neutrals toward the prohibition of trade in ships and munitions of war, an advance beyond the letter of the Rules of Washington.

Closely associated with the question of the private trade of neutral subjects is the larger one of the use of neutral ports by the belligerents. The entrance and sojourn of belligerent ships in neutral ports are favors granted by neutral states which they can always refuse entirely or conditionally.[13] In 1898 the greater

[11] Proclamations and Decrees, pp. 31, 33, 47, 50, 54.
[12] Le Fur, La guerre hispano-américaine, p. 155.
[13] Revue de droit international public, Vol. V, p. 858.

number of neutral states opened their ports to the war-
ships of the belligerents, subject to the qualification
that they should not remain more than twenty-four
hours except in case of distress caused by bad weather,
lack of provisions, or accident. The declarations of
neutrality generally prohibited the simultaneous departure of ships of both belligerents, exacting an interval
of twenty-four hours between their departures.[14]
Italy made an exception to the twenty-four hour limit
for belligerent ships, provided the object of the mission was exclusively scientific.[15]   The colonial circular
of the Netherlands for the Dutch East Indies changed
the time limit to forty-eight hours, and restricted the
number of ships of each belligerent in its ports at the
same time to two.[16]

Brazil qualified its permission for the use of its
ports with the explanation that the privilege would
be granted only to ships en route and putting into a
port through stress of circumstances, and therefore
repeated visits without a sufficiently justified motive
would authorize suspicion that the ship was not really
en route, but was frequenting the seas near Brazil in
order to make prizes of hostile ships. In such cases
asylum or succor given to a ship would be character-
ized as assistance or favor given against the other
belligerent, being thus a breach of neutrality.[17] The
rule was a good one and expressed very clearly what
should be the practice. The Chinese declaration of
neutrality denied entirely the use of harbors to the

[14] Proclamations and Decrees, pp. 48, 56, 58, 63.
[15] *Ibid.*, p. 43.
[16] *Ibid.*, p. 58.
[17] *Ibid.*, p. 14.

belligerents, but this was unusually severe.[18]   In later circulars of instructions from the imperial government at Pekin to the local governors, ports were opened under the twenty-four hour rule.[19]   Great Britain, Holland and Russia, while making the general limit of the sojourn at twenty-four hours, excepted cases of urgent need for repairs.[20]   France and Brazil made no specific limit to the length of the stay, unless accompanied with prizes, when the twenty-four hour rule was applied.[21]   Haiti placed no limitations on belligerents except the common rule of twenty-four hours between the departure of ships of the different belligerents.[22]

Declarations of neutrality generally distinguished privateers from public ships of war, with heavier restrictions upon the former.   Brazil, which did not limit the sojourn of belligerent ships of war if unaccompanied by prizes, fixed it for privateers at twenty-four hours except in cases where forced to put in because of manifest distress.[23]   The prevailing sentiment hostile to privateering was more closely reflected in the rules of Denmark, the Netherlands, Japan and Portugal, which denied privateers entrance at all except in cases of distress.[24]

[18] However, the Scandinavian states closed certain of their ports entirely, except in case of distress, in the Russo-Japanese war, 1904. Hershey, International Law and Diplomacy of the Russo-Japanese War, p. 199.

[19] Proclamations and Decrees, pp. 19, 20.

[20] Ibid., pp. 31, 53, 63.

[21] Ibid., pp. 12, 29.

[22] Ibid., p. 38.

[23] Ibid., p. 14.

[24] Ibid., pp. 23, 28, 48, 55, 58, 61.

Most naturally a belligerent ship of war in a neutral port forfeits its privileged position when it commits a hostile act, or one forbidden by international or municipal law. Brazil, after forbidding hostile acts, the employment of force to recover prisoners or prizes and the sale of all prize property, went so far as to specifically authorize her military to resort to force to execute the prohibition.[25] Most declarations were content with a general prohibition against hostile acts in territorial waters, leaving the form of redress unstated.

Other clauses of the declarations of neutrality dealt with repairs in neutral ports. They generally permitted belligerent war-ships to enter neutral ports for repairs, subject to the restriction that no increase in armament or effectiveness be made. The declarations of neutrality prescribed no time limit for making the necessary repairs, but several, like those of Great Britain, Denmark, the Netherlands and China, required them to depart within twenty-four hours after completing the repairs. France, Paraguay and England had occasion during the war to apply the rules announced in their declarations. France admitted belligerent ships of war without fixing a limit to the duration of the sojourn. Consequently, when the American auxiliary cruiser *Harvard* went into Fort de France, Martinique, in order to make some repairs, and Spain protested against the length of the delay allowed, France could reply that her neutrality was perfectly regular, and that her neutral obligations were fulfilled so long as the *Harvard* made no addition to her military power under the pretext of repairs.[26]

[25] Proclamations and Decrees, p. 15.
[26] Le Fur, La guerre hispano-américaine, p. 158.

The situation was reversed when the Spanish torpedo boat *Temerario,* reported to have been sent down
the coast of South America to intercept the *Oregon,*
took refuge in a port of Paraguay to effect repairs.
Paraguay did not define in advance its policy, but
when the American consul protested, the *Temerario*
was ordered to disarm if it wished to remain in the
neutral port. The commander of the vessel refused,
representing its unseaworthy condition as the reason
for his delay. The Government of Paraguay appointed a commission to examine into the real condition of the vessel, with the result that a month was
granted for making repairs. The *Temerario* remained tied up in the Paraguayan port in a state of
disability during the remainder of the war.[27]   In the
case of a Spanish gunboat undergoing repairs in an
Irish port at the outbreak of the war, Great Britain
ruled that the boat might depart when the repairs were
effected, without fixing a limit to the length of the
delay.[28]

Another aspect of the length of the sojourn in neutral waters arose in the proposed passage of the Suez
Canal by the Spanish reserve fleet. The Convention
of Constantinople, 1888, which dealt with the use of
the canal in war, stipulated that belligerent ships of
war should pass through as rapidly as possible and
could not stop at Port Said or in the roadstead of Suez
more than twenty-four hours.[29]   But the question
arose whether the convention admitted of delays for

[27] Le Fur, pp. 158, 159, and note 1. See New York Tribune,
June 18; Moore, Digest, Vol. VII, p. 996.

[28] Le Fur, La guerre hispano-américaine, p. 159, note 2.

[29] Bonfils-Fauchille, Manuel de droit international public, no.
512, gives the principal clauses of the convention.

necessary repairs beyond the time limit. Lord Cur-
zon, at the time Under-Secretary of State for the Foreign Office, took occasion in the English House of
Commons to state that the Convention of Constantinople had never gone into force and would not as long
as England remained in Egypt, and therefore that the
question of the permissible delay belonged to the Egyptian Government. The Spanish ship in need of repairs
was permitted to remain until they were completed.[30]

The so-called Rules of Washington declared in
effect that a neutral government must not allow the
ships of belligerents to increase their crew or armament while in its ports. A marked tendency was
shown in the declaration of neutrality of 1898 toward
more severe restrictions upon belligerents' ships of war
in provisioning and coaling in neutral ports. Great
Britain, France, Italy, the Netherlands, Denmark and
China limited the provisions which a belligerent ship
might take on in their ports to the actual needs of the
crew. Japan introduced a more explicit rule limiting
the supplies to those necessary to " enable it to get
back to the nearest port of its own country."[31]

The third rule of the treaty of Washington had limited the coal which neutrals might furnish to belligerent ships of war : " So much coal only as may be sufficient to carry such vessel to the nearest port of her own,
or to some nearer destination, and no coal shall again
be supplied to any such ship of war in the same or in
any other port, roadstead, or waters subject to the territorial jurisdiction of Her Majesty, without special per-

[30] The London Times, July 7, 1898; the New York Tribune,
July 11, 1898.
[31] Proclamations and Decrees, pp. 20, 36, 42, 48, 55.

mission, until after the expiration of three months from the time when such coal may have been last supplied to her within British waters." Great Britain, China and Japan asserted the principle in the third Rule of Washington without modification. Brazil substituted for the definite features more general clauses: a quantity sufficient " for the continuance of their voyage," and not again until the lapse of " a reasonable interval," and " a ship which shall once have entered one of our ports shall not be received in that or another shortly after having left the first, in order to take victuals, naval stores, or make repairs, except in a duly proved case of compelling circumstances, unless after a reasonable interval which would make it seem probable that the ship had left the coast of Brazil and had returned after having finished the voyage she was undertaking."[32] But because these clauses were general and susceptible of various interpretations they were less satisfactory. Japan and Haiti permitted supplying vessels with water, provisions and coal in quantities necessary to reach the nearest home port;[33] Denmark, as much as was necessary to " enable the vessel to arrive at the nearest port of its own country or to some other destination near by." The Netherlands introduced the alternatives, " the nearest port of the country to which it belongs, or *that of one of its allies in the war.*" No exception need be taken to the emendations of Denmark and the Netherlands, but Colombia made the curious innovation that a belligerent ship of war could have only enough coal to

[32] *Ibid.,* p. 14.
[33] *Ibid.,* pp. 39, 48.

"take [it] to the nearest foreign port."[34]   The rule
adopted by Colombia would lead to endless confusion
if applied generally.[35]   Many neutrals omitted direct
allusion to coaling, retaining thus the right to pursue
whatever policy was desired as occasion arose. This
was particularly the case with France, Russia and
Portugal. Italy, without limiting the quantity of coal,
fixed a twenty-four hour delay after arrival before
coaling.

It is manifest that the new doctrine of coaling places
a very important limitation on maritime warfare, and
makes it almost impossible for a nation without coaling stations at frequent intervals around the globe to
conduct widespread military operations on the seas.
It is, therefore, not surprising to note that some states
otherwise entering into full particulars in their declarations were silent on these subjects. The tendency of
the declarations of 1898 to limit the quantity of coal
became the rule adopted in the projected code of maritime law of the Institute of International Law in the
session at the Hague, 1898.[36]   The rule covered only
the practice in supplying ships of war, and the declarations of neutrality left neutral subjects free in supplying merchant ships with provisions. The rule on coaling did not apply to the transport of coal. The con-

[34] *Ibid.*, pp. 15, 20, 23, 36, 42, 48, 55. Le Fur, La guerre
hispano-américaine, Appendix V.

[35] Le Fur, La guerre hispano-américaine, p. 165.

[36] Annuaire, Vol. XVII, p. 273; Revue de droit international
public, 1898, Vol. V, p. 853. Oppenheim, International Law,
Vol. II, p. 354, makes the rule read: "A neutral must prevent
belligerent men-of-war admitted to his ports or maritime belt
from taking more provisions and coal than are necessary to
bring them safely to the nearest port of their home state."

sideration of such subjects belongs properly to the discussion of contraband.

Some minor difficulties arose during the war in the interpretation of neutral obligations regarding coaling. On May 14 the Netherlands refused to allow the Spanish fleet to lay in a supply of coal at the colonial port of Curaçao beyond a small amount estimated to be sufficient to take them to Porto Rico. A report in the latter part of May that the Spanish reserve squadron intended to sail to the United States by way of the Azores led the United States to instruct its minister at Lisbon to make a protest on the ground that these islands were entirely outside the routes to the Spanish West Indies and were about to be converted into a base of hostile operations. The fleet in fact sailed eastward to the Suez. Here in the early part of July Spain found the limit on coaling applied greatly to her disadvantage. Admiral Camara on his way to the Philippines reached Port Said, where his coal supply became exhausted. In the mean time the United States consul purchased nearly all the available supply of coal at Port Said for shipment to the Philippines.[37] On the other hand the English Government refused to allow Admiral Camara to take any coal on the ground that he had enough on board to take him back to Cadiz, and it also denied him the use of Egyptian ports to transfer coal from his own transports except under a written agreement to return to Spain.[38] Admiral Camara was in the end forced to depend on the supply in his accompanying colliers. This was a strict application of the rule announced in the English

[37] London Times, July 1, 1898.
[38] See New York Tribune, July 12, 1898.

13

declaration of neutrality, but it does not appear to be more severe than was required by the spirit of the new doctrine of neutral obligations. Mexico was equally strict in limiting the amount of coal for ships of the United States at Acapulco.[39]

It is a perfectly legal and regular act for neutrals to continue trading with belligerents as they have been accustomed to in time of peace, subject to the restrictions which municipal law prescribes in the case of supplying belligerent ships in neutral ports. Nor does it matter how great are the bulk of the transactions; the obligations of the neutrals have not been contravened. But it is quite a different matter when the neutral subjects themselves engage in the transport of goods for belligerent use. This subject involves the limitations imposed by contraband and blockade. As long as belligerent ports remain unblockaded neutrals may transport to the belligerents lawfully and safely whatever the neutrality laws of the particular neutral and contraband decrees of the other belligerent do not proscribe. This rule was the issue in several instances during the Spanish-American war. Mexico seized several Spanish merchant ships in her ports loaded with cargoes of provisions, under the pretext that the articles were destined to supply the Spanish army in Cuba. Since the owners had not violated the Mexican law of neutrality the seizure was an excess of vigilance on the part of the Mexican Government, and the vessels were soon afterwards set at liberty.

The mere act of transporting goods, contraband or not contraband, from neutral ports to belligerent ports

[39] Foreign Relations, 1898, p. 983; Moore, Digest, Vol. VII, pp. 945–46.

involves no guilt upon the neutral individual engaged as long as he does not violate a statutory act of his own state, and consequently his conduct does not reflect back on the neutral state any guilt for violation of its obligations of neutrality. The owner, of course, runs the risk of forfeiture of goods. The taint is on the goods and not on the person. The Brazilian declaration of neutrality absolutely prohibited "the exportation of material of war from the ports of Brazil to those of either of the belligerent powers under the Brazilian flag or that of any other nation."[40] But general practice does not support so stringent a measure, however excellent it may be in theory. Other powers went no further than to warn subjects of the loss of national protection, incurred as a penalty for engaging in contraband trade. The carrier suffers no further penalty except the loss of time, freight and money. While this is the general rule, many treaties permit the carrying vessel to purchase the right to continue the voyage without the delay of going into port by abandoning the contraband to the belligerent. The United States has such treaties with a great many nations, notably with nearly all the South American and Central American states.[41] The transporting by belligerent subjects instead of by neutrals does not alter the position of the neutral from whose port the goods were obtained. When in the course of the war the English colony of Jamaica became the source of supplies for the Spanish in Cuba, the United States had no just grievance against Great Britain, and the

[40] Proclamations and Decrees, p. 13.
[41] Hall, International Law, pp. 692–93.

incident never met with more than a mild protest from
the American consul at Kingston. In view of the
policy of the United States in the past toward the
freedom of neutral commerce with belligerents, and
during the Cuban filibustering in particular, it could
not consistently make any serious objections in the
matter.

The rights of neutrals to trade with the belligerents
are greatly limited by the risks of trade with blockaded
ports where all trade is forbidden, and with all belligerent ports in those articles made contraband by
belligerent decree. Each belligerent declares its own
list of contraband articles during a particular war.
It is possible for a belligerent to nullify the rule that
free ships make free goods by lengthening the list of
contraband.

In the war of 1898 Spain published in her royal
decree of April 24 a contraband list.[42] It included
" cannons, rapid-firing guns, mortars, muskets and all
classes of firearms; the balls, bombs, grenades, hand
grenades, cartridges, fuses, powder, sulphur, saltpeter,
dynamite, and all classes of explosives; articles of
equipment, such as uniforms, leathers, saddles, and
harness for artillery and cavalry; machinery for ships
and their accessories, screw shafts and screws, boilers
and other articles and effects which serve for construction, repair and armament of war vessels; and in
general all instruments, utensils, supplies and objects
which serve in war, and such as in the future can be
classed under such a denomination." The list proclaimed by the Government of the United States com-

[42] Spanish Diplomatic Correspondence and Documents, p. 157.

prehended two classes of contraband, absolutely and conditionally contraband, and was as follows: " Absolutely contraband.—Ordnance, machine guns and their appliances and the parts thereof; armor plate and whatever pertains to the offensive and defensive armament of naval vessels; arms and instruments of iron, steel, brass, or copper, or of any other material, such arms and instruments being especially adapted for use in war by land or sea; torpedoes and their appurtenances; cases for mines of whatever material; engineering and transport materials, such as gun carriages, caissons, cartridge boxes, campaigning forges, canteens, pontoons, ordnance stores; portable range finders; signal flags destined for naval use; ammunition and explosives of all kinds; machinery for the manufacture of arms and munitions of war; saltpeter; military accoutrements and equipments of all sorts; horses.

" Conditionally contraband.—Coal when destined for a naval station, a port of call or a ship or ships of the enemy; material for the construction of railways or telegraphs, and money, when such materials or money are destined for the enemy's forces; provisions, when destined for an enemy's ship or ships or for a place that is besieged."[43]

In the main the two lists agree on the direct munitions of war, and merely serve to specify what are the prevailing instruments of direct warfare. The Spanish decree is general enough in the concluding clauses to comprehend by the interpretation of prize courts a great variety of objects not specifically listed. The United States adds to the Spanish subjects " horses

[43] Proclamations and Decrees, p. 88.

when destined for an enemy's port or fleet." The most significant departure of the United States is in the list of conditionally contraband. This includes subjects like coal, railways, telegraphs, money and provisions, none of which are mentioned by the Spanish decree. These are contraband only when destined for the enemy's fleet or naval station or a besieged place. Coal is a comparatively new instrument of warfare, and yet it is unquestionably indispensable to the conduct of war. In the two great wars in which France has participated since the era of steam warships began coal was not made contraband. Russia took a similar view in the West African Conference of 1884, though she inconsistently made it, together with all other forms of fuel, as naphtha and alcohol, absolute contraband of war in the recent conflict with Japan.[44] Against the French view, and that of the smaller states of Europe, Germany in 1870 regarded coal as absolute contraband. England held it as such only when bound for a belligerent destination. The great writers on contraband are divided, and usually agree with the national policy of the state of which they are subjects. Several French writers like Hautefeuille, Bonfils-Fauchille and Le Fur condemn the distinction between conditional and absolute contraband.[45]

English and American writers like Hall, Lawrence, Wheaton and Woolsey accept the conditionally contra-

[44] Hershey, International Law and Diplomacy of the Russo-Japanese War, p. 164.
[45] Droits des neutres, Vol. VIII, sec. II, p. 3; Manuel de droit international public, nos. 1535 ff.; La guerre hispano-américaine, pp. 262–63.

band character of coal as the more satisfactory, and
thus support the practice of their own governments.[46]
The United States had made the same distinctions in
the Civil War.   Its policy is greatly more favorable to
neutrals than the German and Russian practice, but
less so than the French and Spanish position.   If coal
should be treated as conditional contraband, materials
for railways, telegraphs, balloons, wireless apparatus
and cables would logically have the same character.
They are all new instruments for use in conducting
military operations.   But the inclusion of provisions
and money as conditional contraband has fewer defen-
ders.   It matters little what is the practice regarding
money, for under modern conditions it is seldom necessary to transport money directly to a fleet or besieged
place.   The inclusion of provisions as conditional contraband was in continuance of a century's practice.

One other aspect of the decrees on contraband was
the penalty prescribed for carrying that class of goods.
Here both Spain and the United States expressed a
rule which is extremely severe for neutrals.   Spain
took the position that the entire cargo and ship should
be confiscated if two thirds or more of the cargo
were contraband.   When the illegal part of the cargo
was less than two thirds, only the contraband part

[46] Hall, International Law, p. 686; Lawrence, Principles of
International Law, p. 613; Woolsey, International Law, p.
324; Wheaton, International Law, par. 369. For history of
theories of contraband consult Manceaux, De la contrebande
de guerre, Paris, 1899; Vetzel, De la contrebande par anal-
ogie, Paris, 1901; Brochet, De la contrebande de guerre,
1901. Rivier, Vol. II, p. 419, makes provisions and coal contraband if destined for enemy forces. But silver coined or
uncoined ought not, in his opinion, to be included.

should be confiscated.[47]   The Spanish rule differs from
the French in substituting two thirds for three fourths.
The rule of the United States was still more severe
on neutral commerce than that of Spain.   When the
cargo of contraband and the ship belonged to the same
proprietor, or when there was an attempt to resort
to fraud in representing the destination or the name of
the owner, both the cargo and ship were declared liable
to seizure, and this without regard to the proportionate
amount of the contraband.   However, in the case of
the English merchant ship, the *Restormel*, captured
in attempting to enter the port of Santiago on May
25, the cargo of coal was condemned, while the vessel
was released to its neutral owners.

During the Spanish-American war resort was had
to the two forms of blockade known to American and
English practice, (1) public and (2) de facto or military blockade.   The first hostile action of the United
States was to proclaim portions of Cuba in a state of
blockade.   This President McKinley did in a proclamation on April 22, 1898, including the north coast
of Cuba from Cardenas to Bahia Honda, and the port
of Cienfuegos on the south coast.   Neutral vessels in
any of the blockaded ports were allowed thirty days
within which to depart.   The principle of a direct
notice in each case was included in the instructions to
the blockading force.   " Any neutral vessel approaching any of said ports, or attempting to leave the same,
without notice or knowledge of the establishment of
such blockade, will be duly warned by the commander
of the blockading forces, who will endorse on her
register the fact, and the date of such warning."[48]

[47] Spanish Correspondence and Documents, p. 161.
[48] Proclamations and Decrees, pp. 75–76.

The commander of the Atlantic fleet in Cuban waters, Admiral Sampson, instituted several blockades outside the limits of the President's proclamation without direct authority from his government and without a public notification to neutrals. In this manner the coast from Nuevitas to Port Nipe was blockaded on July 13. The fall of Santiago, on July 13, ended the value of this particular blockade, and Commander Howell seems to have employed his ships in blockading Sagua la Grande and its environs.[49] The last was abandoned upon the order from Washington, August 10, 1898. The instructions from the Navy Department seemingly condemned the creation of a blockade without a public proclamation.[50]

Santiago, Manila, Guantanamo and Manzanillo were subjected to military blockade during the war, that is, to blockades instituted by order of the commander as a part of a military attack on a fortified place. Spain made no attempt to blockade any American port. Both belligerents accepted the rule of the Declaration of Paris, 1856, relative to blockades, namely, that a blockade to be binding must be effective, that is to say, maintained with a sufficient force to actually prevent access to the enemy's coast. This action was the more important as neither of the bel-

[49] Message and Documents, 1898–99, Vol. IV, pp. 297–98.
[50] The telegram ordering the abandonment of the blockade of Sagua la Grande was in the following terms:
"Replying to the last three lines of your telegram of the 8th instant, it is considered best for a few days not to extend the blockade beyond what has already been proclaimed. Beyond these limits be very careful not to seize vessels, unless Spanish or carrying contraband of war, as neutrals have right to trade with ports not proclaimed blockaded." Message and Documents, 1898–99, Vol. IV, p. 298.

ligerents had ever formally become signatory to the Declaration of Paris. However, the practice of both Spain and the United States in the past had accorded with the spirit and letter of the rule of the great powers of Europe.

On June 27, 1898, the President of the United States extended the blockade to all ports on the south coast of Cuba from Cape Frances to Cape Cruz, and to the port of San Juan, Porto Rico. As before, the neutral vessels in any port were given thirty days within which to depart.[51] The thirty-day period for neutrals already in ports at the time of the institution of a blockade was more liberal than the customary allowance, which is only fifteen days. Besides, under the usual application of the rule the neutral is obliged to depart in ballast unless the cargo had been bought and loaded before the blockade began. The rule of the United States permitted the purchase and loading of the cargo after the announcement within the thirty days.[52]

The general order of the Navy Department of the United States, issued June 20, for the instruction of blockading vessels and cruisers is important for the light it throws upon the views of the executive on an " effective blockade," " necessary notification to the neutrals," and the " proper treatment for blockade runners." " A blockade to be efficient and binding must be maintained by a force sufficient to render ingress or egress from the port dangerous." The Declaration of Paris uses the words, " blockades to be binding must be effective, that is to say, maintained

[51] Proclamations and Decrees, p. 79.
[52] Moore, American Review of Reviews, Vol. XIX, p. 566.

by a force sufficient really to prevent access to the coast of the enemy." The American rule, which is the English and which is the interpretation by the courts of both, is, it would seem, somewhat less rigorous on belligerents than the continental theory upon " due notification " and " effective blockade." Writers like Heffter, Ortolan and Hautefeuille would require the actual closure of the harbor by vessels anchored near together, at least enough so that any vessel attempting to enter will be subject to a cross fire from two blockades.[53]

From this view one vessel blockading a port, as at San Juan, would be inadequate. The French writers, Le Fur and Paul Fauchille especially, condemn the American blockade with one cruiser. Spain, in line with the continental theory, protested against the American blockades as ineffective.[54] The blockade until the middle of June was very loose, and came within the definition of a lawful blockade only by a liberal interpretation. The whole subject of blockade is in a confused state. Neutrals almost invariably protest against any blockade, and a strong sentiment demands their abolition. The necessities of the siege of Santiago de Cuba and the transportation of troops to Cuba greatly weakened the effectiveness of the

[53] Hall, International Law, p. 728; Heffter, Droit international, p. 373; Ortolan, Vol. II, p. 328; Hautefeuille, Vol. IX, ch. II, sec. 1; Yale Law Journal, Vol. XII, April, 1903, p. 339; Bertin, Le blocus continental, Paris, 1901.

[54] Spanish Correspondence and Documents, p. 164. See Fauchille, Du blocus maritime, Paris, 1882, and E. G. Boissière, Du blocus maritime, Rennes, 1898, for history and theory. The former is especially valuable for its exhaustive study of the practice of nations and the treaty conventions in force in the same.

blockade of Cienfuegos and of Havana for a considerable portion of the months of May and June. Spain declared that the blockade was entirely illegal because ineffective. The United States constantly maintained the contrary. The question is one which rests ultimately with the courts of the belligerents to determine in the case of each capture. A neutral vessel that has been captured in running a blockade has by the very fact of its own failure a poor defense, and naturally can seldom convince the judiciary of its captors that an ineffective blockade existed. It may be said here that a commercial blockade to be binding does not have to stop every ship that attempts to enter a port. Spain's protest that certain ships had successfully run the blockade was not likely in the present state of the law of blockade to have a sympathetic hearing. A commercial blockade is entirely too likely to become a paper blockade. A belligerent ought to avoid all suspicion of this character, and it may be admitted that the United States did not do this in the cases cited, though the prompt withdrawal by Admiral Sampson of the expanded blockade on the north was just and creditable. No question could be raised against the effectiveness of the other blockades; Manila, San Juan and Santiago especially were at an early date entirely closed to all commerce.

Spain took exception to the practice of the United States in another particular. The proclamation of President McKinley, in defining the character of the notification to neutrals of a blockade, said: "It may be actual, as by a vessel of the blockading force, or constructive, as by a proclamation of the Government maintaining the blockade, or by common notoriety.

If a neutral vessel can be shown to have had notice of a blockade in any way, she is good prize and should be sent in for adjudication; but should formal notice not have been given, the rule of constructive knowledge arising from notoriety should be construed in a manner liberal to the neutral."[55] The Spanish view was that both a diplomatic and a special notification are necessary. That is, a vessel is not legal prize until it tries to violate a blockade after a diplomatic notification has been given to its government and the vessel itself has had a direct notification. The United States in effect made the special or direct notification necessary only when the vessel had left port before the authorities there had had notification. The two opposed positions illustrated here reflect again a hopelessly conflicting practice in Europe.[56]

The French liner *Lafayette*, loaded with a miscellaneous cargo, was captured on May 6 as she was entering Havana harbor, and was sent into Key West under a prize crew and the escort of a man-of-war. The *Lafayette* had made her last call at port on April 23. She left Saint Nazaire_on April 21, stopped at Santander on April 22 and at La Corogne on April 23, and then proceeded directly to the next regular port in her route, Havana. The question of dispute was that of the adequateness of her notification of the blockade. The blockade, be it remembered, was pro-

---

[55] Proclamations and Decrees, p. 85.
[56] Hall, International Law, p. 720. French writers like Paul Fauchille, Du blocus maritime, p. 214, and Rivier, Principes du droit des gens, Vol. II, p. 296, insist upon a special notification, in addition to the general diplomatic notification, to be given to each ship which presents itself at the line of blockade at least once in the course of the blockade.

claimed on April 22. War was formally declared on April 25, but was made to begin on April 21 by a retroactive process. The *Lafayette* could not be held to have knowledge of the blockade before her departure from the last port, and was according to the American practice entitled to a special notification. It was admitted that she had not received this at the time of the capture. Moreover, the French General Transatlantic Company, the owners of the *Lafayette*, foreseeing possible complications, had taken steps at Washington in advance of her arrival at Havana to prevent her seizure. Ambassador Cambon had requested leave of entrance for the *Lafayette*, and orders had been sent to Admiral Sampson to grant the request. The capture was therefore an unfortunate incident resulting from the eagerness of the fleet to enforce the new orders and acquire prizes and from the mischance of a belated order. The prompt release of the *Lafayette* closed the incident.

The decisions of the American judiciary during the war made clearer the principles which obtain in that difficult branch of international law. In the seizure of the *Olinde Rodriguez* the court considered the question of an "effective blockade" and the meaning of "intent to enter" on the part of the blockade runner. The *Olinde Rodriguez* was a French transatlantic steamship which eluded the blockading vessel at San Juan on July 4 and entered port. The following day, as she emerged from the harbor, she was stopped and an official warning of the blockade entered on her log book. She was seized on her return trip, when off San Juan, July 17, on the charge of attempting to run the blockade, and was sent into Charleston. The cargo was released, and the District Court on December 13, 1898, ordered the vessel to be restored to her owners. The action rested on the ground that the blockade of San Juan was ineffective and therefore illegal.[57] The Government appealed to the Supreme Court, where the subject was thrashed out again with a different opinion upon the effectiveness of the blockade. The court said that the test was whether the blockade was "practically effective," and that the question was not controlled by the number of ships in the blockading force. One modern armed cruiser is enough if it is so placed as to make it dangerous to attempt to enter. A distinction was made between a commercial blockade and a military blockade, with the conclusion that a blockade might be practically effective as a case of the former kind and not of the latter. A blockade is not necessarily effective in a military sense against a possible enemy's force. But on the other issue—the fact of "intent to enter"— the court required that proof of actual intent must be clear and decisive. Only one justice dissented, on the ground that the evidence justified condemnation. The results of the case were to declare the blockade of San Juan effective, but to affirm the lower court's action on the restitution of the neutral vessel. In view of the suspicious circumstances of the capture, however, the courts refused to award damages.[58]

The *Newfoundland,* a British steamship loaded with provisions, was taken off the coast of Cuba late in

---

[57] 91 Fed. Rep. 274.

[58] 174 U. S. 510; Moore, Political Science Quarterly, Vol. XV, p. 420; Revue de droit international public, Vol. VI, 1899, pp. 441 ff; Le Fur, La guerre hispano-américaine, pp. 190 ff.

July by the blockading fleet on the charge of trying to violate the blockade of Sagua and Caibarien. She was duly sent to Charleston, and there both vessel and cargo were condemned as lawful prize. The case was appealed to the Supreme Court and an opinion given January 15, 1900. This time it was Justice McKenna, who dissented in the *Olinde Rodriguez* case, who delivered the opinion of the court. There was no issue over notification; she had due notice in her own ports before sailing, her sailing orders forbade a violation of the blockade, and, finally, she received a special notice at the hands of the blockading ships on July 18 and again on the day of her capture. The main question raised was that of the " intent " to enter a blockaded port. At the moment of capture she was some thirteen miles from the coast, twenty miles to the northeast of Havana, with her course directed toward Sagua and Caibarien. What were her intentions? As in the preceding case of the *Lafayette,* the court of last resort held that adequate proof was lacking to justify forfeiture, and restored the ship to the defendants, but without allowing damages for the loss of time and services from July 19, 1898, till January 15, 1900.[59]

An interesting aspect of the case arose out of the fact that the ports of Sagua and Caibarien were never subjected to a regular public blockade, but came under the de facto blockades established by the individual enterprise of Commodore Howell, who was stationed on the north coast of Cuba. The blockade of these points, established about the middle of July, was abandoned by an order from Washington of August

[59] 176 U. S. 97.

10, under circumstances which stamped the case with disapproval.[60]

The *Manoubia*, of the French General Transatlantic Company, was seized some days later, July 25, charged with the intent of entering Sagua la Grande. Her captor admitted having some doubt of the validity of the blockade of Sagua la Grande, but gave his government the benefit of the doubt.[61] As the *Manoubia* carried no cargo to add suspicion to its movements and was some distance from port when taken, the evidence against her was slight, and she was released a few days later without any decision from the prize courts.

A third case involving the American system of de facto blockades arose during the war. The *Adula*, a British steamship, was captured while trying to enter Guantanamo Bay, Cuba. She was proceeding from Kingston, Jamaica, to Cuban ports to convey passengers away from such ports. Such an act was a distinct service to the United States in removing a class which was a burden to it. She was without a cargo when captured, and it seems her master was instructed to proceed directly to Guantanamo Bay, where he would probably be stopped by American vessels, in which case he was to state to the commander the object of his voyage, when it was supposed he would be no longer detained.

Guantanamo was not included in the President's proclamation of April 22, but Admiral Sampson had established a de facto blockade there on June 8. Was a blockade proclaimed by an admiral in direct charge

[60] Message and Documents, 1898-99, Vol. IV, p. 298.
[61] Message and Documents, 1898-99, Vol. IV, p. 280.

14

a sufficient act? The prize court at Savannah condemned the *Adula,* and the decision was affirmed by the Supreme Court on February 26, 1900. The more significant points in the opinion were the declaration that " a legal blockade may be established by a naval officer acting upon his own discretion, or under direction of superiors, without Government notification." That is, that an actual or de facto blockade as distinguished from a public or Presidential blockade is legal. There was laid down what seems a very severe rule for a blockade of the kind in question, where it is simply an investment, without the publicity of a Presidential blockade, and where it ceases with a change in conditions, namely, that if a master has actual notice he is not at liberty even to approach the blockaded port for the purpose of making inquiries.[62] Four members of the Supreme Court concurred in a dissenting opinion to the effect that the blockade was not duly constituted, and that Admiral Sampson's order was not competent authority. The dissenting judges granted the validity of a de facto blockade under certain conditions of military necessity, denied that a neutral could be captured except by a special notification, and opposed the severe rule laid down against the right of neutrals to inquire whether the blockade was still in force.

In conclusion, the decisions on neutral prizes established very plainly that the American courts will insist upon clear and decisive proof of an intent to run the blockade; that they will hold valid a blockade de facto established by a naval commander without the express authority of the President; and that a block-

[62] 176 U. S. 361.

ade may be effective, even though carried on by one armed cruiser alone.

The treatment of neutral cables constitutes another aspect of neutral rights affected by war. Enemy-owned cables and even neutral cables connecting enemy ports are outside the scope of a chapter devoted to the relations of belligerents with neutrals. Nearly all the great cables uniting Cuba, Porto Rico and Manila with the outside world were the property of British owners. These lines the United States destroyed one after another, acting on the principle that cables in mid-ocean were the property of the neutral owner, but that the portion within the three-mile limit of a belligerent coast was as destructible as a neutral-owned line on belligerent soil. This rule adopted by the United States formed an important precedent in international law.[63]

[63] The Institute of International Law in session at Brussels, 1902, adopted the following rules:

"1. Submarine cables connecting two neutral territories are inviolable.

"2. Cables connecting the territories of two belligerents or two parts of the territory of one of the belligerents, can be cut anywhere except in the territorial or the neutralized waters of a neutral territory.

"3. The cables connecting neutral territory with the territory of one of the belligerents can in no case be cut in the territorial sea or the neutralized waters of a neutral territory. On the high seas such cable can only be cut if there is an effective blockade and within the limits of the line of blockade and subject always to the reëstablishment of the cable with the smallest possible delay. The cable can always be cut on the territory and the territorial sea of an enemy territory up to within three miles of low-water mark.

"4. It is to be understood that the liberty of the neutral state to send despatches does not imply the right of using them or permitting their usage to lend assistance to one of the belligerents.

The question of liability for damages to neutrals whose property was destroyed was an important one. The most valuable cable from the standpoint of neutral commercial interests was the Hongkong-Manila line, which remained out of service from May 11 until August 22.[64] The cable, the property of British owners, was of great meteorological value for commercial interests in the Orient. Spain proposed at first that the line be neutralized and the station in Manila placed outside the jurisdiction of the United States and open to all parties without any form of censorship. The same solution for all cables was seriously considered by the American authorities at the outbreak of the war. Unfortunately no such action was taken or compact made.[65] The Eastern Telegraph Company subsequently presented claims for damages from the loss of service on the Hongkong-Manila line, but the United States denied any pecuniary liability for neutral cables destroyed in belligerent territorial waters.

In her declaration of neutrality Brazil prohibited all citizens or aliens " to announce by telegraph the departure or near arrival of any ship, merchant or war, of the belligerents, or to give them any orders,

" 5. These rules admit of no distinction between state cables and those belonging to individuals, nor between cables which are enemy property and cables which are neutral property."

See Annuaire de l'Institut, 1902, Vol. XIX, p. 301 ; Wheaton, International Law (Atlay ed.), p. 722; Professor Holland in Journal de droit international privé, 1898, p. 648; Rivier, Principes, Vol. II, pp. 267–68.

[64] Foreign Relations, 1898, pp. 976–80.

[65] Spanish Correspondence and Documents, p. 189; Message and Documents of the United States, 1898–99, Vol. IV, p. 176.

instructions or warnings, with the purpose of prejudicing the enemy."[66] However, Brazil's high conception of neutral obligations in this respect has not yet had any wider acceptance. If the Brazilian practice prevailed generally the complete immunity of neutral cables would readily be conceded.

The use of a neutral cable connecting neutrals or a belligerent with a neutral by one of the belligerents for military purposes, as for the conveying of despatches to its officers, does in effect constitute a serious breach of neutrality. Some authorities treat cable despatches as contraband by analogy.[67] Several causes for complaint by Spain against cable companies arose during the war, and in almost every instance proper satisfaction was made. In the case of the British-owned line from Cuba to Jamaica the Spanish colonial authorities complained that its use by the American admiralty for military purposes was a breach of English neutrality, and they ordered the company to refuse cipher despatches and to reëstablish a censorship.[68]

The question of what measures a belligerent may take to require satisfaction is one that remains unsettled. There is need of some agreement by an international convention supplementary to the Paris Convention of 1884. It would seem that neutral-owned cables, whether in neutral territory or in belligerent, should be permanently neutralized. The operating companies in turn should be under rigid bond to refuse cipher despatches or military despatches of bel-

[66] Proclamations and Decrees, p. 14.
[67] Manceaux, De la contrebande de guerre.
[68] The London Times, June 19, 1898.

ligerents. An international convention putting them in somewhat the same position as the international mails would insure their immunity in war. Cables have become indispensable in modern civilization for commercial and humanitarian purposes, and they should not be allowed to suffer as spoils of war.

Closely analogous to the restrictions upon the use of neutral ports and the abuse of a neutral's hospitality in opening its ports to belligerent ships is the general prohibition against the abuse of neutral hospitality in the use of its soil. The hospitality is abused if belligerents use their position in a neutral territory to give assistance to one of the belligerents. The American newspapers complained loudly of the act of Polo de Bernabé, the former Minister of Spain to the United States, who withdrew to Canada on the conclusion of his official career in Washington, and more particularly of the advantage he took of his position near the frontier of the enemy. The American authorities seem to have protested in London, and they were even supplemented by friends in the Canadian Parliament; but the subject was not pressed, and apparently no official action was taken by the British Government. The right of Polo de Bernabé to an asylum on neutral soil was unquestioned, but a high conception of neutral obligations would restrict the espionage services he might there perform for his own government. A serious complaint in 1898 from the United States of the conduct of Polo de Bernabé for his slight services to his government while in Canada would have come with bad grace in the light of the long and active operations of the Cuban Junta in New York.

Early in April the American Secretary of State requested permission of the English Government to send four revenue cutters, two of them armed, from the Great Lakes through the St. Lawrence to the Atlantic coast. The permission was given, but owing to the state of navigation they were not able to complete the journey before war opened on April 27. Ambassador Pauncefote agreed to allow them to continue the journey provided the United States Government would give assurance that the vessels would proceed straight to a port of the United States without engaging in any hostile operation, and would not be supplied with more coal and stores than necessary to take them to New York or some other port within easy reach.[69]

The present law of neutrality allows great freedom to the subjects of belligerents on neutral soil. It cannot be said that the negotiation of loans from neutral subjects is a breach of neutrality, even when the operators are the agents of a belligerent government. The furor raised by American journals against the popular subscriptions in France in aid of Spain need not be given serious consideration. The law of neutrality never attempts to suppress popular expressions of sympathy and seldom concerns itself with petty cases of assistance. Municipal law deals in detail with the conduct of such persons on neutral soil, and practice differs from state to state, although the general aim is substantially the same. The declarations of neutrality in 1898 expressed in many cases the existing municipal law. Brazil, the Netherlands, France, Great

[69] Foreign Relations, 1898, pp. 968–70; Moore, Digest, Vol. VII, p. 938.

Britain, Haiti, Italy, Japan, Liberia, Portugal, Venezuela, Roumania, Norway and Sweden prohibited recruiting and enrolling for belligerent armies,[70] but this does not imply that the law of the other neutrals admitted the practice. On the contrary, the rule is now well-nigh a universal one. Some applied the principle to aliens residing within their own limits equally with subjects.[71] The principles upon the use of neutral soil had little application during the war. The law of Spain did not admit of the enrollment of aliens in its armies,[72] and the United States had no occasion to resort to foreign assistance. A minor instance of the kind arose at the beginning of the war. Among the vessels purchased from private companies an American torpedo boat, the *Somers,* at Falmouth, was notified that she must leave within twenty-four hours, but she found herself unable to do so owing to an insufficient crew, and the English Foreign Enlistment Act denied to belligerent vessels in port, even within the twenty-four hours of grace, the privilege of enlisting or augmenting her crew. The *Somers* was forced to remain in port until the war was over,[73] and even her release as late as December 8, 1898, long after the war was practically concluded, was upon the express pledge to the British Government that in the event of a renewal of hostilities the *Somers* would not be employed for military purposes.[74]

[70] Proclamations and Decrees, pp. 13, 27, 29, 31, 39, 40, 42, 47, 48, 50, 60, 62, 69; Le Fur, App. XXXV.

[71] This was the case with the declarations of Great Britain, Brazil, Japan, Portugal, and Haiti.

[72] Le Fur, La guerre hispano-américaine, p. 90.

[73] London Times, April 27, 1898.

[74] Foreign Relations, 1898, p. 1007.

A phase of the rights and duties of neutrals that arose in the Spanish war and for a time threatened serious consequences concerned neutral war-ships in belligerent ports. German merchants with a valuable commerce in the Philippines found it interrupted by the blockade of Manila. The German Government, alive to the interest of its own subjects, concentrated almost the entire Asiatic fleet in the waters of Manila in their defense. At the same time rumors became current that Germany meditated intervention.[75]

During this period of suspicion of German motives occurred the affair of the *Irene*. Her commander, Admiral Diedrich, induced by an overweening enthusiasm for the Spanish cause, intervened to prevent Aguinaldo and his insurgent followers from coöperating with the American forces besieging Manila and capturing Isla Grande. American war-ships went to the relief and the German vessel withdrew without a clash.[76] On another occasion the *Irene* was accused of violating the blockade of Manila, of transporting official despatches and troops for the Spanish authorities, and of resisting visit by the United States blockading fleet. Such incidents most naturally raise the question of the rights and duties of the *Irene* and her kind in Manila Bay during the war.

As a matter of international courtesy war-ships of neutrals are admitted into belligerent jurisdiction; they can scarcely be said to have any rights there. The protection of neutral subjects of the states which the war-ships represent gives a semblance of right or at

[75] See New York Tribune, June 11, 1898, a mere hint of which quickly superexcited American journalistic passions.
[76] The London Times, July 16, 1898.

least a reason for their presence. But if the right to
be there at all is doubtful, when once there the obligation to adhere to a strict neutrality is a preëminent
obligation.

In general the war was noteworthy for the small
degree of friction with neutrals. Such regrettable
incidents as the tactless toast of Admiral Diedrich for
the success of the Spanish arms and the heated after-
dinner invectives of Captain Coglan deserve no notice.
They should have been allowed to pass into oblivion
as soon as uttered, and but for a sensational press
would never have engaged the attention of the two
governments. A misunderstanding in American and
English newspapers as to the part of the German
Government in transporting General Augustin from
Manila to Hongkong several days after the surrender
of Manila reawakened the journalistic controversy.
The fact was that General Augustin had been displaced by his government and ordered home, and with
Admiral Dewey's consent the commander of the
cruiser Kaiserin-Augusta had undertaken to transport
him to Hongkong.[77] These matters never strained
diplomatic relations to any noteworthy degree. Some
of the representations of the newspapers, had they
been founded on facts, were serious enough, but an
exchange of diplomatic explanations fully satisfied the
governments involved. Other neutrals were in belligerent ports regularly during the war without any
protests on account of non-neutral conduct.

[77] Le Fur, La guerre hispano-américaine, pp. 140–41, notes.
Full newspaper accounts of incident quoted.

CHAPTER VIII

Negotiations of Belligerents During War. Restoration of Peace.

The moment when a worsted belligerent becomes conscious of the failure of its cause and desires to enter into negotiations for returning to a peace basis is always a critical one and tries the most resourceful diplomacy to the utmost. The destruction of the Spanish fleet on July 3, the surrender of Santiago on July 16, and the threat of a visit from a hostile fleet to the islands and harbors of peninsular Spain offered grim prospects for any government that would try to prolong the conflict. Only a few military officials in Spain advised that the war be carried on. The practical question for the Government was how to initiate direct negotiations when the ordinary channels of diplomatic intercourse were closed, and the resort to the mediation of one of the great powers was a most logical one. The French Ambassador in Washington, in common with the Austro-Hungarian Minister, had been charged from the first with the interests of Spanish subjects within the United States. The French Ambassador had acted for Spain in several unimportant communications regarding persons taken on Spanish prizes captured during the war. After the naval battle of Santiago he had been charged with the interests of the prisoners taken there.[1] The deli-

[1] Correspondence of the Embassy of France representing the interests of Spain, Treaty of Peace and other Papers, pp. 285 ff. Foreign Relations, 1898, pp. 785 ff.

cate question of procedure was thus in part solved for Spain in advance. Her wish for peace could be made known through France acting as an intermediary without the suspicion of French intermeddling or intervention, either of which would be resented by the American people, influenced by an injudicious journalism.

Preliminary negotiations were begun on July 18 with a telegram from the Minister of State at Madrid addressed to the Spanish Ambassador at Paris. It read in part: " Thinking it feasible that the French Government may help us (if they have the disposition) to open up communication with the American Government, I beg your excellency to ascertain if the Ambassador of France in Washington, who has charge of Spanish affairs and possesses key No. 74, would be able to present to the Secretary of State, Mr. Day, a communication from the Spanish Government, directed to the President of the Republic of the United States, in which he is invited to put an end to the painful situation of the island of Cuba." Thereupon followed an explanation of the state of affairs in Cuba and a statement that the proposed communication would at the same time solicit an immediate armistice.[2] Some slight delays in Paris caused a second message, on July 20, urging haste. The situation in Manila and Porto Rico was advanced as a reason for concluding a suspension of hostilities at the earliest possible moment, and this was set forth, it was manifest from the tenor of the communication, in order to save something from the wreck of colonies. On July 21

[2] Spanish Diplomatic Correspondence and Documents, 1896–1900, p. 200.

the French Government authorized the Ambassador in
Washington to act as a medium of communication
between the belligerents. The introductory communication asking for peace was sent to Ambassador Cambon on July 22, but several days elapsed before it
could be delivered in Washington—and critical days
they were for Spanish interests, for on July 21 Major-
General Miles sailed for Porto Rico, where he made
a landing on July 25, and in the two days following
took Ponce and began the march across the island to
San Juan. The first delay at Washington arose from
the fact that the Spanish archives, including the cipher
key, were stored in the offices of the Austro-Hungarian Minister, who was at the time away from the
city, and several days were consumed in getting a
cipher key from the consul-general in Montreal,
Canada. On July 26 the Spanish message was duly
transmitted to President McKinley.

In brief, the message which opened direct communication between the belligerents, though padded with
much about the motives of Spain in the war, was a
request for information upon the terms of peace which
the United States would offer.[3] President McKinley
withheld an immediate reply, awaiting a conference
with his cabinet. That Spain was anxious for peace
is hardly to be doubted now; that the United States
was uncertain of its proper policy is no less evident.
No suspicion of undue haste could attach to the studied
deliberateness of American action during the days
following July 26. Military reasons gave the United

[3] The correspondence is in Foreign Relations of the United
States, 1898, pp. 819 ff., and in Spanish Diplomatic Correspondence and Documents, 1896–1900, p. 206.

States increasing advantage with each hour of delay. The situation in Manila was no less critical than that in Porto Rico. The army of invasion began landing on July 19, and on July 30 Washington learned from Admiral Dewey that the surrender of the Spanish forces was momentarily expected. But there were other reasons adequate in themselves to warrant hesitation. The prevailing ignorance regarding the Philippine Islands and the temper of the Philippine people embarrassed the Government to no little degree. It was known that the insurgents, who had proclaimed their independence, were becoming aggressive and threatening toward the American army.[4] Besides, there was a considerable element of the American people which was suspicious of the expanding military operations and strongly opposed to territorial expansion. While domestic conditions and self-interest led the United States to proceed slowly, Spain felt the more impatient at the delay. From the standpoint of international law the task of formulating the terms of peace devolved upon the United States, and no ground of complaint resulted from any reasonable delay. Military operations were justifiable until the two governments had agreed upon a common basis of negotiations or upon the suspension of hostilities.

The reply of the United States to the overture of Spain as finally submitted on July 30 enumerated three conditions: (1) the relinquishment by Spain of all claim of sovereignty over or title to Cuba, and the immediate evacuation of the island; (2) the cession of Porto Rico and an island in the Ladrones to be

[4] Message and Documents, 1898–1899, Vol. IV, p. 118.

selected by the United States, both as indemnity in lieu of any pecuniary indemnity; (3) the occupation and holding of the city, bay and harbor of Manila pending the conclusion of a treaty of peace which should determine the control, disposition and government of the Philippines.[5]

In the first conference Ambassador Cambon had participated no farther than to transmit the message of Spain. In the subsequent conferences he had been acquainted in advance with the position of Spain and was authorized to participate in the defence of her interests.[6] On July 30 he had been able to induce President McKinley to modify the third article of the demand by the substitution of the word " disposition " for the original " possession," which seemed to Ambassador Cambon to leave the negotiations slightly more freedom in the final settlement of the Philippines. Spain also preferred the annexation of Cuba to the United States, and Ambassador Cambon urged that action upon the United States, conditioning it only by the suggestion of the moral necessity of a final appeal to a plebiscite of the Cuban population.[7]

The terms proposed by the United States seemed severe to Spain. Her representatives naturally wished to limit the indemnification demanded by the conqueror to a sacrifice of Cuba. Several days of August were consumed in the efforts to secure some modifications in this respect, particularly to retain Porto Rico, but without avail. President McKinley readily acceded to

[5] Foreign Relations, 1898, p. 820; Spanish Diplomatic Correspondence and Documents, 1896–1900, p. 213.
[6] Spanish Diplomatic Correspondence and Documents, 1896–1900, pp. 208–9.
[7] Ibid., pp. 209, 213.

the wishes of Spain that the peace negotiations be transferred to neutral soil, and Paris was selected. Further negotiations fixed the number of commissioners for each at five. On the question of concessions the firmness of the United States convinced Ambassador Cambon of the futility of delay, and he politely informed Spain that in his opinion "all vacillation will further aggravate the severity of the conditions."[8] The second direct communication from Spain to the United States, in the form of a reply to the terms of peace proposed on July 30, was not received until August 9, though sent from Madrid on August 7. The transmission of messages was slow, owing to the circuitous route employed in sending them first to the Spanish Ambassador in Paris, and from him to the French Minister of State, who in turn despatched them to the French Ambassador in Washington. The latter was in turn obliged to await the opportunity for a conference with the President. The reply of Spain accepted the general terms of the demands of the United States, but antagonized the President and Secretary by the reservation upon the evacuation of Cuba and Porto Rico to the effect that the approval of the Cortes would be necessary. President McKinley had demanded immediate evacuation in both cases. During the conference the expedient was suggested of embodying the differences in a protocol to be signed by the Ambassador of France in the name of Spain, and the conference adjourned for its formulation, while Ambassador Cambon communicated the grim facts of the unalterable conditions of peace to the Government in Madrid. His communication transmitted

[8] *Ibid.*, p. 217; Foreign Relations, 1898, p. 823.

frankly and clearly the necessity of accepting as inevitable the rigorous terms already advanced, and the hopelessness and danger of further delay. The following day, or August 10, the protocol, an outline draft of the basis for negotiating a treaty of peace, was submitted to Ambassador Cambon.

The protocol made no changes in the three articles proposed on July 30,[9] but added articles upon the evacuation of Cuba and Porto Rico, the peace commission, and the suspension of hostilities. The first and last of these had been the occasion of the differences of the preceding ten days. The additional articles which went to make up the protocol were as follows:

"Article IV. Spain will immediately evacuate Cuba, Porto Rico, and other islands under Spanish sovereignty in the West Indies, and to this end each Government will, within ten days after the signing of this protocol, appoint commissioners, and the commissioners so appointed shall, within thirty days after the signing of this protocol, meet at Havana for the purpose of arranging and carrying out the details of the aforesaid evacuation of Cuba and the adjacent Spanish islands; and each Government will within thirty days after the signing of this protocol meet at San Juan, in Porto Rico, for the purpose of arranging and carrying out the details of the aforesaid evacuation of Porto Rico and other islands under Spanish sovereignty in the West Indies.

"Article V. The United States and Spain will each appoint not more than five commissioners to treat of peace, and the commissioners so appointed shall

[9] Ante, p. 222.

meet at Paris not later than October 1, 1898, and
proceed to the negotiation and conclusion of a treaty
of peace, which treaty shall be subject to ratification
according to the respective constitutional forms of the
two countries.

" Article VI. Upon the conclusion and signing of
this protocol hostilities between the two countries shall
be suspended, and notice to that effect shall be given
as soon as possible by each Government to the commanders of its military and naval forces."

In one feature the Spanish Government had won a
slight victory. The note of July 30 required an immediate evacuation of the West Indian possessions of
Spain; the protocol, while retaining the principle, introduced a futurity by the thirty-day period and the
control of details by the commissioners. The last
article made the protocol an armistice as well. Without delay Spain, through the circuitous Paris route,
transmitted authority to the French Ambassador to
accept and sign the protocol in all parts as proposed
by the United States. Accordingly on August 12 the
protocol was jointly signed, hostilities were nominally
suspended, and the peace mission of Ambassador Cambon ended.

A moment's consideration may be given here to the
legal significance of a protocol. In concluding a war
three distinct instruments are recognized in international practice—the armistice, the protocol or prelim-
inaries and the definitive treaty of peace. The protocol may act as an armistice, or as in 1898 the two
may be combined in one act. A war from the standpoint of neutral rights and obligations—from the
standpoint of international law—is not ended in real-

ity until a formal treaty of peace is concluded. In usual practice, however, the belligerents restore commerce as quickly as possible after hostilities cease. In 1898 the blockade of Cuban ports was raised on August 13 and authority was soon given to the subjects of the belligerents to engage in trade.[10]

A protocol or preliminary settlement becomes frequently, as it was in 1898, a means of ending the useless effusion of blood when an immediate definitive treaty would be impossible, a means of suspending hostilities while resort is had to deliberation. It is not a treaty of peace. In American constitutional practice it does not require a ratification by the Senate. The Cortes of Spain, however, met in special session on September 5, and after a brief and stormy discussion gave its sanction to the continuation of negotiations on the basis of the protocol.[11] The peace protocol was a most striking illustration of the power of the President to enter into international agreements without the consent of the Senate. It was more than a preliminary treaty of peace. In the stipulations for the immediate evacuation of Cuba and Porto Rico it went further and in a sense anticipated the definitive treaty of peace.[12] Otherwise the protocol, like the armistice, has no more than a temporary character and effect. Both are devices of the executive department for reaching a basis for negotiations without awaiting the difficult and often delayed conferences necessary for a final treaty and for a ratification by the other branch of the Government.

[10] Spanish Diplomatic Correspondence and Documents, p. 228; Message and Documents, 1898–1899, Vol. IV, p. 124.
[11] See Times, London, September 16, 1898.
[12] Moore, Digest, Vol. III, p. 213.

A protocol pledges the Governments to negotiate along certain specified lines, nothing more. It is superseded when the final treaty is signed. In default of agreement the very fact of suspension of negotiations reanimates the suspended hostilities. It is scarcely necessary to add that the protocol placed the Governments under obligation to refrain from all acts calculated to change the military situation, such as reënforcements in the field or increase of the naval force in the neighborhood of disputed territories.

The execution of the protocol involved a great amount of detail upon which it had been insufficiently clear in some cases. There was the suspension of hostilities, the abandonment of the blockade, the temporary resumption of commercial and postal communication between belligerent territories, the treatment of subsequent captures, the occupation of Manila, the evacuation of Cuba and Porto Rico, and the appointment and meeting of the Peace Commission.

The protocol seemingly provided for an immediate suspension of hostilities. Unfortunately there was an indefiniteness in its wording which brought up differences of interpretation. The words were: " upon the conclusion and signing of this protocol hostilities between the two countries shall be suspended, and notice to that effect shall be given as soon as possible by each Government to the commanders of its military and naval forces." The question is as to the precise moment for the dating of the suspension of hostilities, the moment for beginning the new condition of the armistice. Should it be the moment the protocol was signed, as Spain subsequently claimed, or should it vary with the locality, depending on the receipt of the notification by the commanders in the field? That is, should the evacuation take place gradually? The differing constructions involved diverse legal consequences. The statement in this particular should have been more precise.[13]

The request for an armistice originated with the first Spanish overtures, and its concession by the United States was favorable to Spain. The latter desired it immediately for the reason that delay daily prejudiced her military position. From Ambassador Cambon's reports of the several conferences it would seem that the element of immediateness was emphasized in two particulars—in the suspension of hostilities and in the evacuation of Cuba and Porto Rico— but that in the final settlement the immediate evacuation was modified in detail without destroying the principle.[14] Both from the wording of the protocol and from the spirit of the negotiations the suspension of hostilities would seem to date from the signing of the protocol. In fact, the American commanders in the Philippines did not receive the notification until August 16. In the mean time Manila had been bombarded (August 13) and articles of capitulation executed (August 14).[15] Before August 16 the Amer-

[13] In the case of the Franco-Prussian war the armistice agreed upon on January 28, 1871, took effect immediately in Paris and three days later in the departments.

[14] See Spanish Diplomatic Correspondence and Documents, 1896-1900, pp. 200-27.

[15] An engagement between a vessel of the blockading force and two Spanish gunboats took place on August 14 off Caibarien, Cuba, before the respective commanders had notification of the armistice, but as the incident was without serious consequences, either in the destruction of private property, captures or the loss of life, it involved no legal action or controverted consequences.

ican troops had occupied Manila City and were entering into full possession as rapidly as possible.

It is a principle consecrated by practice and by the concurrence of jurists that captures made after the moment fixed for the termination of hostilities, though made in ignorance of the true state of belligerent relations, must be restored. Opinion does not differ. Territory which has been occupied must be given up; ships which have been captured must be restored, and damages from bombardment must be compensated for.[16]

Curiously enough, the different interpretations of the protocol did not in this particular case affect the security of the American position in Manila. If the city was not held by right of the military convention of capitulation, it was held legally by the third article of the protocol.[17] It did affect the title to the territory. In one case Manila was temporarily American by the right of military conquest in public war; in the other it was temporarily American under the terms of a preliminary peace protocol.

Both Governments defended their positions with becoming vigor.[18] If it was the original intent to suspend hostilities immediately on the agreement upon the protocol, as the spirit of the negotiations seemed to indicate and as the letter of the protocol indicated, the technical contention of Spain was the stronger.

[16] Hall, International Law, p. 586; Heffter-Geffcken, Droit international, p. 331.

[17] " The United States will occupy and hold the city, bay and harbor of Manila pending the conclusion of a treaty of peace which shall determine the control," etc.

[18] Spanish Diplomatic Correspondence and Documents gives fullest accounts, pp. 237–50.

The Duke of Almodóvar del Rio, Minister of State, contended that the United States occupied Manila by virtue of the protocol and not by the right of conquest; that any right conferred by the protocol did not include the right to alter the Spanish laws in force there; that the Spanish troops in Manila were not properly prisoners of war, but at liberty to go to other Spanish territories in the continuation of their military service, and that the United States had no power to make changes in the economic and fiscal system of the city, or to divert its customs receipts to other purposes than those for which they were engaged under Spanish control. All these the Secretary of State of the United States denied categorically. The reply assumed that it was immaterial whether the occupation was by virtue of the capitulation or of the protocol, since in either case the powers of the military occupant are the same. To the last statement there is no dissent among writers. The obligations of the United States in Manila City—obligations of the protection of property and the preservation of life—were those of the military occupant. The rights could be no less sweeping. Consequently local law and government yielded to military law and administration except where the old was not specifically displaced. In one particular the American contention was indefensible. Manila was American under the protocol and not by conquest, though the distinction was one in name only. The Spanish forces were virtually prisoners in either case, in the absence of a definition of their status in the protocol. Besieged and shut off from other territories, they could not claim liberty of action, nor could their government avail itself of their services until a treaty of peace set them at liberty.[19]

The blockade, being a part of the military operations of the United States, ceased with the proclamation of the armistice. The abandonment of the blockade automatically opened the ports of Cuba to noncontraband neutral commerce. It was not so with belligerent subjects and their commerce, which were not included in the protocol and remained for separate adjustment, but on August 22 and 23 Spain and the United States agreed to open their ports to belligerent commerce subject to certain conditions. Cuba, the Philippines, and American ports were opened freely and unconditionally to all merchant trade. The importation of food into Porto Rico was reserved to American vessels alone. Spanish ports were opened to American vessels under the condition that in case hostilities were reopened the vessels in Spanish ports would enjoy the immunities conceded to Spanish vessels by Articles 4 and 5 of the proclamation of April 26. That is, the two reciprocally agreed to extend to vessels in port on the outbreak of hostilities a period of thirty days within which to purchase and load cargoes and depart.[20]

The Fourth Article of the protocol required the appointment, within ten days, of commissioners to formulate the details in the evacuation of Cuba and of Porto Rico. They were to meet at Havana and

[19] The American Commission at Paris reached the conclusion just stated regarding the title to Manila. Foreign Relations, 1898, p. 940. Treaty of Peace and Other Papers, p. 146, gives a full statement of the American position. Le Fur, pp. 255–56, holds the opposite view.

[20] Spanish Diplomatic Correspondence and Documents, 1896–1900, pp. 230–31.

at San Juan within thirty days.[21] Both joint commissions began their sessions on September 12, and eight days later Spanish troops began to depart from Porto Rico. No difficulties arose in the details of evacuation of Porto Rico, and the troops were made ready and transported as rapidly as ships could be secured by Spain. The last left on October 24. The maintenance of harmony proved more difficult in the execution of the protocol in Cuba. Differences arose over the meaning of "evacuation," whether in the sense of a "military evacuation" or both "military and civil evacuation," over the property rights of Spain in Cuba, and over the legal status of Cuba if abandoned before the conclusion of a treaty of peace. These technical quibbles, unquestionably inserted to conserve some advantages in the discussions in Paris, have little other significance. The legal status of Cuba may be postponed for consideration in the next

[21] The United States appointed a military commission for Cuba, Major-General Wade, Rear-Admiral Sampson, and Major-General Butler; for Porto Rico, Major-General Brooke, Rear-Admiral Schley, and Brigadier-General Gordon, all connected with the military operations during the war. Spain designated a similar number for each commission. For Cuba, General Don Julian Gonzales Parrado, next to General Blanco in command in Cuba, Don Luis Pastor y Landero, Rear-Admiral, and the Marquis of Montoro, the leader of the Cuban autonomists; for Porto Rico, General Don Ricardo Ortega Diaz of the Spanish troops in the island, Captain Don Eugenio Vallarino y Carasco, commander of the naval station of Porto Rico, and His Excellency Don José Sanchez del Aguila, auditor of division. On account of illness Rear-Admiral Luis Pastor y Landero did not serve, and was superseded by Rear-Admiral Don Vicente de Manterola y Tasconera. Later on General Parrado was superseded for the same reason by Lieutenant-General Don Adolfo Jimenez Castillanos. Spanish Diplomatic Correspondence and Documents, pp. 229, 244, 258.

chapter. Finally the United States Government interfered with the unprofitable discussions in Havana, fixed the date of evacuation at December 1, and later, upon application from Madrid, extended it to January 1, 1899, when the formal transfer of Cuba to the American authorities took place. The last Spanish soldiers left Cuba in February, 1899.[22]

The protocol had called for the meeting of a Peace Commission at Paris not later than October 1, 1898. Premier Sagasta named Don Montero Ríos, President of the Senate; Don Buenaventura de Abarzuza, former Minister of Colonies; Don José de Garnica y Diaz, Magistrate of the Supreme Tribunal of Justice and Deputy in the Cortes; Don Wenceslao Ramirez de Villa-Urrutia, Minister of Spain to Belgium, and General Don Rafael Cerero y Saenz. President McKinley appointed his Secretary of State, Judge Day; Senator Davis, Chairman of the Foreign Relations Committee; Senators Gray and Frye, also of the Foreign Relations Committee, and Mr. Whitelaw Reid, editor of the New York Tribune and former Minister to France. Don Emilio de Ojeda and Professor J. B. Moore, Assistant Secretary of State, were made secretaries of their respective commissions.

The commissioners met in Paris at the Hall of the Ministry of Foreign Affairs for the first conference on October 1, and at intervals thereafter until December 10. At the first session, after the necessary steps in organization, the Spanish Commission presented as preliminary to any discussion of a treaty the demand that the status quo in the Philippines at the time of

[22] Spanish Diplomatic Correspondence and Documents, pp. 232, 250; Moore, Digest, Vol. I, pp. 286-87.

the signing of the protocol be restored. They referred to the progress of the insurrection throughout the
group, and they wished the United States to take
measures to release Spanish soldiers taken prisoners
by the insurgents and to aid in suppressing the rising
rebellion, or at least to set at liberty the prisoners in
Manila held under the capitulation of August 14,
which was considered void by Article 6 of the protocol.[23] As anticipated by the Spanish Commission, the
reply made by the American Commission at the second
conference (October 3) viewed the demands as outside the jurisdiction of the Commission, belonging
rather to the direct diplomatic relations of the Governments in executing other clauses of the original
protocol,[24] and in this position they were unquestionably justified. The subject belonged to the fulfilment
of the protocol. Differences of fact and law had
arisen and the Governments had taken diametrically
opposite views. The transference of such questions
to Paris must have hopelessly entangled relations and
prevented progress toward the object of the conference.[25]

At the same session the American commissioners
presented several propositions for the basis of a treaty.
Spain should relinquish all claim of sovereignty over
Cuba and all title to fixed property in the island, and
should cede Porto Rico and other islands of Spain in
the West Indies and the Island of Guam in the

[23] Treaty of Peace, Protocol and Other Papers, p. 15.
[24] Ibid., p. 21 ; Spanish Diplomatic Correspondence and Documents, p. 275.
[25] Cf. discussion of positions and fulfilment of protocol,
ante, pp. 232–233.

Ladrones. Nothing was said about the Philippines. The policy manifestly was to proceed from the easy to the difficult problems, from the certain to the uncertain, from the propositions upon which American conviction was well known to those upon which it was unknown.

When the Commission met in the third session on October 7 the members for Spain presented a counter-project for a treaty. The seven propositions submitted on that occasion, like the American ones, avoided the Philippine problem and made no allusion to an island in the Ladrones. Articles 6 and 7 ceded Porto Rico and the other islands belonging to Spain in the West Indies. Five articles dealt with Cuba and departed widely from the American project. Spain proposed to transfer sovereignty over Cuba to the United States, which in turn should at the proper time transfer it to the Cuban people. With the transfer of sovereignty were to pass all charges and obligations imposed in a constitutional manner for the services of the island or chargeable to its own individual treasury, including salaries or allowances due civil or ecclesiastical employees of the insular government and all pensions in the civil or military service. This was the appearance of the much-mooted Cuban debt.[26]

At the fourth session on October 11 the American members refused to accept the Spanish proposal, objecting to the conditional character of the relinquishment of sovereignty over Cuba, to the transfer of sovereignty itself to the United States ad interim, and more especially to the heterogeneous burdens to be

[26] Treaty of Peace and Accompanying Papers, p. 27.

assumed. The Spanish Commission attempted to conciliate them by interpreting the article regarding the final transfer of sovereignty over Cuba as optional, and by saying that it was possible for the United States to retain it permanently.[27] The American commissioners stood firmly on the exact language of the protocol: " Spain will relinquish all claims of sovereignty over and title to Cuba," no more and no less.

A memorandum of the Spanish members defended the contention that the debt belonged of right and in law to sovereignty. It is needless to review the successive sessions given to the merits of the debt controversy. It was an ever recurrent topic, and threatened for a time to break up the Conference. Both commissions turned for counsel to the principals at home.[28] Unquestionably from the standpoint of international law the contention of Spain was technically correct. The American commissioners recognized the principle that local debts incurred for the benefit of the transferred territory pass with the sovereignty, and they felt the embarrassment of the situation.[29] On October 25 the President of the Commission telegraphed to Secretary Hay asking if the Government would approve an article in the treaty in which the United States, without contracting any liability of its own, would pledge itself to use its good offices with the Cuban people to induce them to assume any debts incurred for existing internal improvements, the amount of the debts to be determined by a mixed commission.

[27] Spanish Diplomatic Correspondence and Documents, 1896–1900, p. 286.
[28] Ibid., pp. 293, 296; Foreign Relations, p. 930.
[29] Foreign Relations, 1898, p. 931.

This idea was suggested by the memorable compromise of the Peace Conference in Paris at the close of the American Revolution, when Great Britain was pressing the new-born republic to assume the debts of the separate colonial governments.

The conciliatory measures proposed in Paris were, however, promptly rejected by Secretary Hay. He wrote: " The United States will neither assume nor use its good offices to induce any other government to assume such a debt. It is not believed that there are any such debts outstanding incurred for existing improvements." Such was the spirited reply. Any justification for the United States in making an exception to the rule of international law must rest upon the distinction between bona fide debts incurred for the benefit of Cuba through internal improvements and debts incurred for other purposes but fictitiously charged to the Cuban debt. It was held by the American authorities charged with responsibility at the time, and it has been the universal conviction in America, that the so-called debt was a debt of Spain charged to Cuban customs revenues for the convenience of offering security to loan agents.[30]   Mr. Le Fur[31] has laboriously endeavored to show the reality of an obligation upon the United States or the Republic of Cuba to assume the part of the Spanish debt charged to Cuban revenues. No one takes exception to the principle. Debts created for the general good of a state and secured to the creditors by the customs revenues

[30] Treaty of Peace and Accompanying Papers, p. 49, for views of American commissioners on origin of the debt charged to Cuba; Moore, Digest, Vol. I, pp. 351–85.

[31] La guerre hispano-américaine, p. 288.

of the state have, in the practice of the past, been
apportioned to the parts of the state upon a territorial
division of the original state. American and European practice has recognized the principle as one of
primary importance,[32] but it presupposes a bona fide
debt in the interests of the whole state. The so-
called Cuban debt was, as a matter of fact, the fruit
of accountant jugglery. The obligation upon the assumption of the debts of annexed territories must not
be pressed to absurd extremes. Van Bar, in a monograph on "Die cubanische Staatschuld," reaches the
conclusion that debts created for Kultur-objects, such
as works of civilization, railroads, and ports, pass with
a transfer of sovereignty, while debts caused by engagements for political objects, such as the suppression
of insurrection, do not. The difficult and almost in-
surmountable problem of determining the bona fide
character of the former in 1898 made the United States
unwilling to give the distinction any consideration. It
was known that the great proportion of the debt was
created for political purposes, as in the attempt to rein-
corporate Santo Domingo into the Spanish dominion,
the expedition to Mexico, and the cost of the attempt
to conquer Cuba in revolt.

To Americans it appears to follow from these facts
that no moral or legal obligation rested on either the

[32] Moore, Digest, Vol. I, pp. 339 ff., cases illustrative of practice. Whitcomb, La situation internationale de Cuba, pp. 41–43,
condemns the United States for its failure to recognize the
principle. There is an excellent discussion of the subject in
its theoretical aspects in Cabouat, Des annexions de territoires
et de leurs conséquences; René Selosse, Traité de l'annexion
au territoire français et de son démembrement; Appleton, Des
effets des annexions de territoires sur les dettes de l'état
démembré ou annexé, Paris, 1894.

United States or Cuba to shoulder such a burden. On the other hand, any internal improvements of a pacific character were reasonably a subject of consideration before the conference, and the problem was to determine these, if any existed. The difficulty at the time grew out of the failure of Spain to make such a distinction. All the European writers deal with a different set of facts. It is not correct to say that the American Government in its conduct in 1898 violated the sanctity of public debts, for in the clauses dealing with the Philippines the debts incurred for pacific improvements were acknowledged and virtually assumed.

The situation had become so unpromising by October 24 and 25 that recourse was had to the remarkable expedient of the services of the ambassadors in Paris, M. Leon y Castillo for Spain and General Porter for the United States. The American demand for a rejection or acceptance of their demands on the Cuban debt was an ultimatum. In view of the entanglements in Paris the Spanish Minister of Foreign Affairs had ordered a suspension of the conferences. Ambassador Castillo, a staunch supporter of peace, held conferences with the American Ambassador at Paris, and represented to his own government the inflexible position of the United States. It was upon his suggestion that the fertile hint of a possibility of securing concessions elsewhere equivalent to the Cuban differences, particularly in the Philippine question, was adopted.[33]

[33] Spanish Diplomatic Correspondence and Documents, pp. 299, 300, 302; Foreign Relations, 1898, p. 936.

At the conference on October 26, the ninth in order, the Spanish commissioners agreed to suspend the demands on the Cuban debt and to accept the first two articles of the protocol for the treaty, and they asked for the American terms for the Philippines. The original instructions of President McKinley had drawn a sharp distinction between the duty of the United States in the West Indies and in the Orient; the Government stood prepared to recognize the new duties and responsibilities in the latter regions, but in other respects the administration appeared to be deeply embarrassed. The disposition at that time was toward contentment with Luzón, coaling stations, and the "open door" doctrine in the commerce of the entire archipelago. The Commission went to Paris instructed to accept no less than the cession of Luzón. Once in Paris it busied itself with conducting elaborate inquiries into the Philippine situation in every aspect. General Merritt left his post in Manila and went to Paris to give evidence based on his own knowledge, and to carry the personal statement of Admiral Dewey and some half dozen others in Manila, American and foreign. Other witnesses appeared before the commission for the same purpose. During the earlier conferences, while the American commissioners were silent upon their terms regarding the Philippines, they had been endeavoring to determine their own views, with the result that by the time the Spanish members asked for their terms the former were as much divided in opinion and in as great a quandary as was the American public at the same moment. On October 25 the American commissioners reported their differences to

16

Washington and asked for explicit instructions. Senators Davis and Frye and Mr. Reid saw no half-way solution in dealing with the archipelago. To them commercial, military and moral necessities and obligations happily joined in pointing to the annexation of all the islands. Cuban experience was a protest against dividing asunder a group which for centuries had been in political affiliation. Senator Gray stood alone in holding that the United States had no obligations in the Philippines as a result of its position. He argued for magnanimity to Spain and for the strict adherence to the letter of the oft-repeated motives of the war, which were devoid of all spirit of aggrandizement and conquest. President Day was impressed by the experimental nature of American colonial administration in the Orient and by the desirability of keeping acquisitions within reasonable bounds. His plan called for the cession of Luzón, Mindoro, Palawan and a few minor islands which controlled the entrance to the China Sea, with treaty stipulations for the rest providing freedom of trade and non-alienation engagements.[34]

The result of the appeal for further instructions was an unqualified, uncompromising message from Secretary Hay. " The information which has come to the President since your departure convinces him that the acceptance of the cession of Luzon alone, leaving the rest of the islands subject to Spanish rule, or to be the

[34] Foreign Relations, 1898, p. 932. Compare second statement of differences of views on the disposition of Philippines, November 11, where Senator Frye suggests a payment of $10,000,000 for the Philippine debt and Senator Davis, also still in favor of taking the whole group, opposes entirely any money payment whatsoever. *Ibid.*, p. 947.

subject of future contention, cannot be justified on political, commercial, or humanitarian grounds. The cession must be of the whole archipelago or none. The latter is wholly inadmissible, and the former must therefore be required. The President reaches this conclusion after most thorough consideration of the whole subject, and is deeply sensible of the grave responsibilities it will impose, believing that this course will entail less trouble than any other, and besides will best subserve the interests of the people involved, for whose welfare we cannot escape responsibility."[35] Other communications of the time further indicated that the President had become the staunchest supporter of territorial expansion. While the commissioners sought to rest the claim to the Philippines on the ground of indemnity, the welfare of the islands in view of the conditions there, and inability to restore Spanish sovereignty, the President sought to press the untenable claims of right through conquest.[36] The theory was stretched so far as to maintain that the conquest was accomplished by the destruction of the Spanish fleet on May 1.[37]

It was no wonder that the Spanish commissioners were amazed when confronted on October 31 by the American terms. They had come to negotiate on the Philippines, and looked for concessions only to find the ground taken from underneath by a sweeping demand for all.[38] One crumb of concession was found at the

[35] *Ibid.*, p. 935.
[36] Post, p. 251.
[37] Foreign Relations, 1898, p. 940.
[38] Spanish Diplomatic Correspondence and Documents, 1896–1900, pp. 308–10.

end—to assume the " debts of Spain contracted for
public works or benefits of a pacific character for the
Philippines." Spain complained that the terms were
harsh beyond international precedents. The grounds
of the claim—the welfare of the islands—were naturally not admitted by her. Again for weeks her
representatives hurled themselves against terms which
they regarded as unjust. Conference succeeded conference without any change in front. The hope of
Spain was to prolong negotiations by successive alternatives until some change favorable to herself should
occur. The growth of anti-expansion sentiment in
America, a menacing continental opposition to the
American pretensions, and particularly the outcome of
the November elections in the United States were the
only hopes.[39]

Spain rested its case mainly on the contention that
the American terms were in violation of the protocol.
Article 3, it will be remembered, reserved for the
Peace Commission the right to " determine the control,
disposition and government of the Philippines." In
the negotiations with Ambassador Cambon the latter
had secured the substitution of " disposition " for the
original " possession." Now the claim was advanced
that the " sovereignty " of Spain in the Philippines
was not a proper subject of negotiation; that only
the disposition—the necessary reforms and limitations
of the future government—were before the commissioners. The differences involved the precise meaning of English words and the purpose of their use.
It would seem that Ambassador Cambon sought the

[39] Spanish Diplomatic Correspondence and Documents, p. 312.

use of the word which would not seem to prejudge the results. If this view is true the interpretation works both ways. If it did not prejudge the results against Spain, it did not preclude negotiations upon results. A careful reading of the published reports of the interview between Ambassador Cambon and President McKinley gives not the slightest warrant for doubt of the intention on August 12 to leave the Philippine question open for the fullest and freest consideration in the peace conferences.

However, on November 12 the Minister of State instructed the Spanish delegates to ask for an arbitration on the meaning of the third and sixth articles of the protocol, which they did on November 16. The appeal for arbitration was rejected in the answer of November 21.[40] The defense was that "arbitration precedes war, to avoid its horrors; it does not come after the trial by battle to enable either party to escape its consequences. . . . In such an event, nothing remains but for one of the contesting parties to yield its opinions in order that a peaceful solution may be reached."[41]

In other portions of the memorandum of the American commissioners of November 21 the concessions which the United States was willing to make were given: to admit Spanish ships for a certain number of years into the Philippines on the same terms as American; to relinquish mutually all claims for indemnity, public or private, other than the cession of territory exacted; and to offer to Spain twenty million dollars in case the cession of the Philippines was agreed to. The state-

[40] *Ibid.*, pp. 322, 324; Treaty of Peace and Accompanying Papers, pp. 196, 198.
[41] Treaty of Peace and Accompanying Papers, p. 208.

ment was, moreover, couched in terms which made it an ultimatum—to be accepted or rejected before November 28. If the Spanish commissioners were in any doubt as to the final character of the American communication, Mr. Reid left no opportunity for any uncertainty, for early the next morning in a conference with Ambassador Castillo the true character to be attributed to the American position was restated in courteous terms but with an unmistakable frankness.[42] The Spanish commissioners and the Council of Ministers in Madrid hesitated, haggled, bargained, and talked of yielding all, breaking off communications and making no effort to conclude a treaty of peace.[43] Señors Garnica and Cerero were opposed to the pecuniary compensation as insignificant in quantity and as otherwise prejudicial to future action on the colonial debts. There was a faint hope that the terms of peace might be so guarded that Spain would be left free to settle the debt problem with the Cubans at a later time, when America should be eliminated by a treaty of peace.[44]

A perusal of the communications at this time emphasizes the constant and close communication with the home government and the helpless, hopeless situation of Spain. It dared not return to hostilities, it could not face the humiliating inevitable. Squirm as their responsible authorities would, cast about for alternatives as they tried, there was nothing to do against the inexorable finality of the American propositions; longer resistance had become useless. Long before this the November elections in the United States

[42] Spanish Diplomatic Correspondence and Documents, p. 326.
[43] *Ibid.*, pp. 326–27.
[44] *Ibid.*, p. 319.

had destroyed any flickering hope of dissensions in that quarter.

On November 25 the Council of Ministers in Madrid painfully submitted, and ordered the commissioners in Paris to yield to the American terms of peace.[45] Only subsidiary matters remained to engage the attention of the Peace Commission after the conference on November 28. The American commissioners sought to secure an island in the Carolines, liberty of worship throughout the group, rights of landing cables on Spanish territories, and the renewal of treaties suspended by the war, but they found the Spanish Government unwilling to consider them until a treaty of peace was concluded. The matters were suitable subjects for negotiations, but were all outside the subjects of the protocol and alien to the true work of the conference. This was the view of Spain. On the other hand the American commissioners were divided upon the character of the concessions to be made in return, and nothing came of the attempt to widen the scope of the treaty. The treaty of peace was finally concluded along the lines laid down in the ultimatum.

The indelicate allusion to the *Maine* affair in the President's message to Congress on December 7 led to the final effort of Spain for an international inquiry into the causes of the *Maine* catastrophe. The subject was like the American visions of territories in the Carolines—well outside the lines of negotiations laid down in the protocol, and the same reasons that cut short discussion on the one acted on the other. The final draft of the treaty was signed by the Peace Commission on December 10. The ratification in the Senate met with opposition from those opposed to the

[45] *Ibid.*, p. 334.

annexation of territory included in the treaty. An effort was made to secure legislation which would give the Filipinos ultimate freedom, but the treaty was finally ratified by the Senate on February 6, 1899. In Spain the Government met with far greater difficulties. The violent opposition frustrated all efforts to secure the assent of the legislative branch, and the constitutional alternative—the signature of the Queen Regent —was submitted on March 19, 1899. Final ratifications were exchanged on April 11, 1899, and then and not till then was it possible to declare the war formally at an end. On March 2 Congress voted the sum to be paid to Spain under the treaty, and on May 1 this was formally paid over. On June 3 the diplomatic relations were fully restored by the receiving in Washington of a minister from Spain.

The treaty of peace made no reference to such important matters as the status of treaties declared broken at the beginning of the war, extradition, postal relations, copyright regulations, commerce, amity and general relations, all of which it is quite proper for a treaty to deal with, either by declaring the old treaties revised or by substituting new ones. Several years elapsed before the first action. On July 3, 1902, Bellamy Storer, Minister to Spain, concluded with the Duke of Almodóvar del Rio, Minister of State, a treaty of friendship and general relations for a term of ten years. The twenty-ninth article abrogated all treaties, agreements, conventions and contracts made prior to 1898 save the claims treaty of 1834. Otherwise the treaty relates almost exclusively to commerce and the consular service.[46]

[46] Compilation of Treaties in Force, United States, 1904, p. 732.

CHAPTER IX

Interpretation and Fulfilment of Treaty of Peace

There is no better place to test the spirit of a government than in its conduct as a conqueror after the formal conclusion of a war. Its animus will appear again and again in the execution of the treaty of peace, and the perfection of its governmental institutions be the most severely tried. Law is provided with some of its richest precedents at such times. The Spanish-American war was virtually closed with the treaty of Paris, signed December 10, 1898, but from the standpoint of general international law and from that of American administrative law there remained many difficult problems. At the close of the war there were obligations toward neutral powers to be observed; obligations toward the vanquished to be carefully regarded; obligations toward those whom fate had thrown under the jurisdiction of the United States to be sacredly administered.

The first three articles of the treaty of peace have to do with the territorial changes which Spain was called upon to recognize.[1] By the first article Spain

[1] Treaty of Peace, Senate Document 62, 55 Cong., 3 Sess.
" Art. 1.—Spain relinquishes all claim of sovereignty over and title to Cuba. And as the island is, upon its evacuation by Spain, to be occupied by the United States, the United States will, so long as such occupation shall last, assume and discharge the obligations that may under international law

relinquished all claim to sovereignty in Cuba. The
United States at the same time assumed and agreed
to discharge such obligations as might arise under
international law in respect to that island, but the question of its ultimate disposal remained unsettled in the

result from the fact of its occupation, for the protection of
life and property.

"Art. 2.—Spain cedes to the United States the island of
Porto Rico and other islands now under Spanish sovereignty
in the West Indies and the island of Guam in the Marianas,
or Ladrones.

"Art. 3.—Spain cedes to the United States the archipelago
known as the Philippine Islands, and comprehending the
islands lying within the following line: A line running from
west to east along or near the twentieth parallel of north
latitude and through the middle of the navigable channel of
Bachi, from the one hundred and eighteenth (118th) to the
one hundred and twenty-seventh (127th) degree meridian of
longitude east of Greenwich, thence along the one hundred
and twenty-seventh (127th) degree meridian of longitude east
of Greenwich to the parallel of four degrees and forty-five
minutes (4° 45') north latitude, thence along the parallel of
four degrees and forty-five minutes (4° 45') north latitude
to its intersection with the meridian of longitude one hundred
and nineteen degrees and thirty-five minutes (119° 35') east
of Greenwich, thence along the meridian of longitude one
hundred and nineteen degrees and thirty-five minutes (119°
35') east of Greenwich to the parallel of latitude seven degrees
and forty minutes (7° 40') north, thence along the parallel of
latitude seven degrees and forty minutes (7° 40') north to
its intersection with the one hundred and sixteenth (116th)
degree meridian of longitude east of Greenwich, thence by a
direct line to the intersection of the tenth (10th) degree parallel of north latitude with the one hundred and eighteenth
(118th) degree meridian of longitude east of Greenwich, and
thence along the one hundred and eighteenth (118th) degree
meridian of longitude east of Greenwich to the point of
beginning.

"The United States will pay to Spain the sum of twenty
million dollars ($20,000,000) within three months after the
exchange of the ratifications of the present treaty."

treaty. The second article ceded to the United States
Porto Rico and the other islands in the West Indies
belonging to Spain, of which the Isle of Pines is the
most important, and the island of Guam in the Ladrones group as well. The third article ceded the
Philippine Islands to the United States, which power
agreed in turn to pay twenty million dollars to Spain.
This money payment was a reimbursement to Spain
for the surrender of what was assumed to be an equivalent value in public property owned by that power in
the Philippines, together with improvements of a
pacific character, and was in no sense a purchase price
allowed for the group.[2]

But upon what ground within international usage
could the United States demand the cession of these
territories? The act of Spain in yielding sovereignty
over Cuba accomplished the end for which the war was
begun. The inquiry becomes directly, What was the
rule of international law under which the annexation
was made?

Five modes of acquiring territory have been recognized: occupation, prescription, accretion, conquest
and cession. As the Spanish colonies were already
the possession of a civilized power none of the first
three modes would apply. Transfer of title by conquest indicates that the basis is not a treaty, as it must
be in cession. No serious writer holds any longer to
the theory that conquest alone is sufficient justification for territorial annexation. In the last century
there have been some notable examples of resort to
the right of conquest as a sufficient title,[3] but these

[2] The Treaty of Peace and Accompanying Papers, p. 109.
[3] The case of Hesse-Cassel, annexed to the Westphalian
territories by Napoleon.

have been relics of the old system when states and their inhabitants were held to be the patrimony of their sovereigns. No nation now holds to the bald doctrine of an adequate title by the fact of conquest alone, and recent practice indicates that it must give way entirely to a dependence upon some form of cession by treaty. Besides, the United States had not conquered the Philippines, and possessed no rights whatever of that kind. All the territorial changes effected by the treaty of 1898 were the application of the latter mode of acquiring territory, and they took on the special form of forced gifts of territory in lieu of other indemnity, sanctioned by a special deed of cession.

So much was the forfeit demanded from Spain for resorting to the arbitrament of war. The territories ceded were accepted by the United States as compensation in full for the losses and expenses occasioned by the war and for the claims of its citizens by reason of the injuries and damages they might have suffered in their persons and property during the Cuban insurrection. Spain made no denial of the right of the United States to demand a territorial indemnity, but confined its efforts to an attempt to retain sovereignty over the Philippine archipelago, and failing that the Sulu Islands, and to an attempt to secure more liberal privileges and concessions in those yielded.[4]

The United States might have chosen to set an example of unprecedented magnanimity in accepting no indemnity for its work of philanthropy in Cuba's behalf. Many of its people thought this course the only consistent and honorable one. In choosing to exact

[4] The Treaty of Peace and Accompanying Papers, Washington, 1899, pp. 58, 92, 95, 209, 219.

the customary penalty in such cases the United States was acting strictly within its legal rights as understood by the current principles of international law.[5] It is quite another question whether the United States was justified in exacting so high a price. International law prescribes no definite limits to the amount of the indemnity, but it must be reasonable in amount. To go beyond that would be to array neutral powers against the offender, and to defeat the aim of the demand for indemnity, namely, permanence of the peace. It has been maintained that a power like the United States, so thoroughly committed to the right of the individual to decide by what government he would be ruled, should have submitted the question of change of sovereignty in the islands annexed to a popular ratification by their inhabitants.[6] The United States acted on the presumption that an application of the popular plebiscite even to Porto Rico was not feasible. The time, however, has certainly come when popular sanction must be secured in all changes of territory affecting civilized peoples. The treatment of civilized inhabitants and their territories as so much property to be given as an indemnity is a political absurdity.

There were numerous precedents for a plebiscite. In 1860 Sicily, the Marches and Umbria were annexed to the Kingdom of Italy by direct and universal suf-

[5] For general subject see the monograph of Cassan, Les cessions de territoire, Paris, 1900; Westlake, Law Quarterly Review, Vol. XVII, p. 392, an article on "The Nature and Extent of the Title by Conquest." The latter is in the main a criticism of the conclusions of Rivier, Principes du droit des gens, on the effect of conquest and the rights of the conquered, illustrated by the South African war.

[6] For this view see Le Fur, La guerre hispano-américaine, p. 278.

frage. Savoy and Nice were united with France upon the condition that the consent of the inhabitants be obtained.[7]

A plebiscite in Porto Rico might not have changed the result. The island offered no resistance to occupation by the United States, and the conduct of the inhabitants expressed in more ways than one their virtual consent to the change of régime as it was made. The rule presupposes the existence of a reasonable degree of political intelligence and experience, and the people should have reached that state where they either know what they want or have the ability to determine it for themselves and can fulfil international obligations. Opinion in the United States has differed upon the possession in Porto Rico of the adequate political experience.

It is more doubtful whether the same moral obligation to consult the natives existed in the Philippines, where the ballot was unknown and where a minority sought independence in the interest of self-aggrandizement and for the exploitation of the majority. The islanders had been for centuries under the tutelage of Spain, and the destroyer of those bonds could not in moral right or in respect of international obligations leave them adrift. In fact, the Philippines offered unique aspects in the history of transfers of sovereignty. The United States could make no pretensions to an effective occupation of the archipelago at the conclusion of the war; up to the signature of the treaty of peace it never possessed more than the mili-

[7] For a special treatise on annexation conditional upon popular approval see Solière, Le plébiscite dans l'annexion, Paris, 1901.

tary occupation of the arsenal of Cavite, and the bay and city of Manila. It could scarcely be maintained that this was an occupation of a vast territory such as the Philippine group. The Hague Conference of 1899 included in the projected second convention on the law and custom of war on land the rule that a territory to be occupied must be actually under the authority of the hostile army, which is in a position to assert itself.[8] It was not necessary that there should be an occupation as against a title by cession from Spain. The rule of international law is that the conqueror must show effective occupation of such territory as he claims to be entitled to retain by virtue of occupation.[9] The Philippine insurgents formed a third party in actual possession of a larger part of the territory.

The question whether the conquest of a capital or a principal part of the territory gives a title to the whole of the territory as against the occupation of a larger part of it by a third power has been so rarely raised that there can scarcely be said to be any rule of international law formulated to meet it. Only one other case at all analogous to that in the Philippines is recalled. That was the conquest of the Soudan by British and Egyptian troops at Omdurman, while France occupied a part of this territory at Fashoda; and even here the situation is not exactly analogous, for the British Government acted for the Egyptian Government and not in its own right.[10] It seems that

[8] Holls, Peace Conference at The Hague, p. 445.
[9] Le Fur, La guerre hispano-américaine, p. 280.
[10] Westlake, "The Nature and Extent of the Title by Conquest," Law Quarterly Review, October, 1901.

a candid examination of the facts will show that the insurrection of 1896 had ceased before the Spanish-American war broke out; that Spain at that time was in the exercise of its sovereignty over at least the portions occupied by civilized peoples, however grievous or oppressive this sovereignty may have been; that the insurgents took advantage of the preoccupation of the Spanish forces in defending Manila against the American forces; that the insurgents became alienated from the American allies in this period, but that they did not win their independence by the only means by which it can be won, namely, successful revolt; and that independence must be actually established before the insurgent government is entitled to a recognition of any sovereign rights over territory which may be in its power.[11]

Some outlying islands belonging properly to the Philippine archipelago but outside of the boundaries set in Article 3 of the treaty of peace became the subject of a separate treaty of cession. They were located to the west of the Sulus and had been recognized as a part of Spain's Philippine territories. The United States took possession of them along with the remainder of the group, but Spain contested the rights claimed by the American Government. They were clearly Spanish territory, but on November 7, 1900, Spain ceded the islands of Cagayán Sulu and Sibutu and their dependencies to the United States. In consideration of this the United States paid that power one hundred thousand dollars.[12]

[11] Hall, International Law, p. 87; Wharton, Digest, par. 70.
[12] Treaties in Force, 1904, pp. 728–29; Moore, Digest, Vol. I, pp. 530–31, note *b*. Germany acquired from Spain in Feb-

Under the protocol Spain was pledged to transfer the control of Cuba to American forces, but the actual abandonment of Cuba did not take place until January 1, 1899. The treaty of peace signed on December 10, 1898, gave a formal and final sanction to the arrangements of the protocol. In the interval of something more than three years which elapsed before the Cuban Republic was established sovereignty was exercised by the American Government in trust for the Cuban people, for the avowed object of assisting them in establishing a government of their own. The military government maintained by the United States in Cuba constituted the agency for the exercise of their sovereignty, which passed to them automatically with the departure of Spain's representatives. It would be incorrect to speak of sovereignty as dormant. Sovereignty is not a matter *de jure,* but *de facto.* An agency for expressing the sovereign will must exist somewhere; it cannot be destroyed or put to sleep. The temporary and limited character of the occupation cannot alter the fact that for its duration, brief or long, temperate or licentious, there must needs be sovereignty somewhere. During the military government of a territory sovereignty—however distributed by the exigencies and peculiar constitutional forms of the conqueror, and however limited by the extra-legal restraints of international law—is actually exercised by the agencies of the occupant. It must be remembered that the sovereignty so exercised in behalf of the original power or real possessor is of necessity

ruary, 1899, the Caroline Islands and the remainder of the Ladrones upon the payment of $4,825,000. International Year Book, 1899, p. 166.

17

of a temporary nature, liable to revert with the fortunes of war or to follow the determinations of the final treaty of peace. In this particular instance the United States possessed the law-making and law-enforcing parts of government without merging the identity of the new political entity with that of the occupant.[13] The Cuban people formed an aggregation of men living upon a determinate territory fixed by a treaty, with nearly all the characteristics of an organized society—a homogeneous population, a body of laws, a consciousness of a political entity, and certain definite promises of complete independence. For the time being a foreign master constituted the agency to express the popular will. During the period of tutelage the consuls and diplomatic agencies of the United States extended their protection and good offices to Cubans abroad.[14] In the international relations the United States represented Cuba. Other countries having interests in Cuba were obliged to refer them to Washington for settlement.[15]

With reference to the relation of Cuba to the American system the island was " foreign territory . . . under the control of the United States. . . . A citizen of Cuba [was] a citizen of a foreign state."[16] The American authorities submitted the baggage of civilians passing from Cuba to the United States to

[13] Magoon, The Law of Civil Government, pp. 31–34, takes the position that sovereignty in Cuba was dormant.
[14] Foreign Relations, 1898, p. 894.
[15] Moore, Digest, Vol. I, p. 534.
[16] So the Supreme Court in the Neely case, 180 U. S., Jan. 14, 1901; so Congress by an Act of Extradition, 31 Stat. 656, c. 793; also Betancourt v. Mutual Reserve Fund Life Association, 101 Fed. Rep. 305.

the same custom formalities that were required in passing from other foreign territory.[17]

The acts of Spain between the signature of the protocol and the evacuation, done in good faith and in the ordinary exercise of governmental powers, were recognized as valid.[18] The American Peace Commission at Paris, while repudiating all financial obligations resulting from the so-called Cuban debt, consented to add to the first article of the protocol the acknowledgment that concluded the first article of the treaty of peace: "And as the island is, upon the evacuation by Spain, to be occupied by the United States, the United States will, so long as such occupation shall last, assume and discharge the obligations that may under international law result from the fact of its occupation, for the protection of life and property." The anticipated prolongation of military occupation beyond the period of war made a recognition of the consequent international obligations upon the United States more than a mere empty form.

It will be remembered that before the war the Teller Resolution disclaimed any intention of assuming permanent sovereignty in Cuba. The Foraker Resolution, incorporated in the Army Appropriation Act, March 3, 1899, put into practice the substance of the early declaration by the limitation that "no property, franchise, or concessions of any kind whatever shall be

[17] Order of War Department, Dec. 13, 1898. Whitcomb, La situation internationale de Cuba, Paris, 1905, is a painstaking study of the administration of Cuban government during the occupation, commendatory of the achievements of the United States.

[18] Order of Secretary of War, May 29, 1901; Magoon, Law of Civil Government, pp. 594, 602.

granted by the United States or by any military or other authority whatever in the island of Cuba during the occupation thereof by the United States." The apparent self-denial was no more than justice in view of the avowed temporary character of the régime established by the results of war. Any other course would manifestly have violated the letter of the treaty, the principles of belligerent obligations in occupied territory laid down by the laws of war, and the moral responsibilities of the big, overgrown ally of the luckless Cuban insurgents.

In the other insular possessions of Spain there is less doubt regarding the nature of the transfer of sovereignty. The dates on which the military occupation began—in Manila, August 14, 1898, in Porto Rico, October 18, 1898—became the moment for the transfer of the government to a new agency. Sovereignty itself remained with Spain until the treaty of peace was executed. Throughout the remainder of the Philippines Spain retained both sovereignty and the governmental agencies until the evacuation which followed and fulfilled the treaty of peace. The existence of open rebellion did not affect the location of sovereignty, but it made precarious the efficiency of the agencies for administering the new sovereignty over the group.

The avowal on the part of the United States as to the temporary character of its occupation did not release it from the new international obligations which were the result. Spain could point to the treaty of peace in its first article, the rest of the world to the principles of law that bind a would-be civilized power. These obligations endured until the Cuban Republic was formally launched. The international obligation comes simply from the necessity that the destroyer of the authority of a conquered state must put in its place some adequate power to preserve order and protect property and life. The military governments in the several territories affected became merely the representatives of the sovereignty of the United States, and neutrals looked to the United States for the fulfilment of these obligations. In Article 16 of the treaty the United States pledged itself to advise any government established in Cuba to assume the same international obligations.[19]

The nature of the powers exercised by the military governments differed considerably in the territories affected by the treaty of peace. In Porto Rico, where the natives had never offered any resistance, the military department became essentially transitory and provisional, being subordinate to the laws of Congress and in waiting for the creation of a temporary civil government by Congress. The commanding general became a military governor, and all civil affairs came under his supervision and direction. Where existing laws were regarded as detrimental to the public welfare he had authority to change or repeal them. The old local courts ceased to exist only upon the institution of new ones with competent jurisdiction. In the Philippines, where hostilities still existed after the conclusion of peace with Spain, the military government was

---

[19] "Art. 16.—It is understood that any obligations assumed in this treaty by the United States with respect to Cuba are limited to the time of its occupancy thereof, but it will, upon the termination of such occupancy, advise any government established in the island to assume the same obligations."

limited only by the laws and usages of war and the military law of the United States. The conclusion of a treaty of peace had no effect upon the belligerent rights of the United States there, though the insurrection never reached the dignity in international usage that the term belligerency implied. The treaty of peace made no stipulation as to the form of government to be instituted in the acquired and abandoned territories of Spain. Article 9 closed with the words: "The civil rights and political status of the native inhabitants of the territories hereby ceded to the United States shall be determined by the Congress." The United States was left absolutely free to consult its own notions of justice in selecting the time for transferring to Cuba the powers of government requisite to complete her independence, and for according self-government to the other islands. By Article 10 the treaty guaranteed religious liberty. It is entirely probable that the courts would have exacted the same in its absence from the definite treaty of peace.[20]

The insular cases[21] have defined, though far from clearly, the status of the island in the American constitutional system. The Government had insisted "that it never could have been the intention of Congress to admit Porto Rico into a customs union with the United States, and that while the island may be to a certain extent domestic territory it still remains a 'foreign country' under the tariff laws, until Cong-

[20] Willoughby, The American Constitutional System, p. 220.
"Art. 10.—The inhabitants of the territories over which Spain relinquishes or cedes her sovereignty shall be secured in the free exercise of their religion."
[21] 182 U. S. 1–498.

ress has embraced it within the general revenue system." As far as Porto Rico is concerned, from July 26, 1898, to August 19, 1898, import duties were collected under the terms of the proclamation of General Miles, directing the exaction of the former Spanish and Porto Rican duties; from August 19, 1898, until February 1, 1899, under the customs tariff for Porto Rico, proclaimed by order of the President; and from February 1, 1899, to May 1, 1900, under the amended tariff customs promulgated by order of the President. Porto Rico was at the time under the provisional government. The acts indicate the executive interpretation of the status in one aspect—that it was outside the American tax system. The military government of the Philippines imposed both an export and an import duty, and therefore took the position, later upheld by the Supreme Court,[22] that the constitutional prohibition of an export tax applied only to exports from states. Justice Brown, who gave the opinion of the Supreme Court in De Lima v. Bidwell, held that "by the ratification of the treaty of Paris the island became territory of the United States, although not an organized territory in the technical sense of the word," and "that at the time these duties were levied Porto Rico was not a foreign country within the meaning of the tariff laws but a territory of the United States." It follows from this that the duties were illegally exacted.[23] Likewise in Dooley v. U. S.,[24] involving the legality of export duties before Congress had taken action, Justice Brown delivered the opinion

[22] 182 U. S. 244, Downes v. Bidwell.
[23] 182 U. S. 200.
[24] 182 U. S. 222 ff.

that " the order imposing duties upon goods imported into Porto Rico . . . ceased to apply to goods imported from the United States from the moment the United States ceased to be a foreign country with respect to Porto Rico, and that until Congress otherwise constitutionally directed such merchandise was entitled to free entry." The case of Downes v. Bidwell[25] involved the question whether since the passage of the Foraker Act merchandise is exempt from duty notwithstanding the third section of that act, which requires the payment of " fifteen per centum of the duties which are required to be paid upon like articles imported from foreign countries," and also the broader question whether the clauses of the constitution extend of their own force to newly acquired territories. The court held that Porto Rico is a territory " appurtenant and belonging to the United States, but not a part of the United States, within the revenue clauses of the Constitution (" All duties, imports and excises shall be uniform throughout the United States ") ; and that the Foraker act is constitutional so far as it imposes duties upon imports from such islands." So great, however, was the division of the court upon the several insular cases that in effect seven of the justices were of the opinion that the Constitution becomes applicable to a territory whenever such territory is duly organized, and a majority must hold, whenever the question comes before them, that the uniformity clause of the Constitution is applicable, not only to the states, but also to the territories that may have been duly

[25] 182 U. S. 244.

organized.[26] It follows that the majority of the Supreme Court were of the opinion that as soon as a
territory has been given a territorial organization by
act of Congress it comes within the scope of the Constitution, but regarding the period during which a
provisional government exists over annexed territories the opinion of the court was widely divergent.
Four judges held that the constitution passes to annexed territories by a sort of innate force. Three
judges took the ground that territory must be organized under an enabling act of Congress before it
comes within the scope of the Constitution, but that
once so organized it comes immediately within it.
One of the justices assumed the position that the Constitution does not by its own force extend into any
territory, whether organized or not.

The conduct of the United States with reference to
the new territories seems to be a dangerous stretch
of the true intent of the uniformity clause of the Constitution. There was no valid reason for denying the
rule of the Constitution in the Philippines or Porto
Rico, though it is well known that there have been precedents for such practice. The earliest administrative
acts of Louisiana are in evidence, but those preceded
the initiation of civil government. No instance exists
of the incorporation of the principles into an act of
civil government. The doctrine that the Constitution
is limited by purely geographical bounds is inadmissible. On the other hand, the mere fact of annexation
does not signify an ultimate intention to incorporate

[26] See excellent analysis of the decisions by George S.
Boutwell, N. A. R., Vol. 173, p. 154; and by Professor W. W.
Willoughby, American Constitutional System, ch. 14.

the new territory as a state. Until recent years no one could possibly have thought of Alaska as a candidate for statehood. Its inhospitable climate was a greater barrier than the tropical one of the Philippines and Porto Rico. The fact that its population was sparse should not be cited, as the limitations of the Constitution are not subject to variations in numbers. When the Indian Territory was set aside no one foresaw statehood for it, yet the rule of the Constitution has in no way interfered with our government there.

Article 9 of the treaty of peace[27] applied the usage of nations to the inhabitants of the annexed territories, and gave them a year after the exchange of ratifications, in fact to April 11, 1900, within which to elect whether to remain subjects of Spain or to adopt the nationality of the territory. In either case they became entitled under the treaty to all rights in property and to the pursuit of business, always subject to the

[27] " Art. 9.—Spanish subjects, natives of the peninsula, residing in the territory over which Spain by the present treaty relinquishes or cedes her sovereignty, may remain in such territory or may remove therefrom, retaining in either event all their rights of property, including the right to sell or dispose of such property, or of its proceeds; and they shall also have the right to carry on their industry, commerce and professions, being subject in respect thereof to such laws as are applicable to other foreigners. In case they remain in the territory they may preserve their allegiance to the crown of Spain by making, before a court of record, within a year from the date of the exchange of ratifications of this treaty, a declaration of their decision to preserve such allegiance; in default of which declaration they shall be held to have renounced it and to have adopted the nationality of the territory in which they may reside.

" The civil rights and political status of the native inhabitants of the territories herein ceded to the United States shall be determined by the congress."

law of the new state as applied to subjects and aliens.
These were scarcely rights, but they have come to be
the established practice of nations.

In Article 8 of the treaty of peace Spain relinquished
in Cuba and ceded to the United States in the other
islands all the public buildings, wharves, barracks,
forts, structures, public highways, and other immovable property.[28] This introduced no new principle in

[28] " Art. 8.—In conformity with the provisions of articles 1, 2
and 3 of this treaty, Spain relinquishes in Cuba, and cedes in
Porto Rico and other islands in the West Indies, in the island
of Guam and in the Philippine archipelago, all the buildings,
wharves, barracks, forts, structures, public highways and other
immovable property which, in conformity with law, belong to
the public domain and as such belong to the crown of Spain.

" And it is hereby declared that the relinquishment or cession, as the case may be, to which the preceding paragraph
refers, cannot in any respect impair the property or rights
which by law belong to the peaceful possession of property
of all kinds, of provinces, municipalities, public or private
establishments, ecclesiastical or civic bodies or any other asso-
ciations having legal capacity to acquire and possess property
in the aforesaid territories renounced or ceded, or of private
individuals, of whatsoever nationality such individuals may be.

" The aforesaid relinquishment or cession, as the case may
be, includes all documents exclusively referring to the sovereignty relinquished or ceded that may exist in the archives of
the peninsula. Where any document in such archives only in
part relates to said sovereignty a copy of such part will be
furnished whenever it shall be requested. Like rules shall be
reciprocally observed in favor of Spain in respect of documents in the archives of the islands above referred to.

" In the aforesaid relinquishment or cession, as the case
may be, are also included such rights as the crown of Spain
and its authorities possess in respect of the official archives
and records, executive as well as judicial, in the islands above
referred to, which relate to said islands or the rights and
property of their inhabitants. Such archives and records shall
be carefully preserved and private persons shall without distinction have the right to require, in accordance with law,

the law of annexation. The treaty itself so fully defined the exceptions that there could be no serious differences. Article 5 excepted stands of colors, uncaptured war vessels, small arms, guns of all calibre, with their carriages and accessories, powder, ammunition, live stock and materials and supplies of all kinds belonging to the land and naval forces of Spain in the Philippines and Guam, which property should remain the property of Spain. It was agreed that pieces of heavy ordnance, exclusive of field artillery, should remain in their emplacements for six months, with a right to the United States to purchase them if satisfactory agreement as to value proved possible. The same detail regarding the military property in Cuba and Porto Rico was not necessary for the reason that the evacuation commissions under the protocol had already determined the line of demarcation between the public property to be retained by the army of Spain and that to pass to the United States. The distinctions applied in the Philippines were substantially the same as those applied earlier by the evacuation commissioners in the other islands. Other portions of Article 8 dealt with the transfer of archives and public records, and with reciprocal rules for securing authenticated copies of such legal papers in Spain or the islands as might be of value to the subjects of either party.

The treaty of peace provided for two fundamental personal rights of the inhabitants of the island terri-

authenticated copies of the contracts, wills and other instruments forming part of notarial protocols or files, or which may be contained in the executive or judicial archives, be the latter in Spain or in the islands aforesaid."

tories—religious liberty and choice of nationality—
and also included adequate guarantees for the private
property of the inhabitants. Article 9 secured them
in the peaceful pursuit of their ordinary occupations,
commerce and professions. Article 8 provided that
the cession of territory should not "in any respect
impair the property rights which by law belong to
the peaceful possession of property of all kinds, of
provinces, municipalities, public or private establishments, ecclesiastical or civic bodies, or any other as-
sociations having legal capacity to acquire or possess
property in the aforesaid territories, or of private
individuals, of whatsoever nationality such individuals
may be." Article 13 gave the same sanctity to copyrights and patents. Spanish literary, scientific and
artistic property was freed from import duties for ten
years. Another article (12) freed pending civil actions of private parties from interruption by virtue of
territorial transfers.[29]

[29] "Art. 11.—The Spaniards residing in the territories over
which Spain by this treaty cedes or relinquishes her sovereignty shall be subject, in matters civil as well as criminal, to
the jurisdiction of the courts of the country wherein they
reside, pursuant to the ordinary laws governing the same, and
they shall have the right to appear before such courts and to
pursue the same course as citizens of the country to which
the courts belong.

"Art. 12.—Judicial proceedings pending at the time of the
exchange of ratifications of this treaty in the territories over
which Spain relinquishes or cedes her sovereignty shall be
determined according to the following rules.

"1.—Judgments rendered either in civil suits between private individuals or in criminal matters before the date mentioned and with respect to which there is no recourse or
right of review under the Spanish law shall be deemed to be
final and shall be executed in due form by competent authori-

The interpretation of these guarantees caused some conflicts with the United States in both Cuba and the Philippines. Several of the most interesting had reference to the effect of the change of sovereignty upon the vitality of franchises granted by the Spanish Government.

The case of the Manila Railway Company and that of the Eastern Extension Australasia and China Telegraph Company involved the rights of two British corporations under franchises granted by Spain which conferred monopolistic rights in particular fields and necessitated the payment of fixed subsidies. Under such a concession the Manila Railway Company constructed a line from Manila to Dagupan in the island of Luzón, a distance of about one hundred and thirty

ties in the territory within which such judgments should be carried out.

"2.—Civil suits between private individuals which may on the date mentioned be undetermined shall be prosecuted to judgment before the court in which they may then be pending, or in the court that may be substituted therefor.

"3.—Criminal actions pending on the date mentioned before the supreme court of Spain against citizens of the territory which by this treaty ceases to be Spanish shall continue under its jurisdiction until final judgment; but such judgment having been rendered, the execution thereof shall be committed to the competent authority of the place in which the case arose.

"Art. 13.—The rights of property secured by copyrights and patents acquired by Spaniards in the Island of Cuba and Porto Rico, the Philippines and other ceded territories, at the time of the exchange of the ratifications of this treaty, shall continue to be respected. Spanish scientific, literary and artistic works, not subversive to public order in the territories in question, shall continue to be admitted free of duty into such territories for the period of ten years, to be reckoned from the date of the exchange of the ratification of this treaty."

miles. The Spanish guaranty was eight per cent. per annum upon the capital invested, which had been paid by Spain in quarterly installments up to the time of the war. After the treaty of peace the Manila Railway Company entered a claim against the United States upon the ground that by the assumption of sovereignty the United States became bound to respond to the obligations of Spain. The Australasia and China Telegraph Company presented a claim which offered no different legal aspects. It had laid cables connecting various points in the Philippines with Chinese ports, and early in the war the American naval forces cut the cables and interrupted its service. After the conclusion of peace the cable company sought to force the United States to carry out the contract under which Spain paid a subsidy.

Both claims were referred from the War Department to the Attorney-General, who denied any legal binding force to the claims on the ground that they constituted a " general debt " and a " personal contract " of the Spanish Government. He said on the Manila Railway case: " The contract was made by Spain and partly for her own benefit; it was the indivisible personal contract of Spain and of the concessionnaire . . . The concessions here in question are executory contracts not concerning the public domain owned by Spain, but containing many personal obligations of Spain and of other parties . . . The difference between them and what we conceive of as a franchise seems to me to be an obvious one . . . There is no rule of law to the effect that contracts made by the old sovereignty for local and imperial objects shall

be obligatory as such upon the new sovereignty."
The statement may have been good American law,
but it is less certain that it expressed the best opinion
and usage of international law.

Even the contention that the contract with Spain
was an indivisible personal contract, continuing and
executory and therefore not binding on the new
sovereign, had a ragged appearance, with somewhat
the aspect of a technical quibble. The principle that
the obligations of a government for local pacific purposes attach to the new sovereign is too well recognized to need citations from international authorities.
The American Peace Commission at Paris itself recognized the principle. Whether the intention was to
cancel it by the payment of twenty million dollars is
another matter. That merely constituted a particular
way of avoiding an obligation which the very expedient devised tacitly recognized as the usage of nations.
The very fact that the agreement was continuing and
executory would perhaps class it outside of those
comprehended in the ones cancelled by a lump payment, but would leave it a local obligation none the
less. The Transvaal Commission appointed by Great
Britain in 1901 "to inquire into the concessions
granted by the government of the late African Republic" stated the rule of international law: " Though
we doubt whether the duties of an annexing state
toward those claiming under concessions or contracts
granted or made by the annexed state have been
defined with such precision in authoritative statement
or acted upon with such uniformity in civilized practice as to warrant their being termed rules of inter-

national law, we are convinced that the best modern opinion favors the view that as a general rule the obligations of the annexed state toward private persons should be respected."[30]

Happily the Attorney-General concluded with a recognition of a moral, if not a legal, obligation on the United States to furnish relief, and in the claim of the Eastern Extension Telegraph Company he recommended action by Congress, and that body, "as an act of equity and comity," reimbursed the owners for the actual expense incurred in the repair of cables. Upon the question whether the United States should pay the subsidy, which Spain had by the terms of the concession agreed to pay, the Attorney-General advised that the question of subsidy should be treated "as though it was an original application made by a company contemplating the construction of *quasi* public improvement."[31] In a similar manner the United States recognized an equitable liability to the Manila Railway Company.[32]

Another analogous claim brought up the American view of the obligations for the period of its control of the island of Cuba. A British corporation held a concession for a cable system there, and it demanded that the United States protect it and assume the obligations of Spain. The Attorney-General decided adversely to the claimants on the ground that the United States was not the successor of Spain in Cuba, "but merely an intervening power arranging the succession. . . . It did not make the contract of concession.

[30] Moore, Digest, Vol. I, pp. 411–12.
[31] The Law of Civil Government, p. 531.
[32] Moore, Digest, Vol. I, pp. 405–6.

18

It is not the beneficiary receiving the benefits said to
accrue to the island from the cables, nor is it the island,
nor the locality to which the obligations are said to be
locally attached; neither does it appropriate to itself
the revenue of the island." On the other hand, the
exclusive privileges claimed under concessions from
Spain were upheld. The words of the Attorney-General were as follows: " Concessions of this kind, which
carry with them exclusive rights for a period of years,
constitute property of which the concessionary can no
more be deprived arbitrarily and without lawful reason than it can be deprived of its personal tangible
assets."

Two cases in Porto Rico brought about a stronger
recognition of the property rights in concessions. In
the instance of a concession for the use of water-
power it was stated by the Attorney-General that " if
at the time the Treaty of Paris took effect the appli-
cant had a complete and vested right to the use of
the waters of the River Plata, that right would be
respected by the United States." A like opinion was
given upon the application of a concessionary for a
tramway. In both Porto Rico and the Philippines
certain banks were enjoying exclusive banking privileges under Spanish law—the exclusive right to issue
bank notes and, under regulations, to control the
amount of these in relation to the capital, etc. The
Philippine Commission denied any rights conferred by
the Spanish charter and advanced to an application of
the extreme doctrine of the Veazie Bank *v.* Fenno,
" that it was entirely competent for Congress to impose any such tax as it saw fit, upon the issue of cir-

culating notes by State banks, even though such a tax should be prohibitive by reason of its amount."

If the rights of the banking companies were established by bona fide franchises, it is hard to see why they were not entitled to protection in these rights. Franchises are property in Spanish law if not in American, and American courts recognize the law whence they originate as the proper test of their character.[33] The treaty of peace guaranteed the security of property rights, and under what seems a similar circumstance the Supreme Court declared: " If the United States were not content to receive the territory charged with titles thus created, they ought to have made, and they would have made, such exceptions as they deemed necessary."[34]

With respect to industrial property, such as patents, copyrights and trademarks, the United States construed its obligations to extend to such as were recorded in an insular registry or in the national registry at the bureau of the union for the protection of industrial property at Berne, Switzerland, requiring at the same time a certified copy of the patent or of the certificate of registration of the trademark or copyright to be kept in the office of the Governor.[35]

In two instances the American authorities were called upon to decide the property right in public

[33] 16 Pet. 196, 198, 200; 1 Wall, 352; 5 Wall, 326; 11 How. 663.

[34] U. S. v. Clarke, 8 Pet. 436. See the excellent article, " Are Franchises Affected by Change of Sovereignty," Columbia Law Review, April, 1903, Vol. III, p. 241. Magoon, Law of Civil Government, gives legal opinion on these cases; Reports of Attorney-General give opinions of that department and Reports of Secretary of War contain narrative of claims.

[35] Magoon, The Law of Civil Government, p. 395.

offices and the extent of the obligations of the United
States in Cuba in particular. The Countess of Buena
Vista and Dr. Don Gustavo Gallet Duplessis possessed jointly at the moment of the military occupation
of Havana the authority and emoluments of the office
of sheriff. The office under the Spanish system re-
sembled closely in function that of a marshal of a territory in the United States, but at Havana it had been
hereditary in the family of the Countess of Buena
Vista since the year 1728, when it had been bought
at public auction. At a judicial sale in 1895, to satisfy
certain private indebtedness of the high sheriff, Dr.
Don Gustavo Gallet Duplessis purchased a one-half
interest in the emoluments of the office. The com-
plainants contended that the office was property belonging to them when the treaty of peace was ratified,
and that the action of the military government in
depriving them of their property contravened the provisions of Article 8, which pledged the United States
to respect property rights in the islands relinquished
and ceded. The answer of the Secretary of War set
forth that the office was not property in the sense that
any rights to its authority or emoluments survived the
passing of Spanish sovereignty, and that any claim for
indemnity depended upon the personal contract with
Spain, whose obligations did not pass to the United
States with the transfer of sovereignty.[36]

An office-holder in San Juan, Porto Rico, Antonio
Alvarez Nava, presented a claim for indemnity be-

[36] Magoon, pp. 194–209. Spain subsequently made provision
for loyal subjects of the former colonies, so that the pensions
once paid them were continued and in other cases new pensions made available. Report of Premier Sagasta, May 11,
1901. See Foreign Relations, 1901, p. 475; Moore, Digest,
Vol. I, pp. 380–81.

cause he had been deprived of the office of notary, which he had purchased in 1896. He was in fact deprived of his office before the conclusion of the war by the commander of belligerent forces in Porto Rico. The island passed completely to the United States by the treaty of peace. Article 8 stipulated for a mutual relinquishment of all claims for individual indemnity arising since the beginning of the Cuban insurrection. This covered the case completely, and Antonio Alvarez Nava had not the shadow of a legal claim against the United States. The law officers maintained correctly that in time of war the commanding officer is the sole judge of existing military necessity, and cannot subsequently be called to account by the enemy.[37]

A more delicate matter, involving the attitude of the United States toward property rights in the annexed territories and promising to be a difficult agrarian dispute, was that of the disposition of the lands of the friar orders in the Philippines. The property of the friars involved about one third of the total amount within the walls of old Manila and over four hundred thousand acres of the best and most fertile agricultural lands of the island, populated by a vast tenantry of discontented native peasants. Without adjudicating the vexed question of the legality of the title of the friars to their lands, Governor Taft and the Civil Commission, acting with the authority of Congress, happily effected the purchase of the lands for the United States Government, and provided for their sale to the tenants upon long, easy payments.[38]

[37] Magoon, Law of Civil Government, pp. 454–57.
[38] Message and Documents, Report of Governor Taft, 1903, Vol. I, p. 592. The lands were paid for by Philippine government bonds at 4 per cent., payable in ten to thirty years.

Article 7 of the treaty of peace dealt with the interests of American citizens as affected by the Cuban insurrection and the war between Spain and the United States. The property of American citizens in Cuba suffered both from direct destruction and from the interruption of its normal use during the insurrection. In many cases the owners had presented statements of their losses to the State Department, but the intervention interrupted the regular progress of the diplomatic prosecution of the claims.

The American claims came up again in the negotiations at Paris. The question was whether Spain or the United States was under obligation to examine and settle such as were valid. It has been a general practice in the last hundred years to arrange the terms of peace so that each state could assume all liability for the claims of its own citizens.[39] The mode commends itself in avoiding the possibilities of further diplomatic differences at a time when feeling is most easily aroused. According to precedents numerous enough to make that the only natural procedure, Article 7 provided for a mutual relinquishment of all claims of every kind, national or individual, from the beginning of the Cuban insurrection.[40] The United

[39] The United States has entered into such a settlement on ten occasions, and domestic claims commissions have repeatedly been resorted to as a means of adjudication and distribution.

[40] "Art. 7.—The United States and Spain mutually relinquish all claims for indemnity, national and individual, of every kind, of either government, or of its citizens or subjects, against the other government that may have arisen since the beginning of the late insurrection in Cuba and prior to the exchange of ratifications of the present treaty, including all claims for indemnity for the cost of the war. The United

States on its part agreed to "adjudicate and settle
the claims of its citizens against Spain" which were
relinquished by the previous clause. The clause
remained unexecuted for several years. Enormous
claims were involved, and great opportunity for fraud
existed.

Finally, on March 2, 1901, Congress authorized a
Treaty Claims Commission of five members " to receive, examine and adjudicate " the claims of American citizens against Spain for which the United States
was liable under the treaty of peace.[41] As a preliminary to its real work, the Commission devoted much
time and effort to formulating an interpretation of the
obligations of the United States. Leading American
authorities submitted exhaustive written opinions for
its guidance. The conclusions of the preliminary study
were stated in the form of eleven rules. They were:

" 1. Under Article VII of the treaty of Paris, the
United States assumed the payment of all claims of
her own citizens for which Spain would have been
liable according to the principles of international law.
It follows, therefore, that the sole question before this
Commission is that of the primary liability of Spain,
which is not in any way enlarged by the agreement of
the United States to adjudicate and pay such claims.

" 2. Although the late insurrection in Cuba assumed
great magnitude and lasted for more than three years,
yet belligerent rights were never granted to the in-

States will adjudicate and settle the claims of its citizens
against Spain relinquished in this article."
[41] The commissioners were Ex-Senator W. E. Chandler,
Mr. Gerrit J. Diekema, Mr. James Perry Wood, Mr. Wm.
A. Maury, Mr. Wm. L. Chambers.

surgents by Spain or the United States so as to create a state of war in the international sense which exempted the parent government from liability to foreigners for the acts of the insurgents.

" 3. But, where an armed insurrection has gone beyond the control of the parent government, the general rule is that such government is not responsible for damages done to foreigners by the insurgents.

" 4. This Commission will take judicial notice that the insurrection in Cuba which resulted in intervention by the United States and in war between Spain and the United States, passed, from the first, beyond the control of Spain, and so continued until such intervention and war took place. If, however, it be alleged and proved in any particular case before this Commission that the Spanish authorities by the exercise of due diligence might have prevented the damages done, Spain will be held liable in that case.

" 5. As war between Spain and the insurgents existed in a material sense, although not a state of war in the international sense, Spain was entitled to adopt such war measures for the recovery of her authority as are sanctioned by the rules and usages of international warfare. If, however, it be alleged and proved in any particular case that the acts of the Spanish authorities or soldiers were contrary to such rules and usages, Spain will be held liable in that case.

" 6. As this Commission has been directed by Congress to ascertain and apply the principles of international law in the adjudication of claims of neutral foreigners for injuries to their persons and property caused by a parent state while engaged in subduing

by war an insurrection which had passed beyond its
control, it cannot fail, in determining what are and
what are not legitimate war measures, to impose upon
the parent state such limitations as the consensus of nations at the present day recognizes as restricting the
exercise of the right to remove all the inhabitants of
a designated territory and concentrate them in towns
and military camps, and to commit to decay and ruin
the abandoned real and personal property or destroy
such property and devastate such region.

" 7. Adopting, therefore, a wide and liberal interpretation of the principle that the destruction of
property in war where no military end is served is
illegitimate, and that there must be cases in which
devastation is not permitted, it should be said that,
whenever reconcentration, destruction, or devastation
is resorted to as a means of suppressing an insurrection beyond control, the parent state is bound to give
the property of neutral foreigners such reasonable
protection as the particular circumstances of each case
will permit. It must abstain from any unnecessary
and wanton destruction of their property by its responsible military officers. When such neutral foreigners are included in the removal or concentration
of inhabitants, the government so removing or concentrating them must provide for them food and
shelter, guard them from sickness and death, and protect them from cruelty and hardship to the extent
which the military exigency will permit. And, finally,
as to both property and persons, it may be stated that
the parent state is bound to prevent any discrimina-
tion in the execution of concentration and devastation

orders against any class of neutral foreigners in favor
of any other class or in favor of its own citizens.

"8. Subject to the foregoing limitations and restrictions, it is undoubtedly the general rule of international law that concentration and devastation are
legitimate war measures. To that rule, aliens as well
as subjects must submit and suffer the fortunes of
war. The property of alien residents, like that of
natives of the country, when 'in the track of war,'
is subject to war's casualties, and whatever in front
of the advancing forces either impedes them or might
give them aid when appropriated, or if left unmolested
in their rear might afford aid and comfort to the
enemy, may be taken or destroyed by the armies of
either of the belligerents; and no liability whatever
is understood to attach to the government of the
country whose flag that army bears and whose battles
it may be fighting.

"If, in any particular case before this Commission,
it is averred and proved that Spain has not fulfilled
her obligations as above defined, she will be held liable
in that case.

"9. It is the opinion of the Commission that the
treaty of 1795 and the protocol of 1877 were in full
force and effect during the insurrection in Cuba, and
they will be applied in deciding cases properly falling
within their provisions.

"10. As to the first clause of Article VII of the
said treaty, wherein it is agreed that the subjects and
citizens of each nation, their vessels, or effects shall
not be liable to any embargo or detention on the part
of the other for any military expedition or other public

or private purpose whatever, the Commission holds that, whether or not the clause was originally intended to embrace real estate and personal property on land as well as vessels and their cargoes the same has been so construed by the United States, and this construction has been concurred in by Spain; and, therefore, the Commission will adhere to such construction in making its decisions.

" 11. But neither this particular clause nor any other provision of the treaty of 1795 will be so applied as to render either nation, while endeavoring to suppress an insurrection which has gone beyond its control, liable for damages done to the person or property of the citizens of the other nation when found in the track of war, or for damages resulting from military movements unless the same were unnecessarily and wantonly inflicted."[42]

Several of these bear upon unsettled questions of law and have an international interest. Rules 1, 3, 4, 6, 7, and 8 are especially worthy of consideration. Rules 3 and 4 give a definition of liability of the parent state in time of an insurrection ranking between a riot and a formal state of belligerency. The Cuban insurrection had passed beyond the control of Spain. It followed in consequence that Spain was not liable to foreigners for the acts of the insurgents. The Commission decided in effect that damages by insurgents are the unavoidable but not unlawful consequences of war, and that Spain would not have had any liability for the payment of this class of claims. If, however, it could be proved in any particular case that by due

[42] Sen. Doc. 25, 58 Cong., 2 Sess., p. 5; North American Review, May, 1906, p. 738.

diligence the authorities of the parent state might have prevented the alleged acts this immunity would not be tolerable.

Rules 5, 6, 7, and 8 deal with the legality of the concentration orders and formulate the principle that, under certain limitations, concentration and devastation are legitimate modes of warfare where they serve a military end. The limitations are: (1) the parent state must furnish foreigners as reasonable an amount of protection as the circumstances afford; (2) it must abstain from the unnecessary and wanton destruction of neutral property; (3) it must furnish foreigners who are included in the concentration of inhabitants with food and shelter, and it must protect them from cruelty and hardship to the extent which the military exigencies permit; and finally (4) it must not discriminate against any class of foreigners in favor of any other class or in favor of its own citizens. These conditions fulfilled, the liabilities of a state toward foreigners are satisfied. The effect of such rules was to destroy any value at all in the vast majority of the claims against the United States. As the claims amounted to more than sixty million dollars the result was well on the side of administrative economy and approved itself to those who were not claimants. It may be readily conceived, too, that the principles have the endorsement of Spanish publicists. In fact, in the entire litigation Spain was the real defendant. Under the treaty of peace, Article 7, 1898, and the act of Congress of March 2, 1901, it became the duty of the Treaty Claims Commission to determine the liabilities of the United States exactly as it would act were it sitting at Madrid, and to assert no pretensions on the part of the United States which it would not allow Spain under the same circumstances.[43]

Pressure was brought to bear on Congress by the claimants to upset the ruling of the commissioners. A bill to permit appeals to the Supreme Court and secure a judicial interpretation of the obligations of the United States passed the Senate, but was left with the House Committee on Judiciary at the first session of the fifty-ninth Congress.[44]

It is not correct, however, to say that the Commission has reversed the previous conclusions of the political department. The fact is that the validity of the claims was never examined by the State Department, and Spain was never asked to pay them or even to acknowledge their validity. The United States merely notified Spain that claims of such a character had been recorded without endorsing them in any manner.[45] There is not the slightest evidence that the United States would have supported the claims had war not intervened and a treaty of peace taken them outside of diplomacy.[46]

[43] Cf. words of Lord Stowell in the case of the *Maria,* where he said that it was the duty of the court " to determine this question exactly as they would determine the same question if sitting at Stockholm; to assert no pretentions on the part of Great Britain which they would not allow to Sweden in the same circumstances." North American Review, Vol. 182, p. 743.

[44] Congressional Record, 59 Cong., 1 Sess., pp. 8973, 9063.

[45] H. Taylor, Former Minister to Spain, North American Review, Vol. 182, p. 740.

[46] The action of the Commission has been the subject of no little magazine and newspaper controversy; Forum, Vol. 31, p. 713; Vol. 32, p. 414; North American Review, February, 1905, March, 1906.

With reference to the duration of the occupation the treaty of peace used the words: "Spain relinquishes all claim," etc., "and as the island is, upon its evacuation by Spain, to be occupied by the United States, the United States will so long as such occupation shall last assume and discharge the obligations that may under international law result." The treaty of peace was technically fulfilled when the military forces of the United States took possession on January 1, 1899. During the period of occupation as long as international obligations were duly observed by the United States the treaty was properly executed. Article 4 was a concession to Spain to offset the heavy terms exacted by the peace. The United States obligated itself to keep the Philippines open to Spanish ships and to those of its own citizens on the same terms. Articles 5 and 6 treated of the release and return of all prisoners of war held by either state and of the evacuation of the ceded territories of the Pacific. Articles 14 and 15 are consular and commercial clauses similar to the provisions incorporated in all general treaties of peace.[47] In spite of repeated assertions to

[47] "Art. 4.—The United States will, for the term of ten years from the date of the exchange of the ratifications of the present treaty, admit Spanish ships and merchandise to the ports of the Philippine Islands on the same terms as ships and merchandise of the United States.

"Art. 5.—The United States will, upon the signature of the present treaty, send back to Spain, at its own cost, the Spanish soldiers taken as prisoners of war on the capture of Manila by the American forces. The arms of the soldiers in question shall be restored to them.

"Spain will, upon the exchange of the ratifications of the present treaty, proceed to evacuate the Philippines, as well as the island of Guam, on terms similar to those agreed upon by the commissioners appointed to arrange for the evacuation

the contrary, however, all Europe, and Spain in particular, expected the United States to prolong the
occupation indefinitely. The history of the two years
of military occupation is no part of the concern of

of Porto Rico and other islands in the West Indies under
the protocol of August 12, 1898, which is to continue in force
till its provisions are completely executed. The time within
which the evacuation of the Philippine Islands and Guam
shall be completed shall be fixed by the two governments.
Stands of colors, uncaptured war vessels, small arms, guns of
all calibers, with their carriages and accessories, powder,
ammunition, live stock and materials and supplies of all
kinds, belonging to the land and naval forces of Spain in the
Philippines and Guam, remain the property of Spain. Pieces
of heavy ordnance, exclusive of field artillery, in the fortifications and coast defenses, shall remain in their emplacements
for the term of six months, to be reckoned from the exchange
of ratifications of the treaty; and the United States may, in
the meantime, purchase such material from Spain, if a satisfactory agreement between the two governments on the subject shall be reached.

"Art. 6.—Spain will, upon the signature of the present
treaty, release all prisoners of war and all persons detained
or imprisoned for political offenses, in connection with the
insurrections in Cuba and the Philippines and the war with
the United States.

"Reciprocally, the United States will release all persons
made prisoners of war by the American forces and will undertake to obtain the release of all Spanish prisoners in the
hands of the insurgents in Cuba and the Philippines.

"The government of the United States will, at its own
cost, return to Spain, and the government of Spain will, at its
own cost, return to the United States, Cuba, Porto Rico and
the Philippines, according to the situation of their respective
homes, prisoners released or caused to be released by them,
respectively, under this article.

"Art. 14.—Spain will have the power to establish consular
offices in the ports and places of the territories the sovereignty over which has been either relinquished or ceded by the
present treaty.

"Art. 15.—The government of each country will, for the

the present chapter.[48]   From the first the temporary
character of the sojourn was emphasized.

In November, 1900, a Cuban convention met and
began the work of drafting a constitution. The more
difficult part of its work was the formulation of an
agreement with the United States as to the relations
of the two states. After a protracted discussion in
the Cuban convention a committee was appointed
which visited Washington in May, 1901, and entered
into direct negotiations upon the terms of settlement.
Congress had adopted the Platt Resolution in the
form of an amendment to the Army Appropriation
Act, March 2, 1901, as an expression of its views
upon the essential parts of the future relations with
Cuba. The delegates reported back to the convention upon the character of the American proposals
and the temper of the American authorities. The
result was the final adoption of the Platt Resolution
without modification on June 12, 1901. After the
establishment of an independent government in 1902
the Platt Amendment or Resolution was embodied

term of ten years, accord to the merchant vessels of the other
country the same treatment in respect of all port charges,
including entrance and clearance dues, light dues and tonnage
duties as it accords to its own merchant vessels not engaged
in the coastwise trade.
"This article may at any time be terminated on six months'
notice given by either government to the other."
[48] For an estimate of the American administration of Cuba
from 1899–1902, see Whitcomb, La situation internationale de
Cuba, Paris, 1905, ch. 3. The writer considers that the conduct of the United States was correct, appraises very highly
the work of General Wood in the reorganization of Cuban
industries and the reform of social conditions, and incidentally criticizes England for the length of time during which
the occupation of Egypt has been continued.

with minor verbal alterations in a treaty concluded on May 22, 1903, and ratified on July 1, 1904.[49]

The compact contains seven articles, the first three of which are the most important. Article 1 applies the Monroe doctrine to Cuban relations. No government of Cuba shall ever enter into a compact which will impair independence or permit a foreign power to obtain control of any part of the island by colonization or by any other process. Article 2 was intended to save Cuba from the pressure of debt-collecting governments, and supplements the treaty with Spain. At Paris the United States had refused to assume the Cuban debt or to specifically pass it to Cuba. In the new treaty Cuba was forbidden to assume any debt to pay the interest upon which and to provide a sinking fund for which the ordinary revenues, after defraying the current expenses of government, should be inadequate.

Article 3 recognizes that Cuba received her sovereignty under a compact which, if violated, would forfeit all independent sovereign rights. This is accomplished by defining the conditions of American intervention in Cuba as follows:

" That the government of Cuba consents that the United States may exercise the right to intervene for the preservation of Cuban independence, the maintenance of a government adequate for the protection of life, property and individual liberty, and for discharging the obligations with respect to Cuba imposed by the treaty of Paris on the United States, now to be assumed and undertaken by the government of Cuba."

[49] Compilation of Treaties in Force, 1904, p. 952.

19

Article 3 constitutes what is probably the first international agreement formally defining a right of forcible intervention. By the compact with the United States Cuba is bound to maintain a free stable government and to fulfill her international obligations. If she fails she recognizes a right of the United States to help her to do so. Another article deals with sanitation and makes it a duty to maintain such sanitary conditions in her cities as would make life safe there and in the neighborhood as well. This merely supplements the other duty to protect life—a duty common to all sovereign states and intolerable where ignored. Article 5 provides that the title to the Isle of Pines should be left to future adjustment by treaty.[50]

Not one article of the agreement nor all of them together constituted such a limitation on Cuban sovereignty as to make Cuba in any sense a vassal state, or a protectorate, much less a dependency, or even a sphere of influence in the legal sense. Cuba became a sovereign state without hindrance to normal foreign intercourse and the exercise of all the prerogatives of

[50] Subsequently the American Government decided that the island properly belonged to Cuba, and in 1902 Cuban authorities were allowed to take possession of it along with other Cuban territories, and American forces stationed there were withdrawn. A treaty was then negotiated with the Republic of Cuba in which the Isle of Pines was recognized as Cuban territory, but the treaty has failed of ratification by the Senate. The Supreme Court in the case of Pearey v. Stranahan decided on April 8, 1907, that the island is not American territory. See Whitcomb, La situation internationale de Cuba, pp. 139–40; Moore, Digest, Vol. I, p. 536. Senate Document 105, 58 Cong., 2 Sess., pp. 118 ff.

sovereignty.[51] The failure of any state to fulfill the same conditions prescribed in the treaty causes it to forfeit all rights as a member of the community of states. They are the essential elements of statehood itself. The completion of Cuban independence in 1902 fulfilled the objects of the Spanish-American war and executed the spirit and letter of the treaty of Paris. The occasion of the recent intervention provided for in the Platt Amendment is outside the scope of this work. Incidentally it would seem to illustrate the truth of a contention set forth by Spain in defense of the form of autonomous government offered to Cuba in 1897, namely, that the Cubans were unprepared for more. Beyond this, recent experience has shown the wisdom of the conditional restraint of the Platt Amendment, under which Cuba may continue in the future to enjoy independence.

[51] Consult the article by C. F. Randolph, Columbia Law Review, Vol. I, p. 352, "The Joint Resolution of Congress respecting the Relations of the United States and Cuba." Whitcomb, La situation internationale de Cuba, ch. 5, compares the situation of Cuba with the relation to Turkey of Bulgaria under the treaty of Berlin and of Crete, but the similarity is very slight. Cuba possesses the name and position of an independent republic; the other cases cited are of states tributary to Turkey in the clearest manner. Cuba conducts its own foreign relations, the others have not been allowed the privilege.

INDEX

293

INDEX 297

191; action on coaling of Spanish fleet at Curaçao, 193, 215.

Neutrality, effect of inhumanity of belligerents on, 34; rules of international law on declarations of, 179–81; declarations of, 125, 181, 185 ff., 212–13, 215–16; obligations of, 182 ff.; charge against Polo de Bernabé for alleged violation of, 214.

Neutrality act, violations of, 46 ff.; principles of interpretation established by filibustering cases, 58.

Neutralization, attempt to establish zone at San Juan, 126–27; of hospital ships, 157; of transports with prisoners, 158; status of Suez Canal as to, 190.

Neutrals, part of, in insurrection of 1895, 25; effect of policy of concentration on attitude toward Cuban insurrection, 34; rights of, affected by war in Cuba, 37; obligation of notification to, 123; sale of ships and supplies by, 185; belligerent use of ports of, 185; carrying of contraband by, 195 ff.; capture of ships of, 205 ff.

Newfoundland, decision of prize court in case of, 207–8.

Non-combatants, effect of concentration on Cuban, 29.

Norway, declaration of neutrality by, 216.

Olinde Rodriguez, decision of prize court in the case of, 206–7.

Ostend Manifesto, relation to national policy, 16.

Palma, Tomas E., letter of, on causes of insurrection, 23–24.

Panama, decision of prize court in case of, 168–70.

Paqueta Habana, decision of prize court in case of, 174–75.

Paraguay, declaration of neutrality of, 188; *Temerario* disarmed by, 189.

Paris, negotiations of peace transferred to, 224, 226; meeting of peace commission in, 234; treaty of, signed, 247.

Pauncefote, Sir Julian, spokesman for European powers in appeal for peace, 90; agreement for passage of Saint Lawrence, 215.

Peace Commission, membership of, 224; meeting of, 234 ff.; treaty of peace concluded by, 247.

Pedro, decision of prize court in case of, 170, 171.

Philippines, employment of insurgents in belligerent operations in, 144; treatment of prisoners by insurgents in, 159; peace negotiations concerning disposition of, 228; capture of Manila in, 229; demand of peace commissioners of Spain as to, 234; change of policy of United States toward acquisition of, 241–43; cession of, 250.

Platt Resolution, 288–90; legal effect of, 290.

Polk, James K., offer to purchase Cuba, 16.

Pope Leo XIII, offer of services as mediator, 86; action through Archbishop Ireland for peace, 89.

Porto Rico, invaded, 126; peace negotiations concerning, 225, 227; commissioners for evacuation of, 232; cession of, 250–51; transfer of, to United States, 260, 261.

Portugal, declaration of neutrality of, 187, 192, 216.

Prisoners of war, conduct of United States toward, 158–59; exchange of, 160.

Privateering, rejected by the United States, 128; right reserved by Spain to issue letters of marque for, 133; relation of auxiliary naval service to, 133–37.

Prize, rules of war on taking enemy

www.ingramcontent.com/pod-product-compliance
Lightning Source LLC
Chambersburg PA
CBHW030258100426
42812CB00002B/485